Just me
At sea

Just me
At sea

Jacqueline Hope

eQuil Books

Copyright © Jacqueline Hope 2020

All rights reserved. The moral right of the author has been asserted. No part of this book may be reproduced by any means, other than as brief quotations in other works or reviews without written permission of the publisher.

First published in 2020 by eQuil Books
16 Cooke Ave
Hampton East
Victoria 3188
Australia.
Email: equilbooks@fastmail.fm

 A catalogue record for this work is available from the National Library of Australia

ISBN 978-0-9874711-2-3

Front cover photograph: Chris Glaves
Back cover photograph: Nick Young

For my children and theirs
And for the dreamer in all of us.

Contents

Prologue	1
Chapter 1 - Pivotal Moments	3
Chapter 2 - Never Quite Ready	9
Chapter 3 - The Push to Darwin	19
Chapter 4 - Turning Back	31
Chapter 5 - Better Prepared	41
Chapter 6 - Solo Departure	51
Chapter 7 - Confidence Restored	65
Chapter 8 - This Is It	73
Chapter 9 - Stay on the Boat	83
Chapter 10 - Calling All Angels	93
Chapter 11 - Digging Deeper	103
Chapter 12 - Cape of Storms	113
Chapter 13 - Vertical Time	125
Chapter 14 - Close Encounters	137
Chapter 15 - Homeward Bound	151
Chapter 16 - No-Go Zone	163
Chapter 17 - Time and Motion	173
Chapter 18 - Still Waiting for my Epiphany	183
Chapter 19 - Four Single-Handers	195
Chapter 20 - The Pragmatism of Age	205
Epilogue	221
Appendix 1 - Glossary	223
Appendix 2 - Layout of Shanti	227

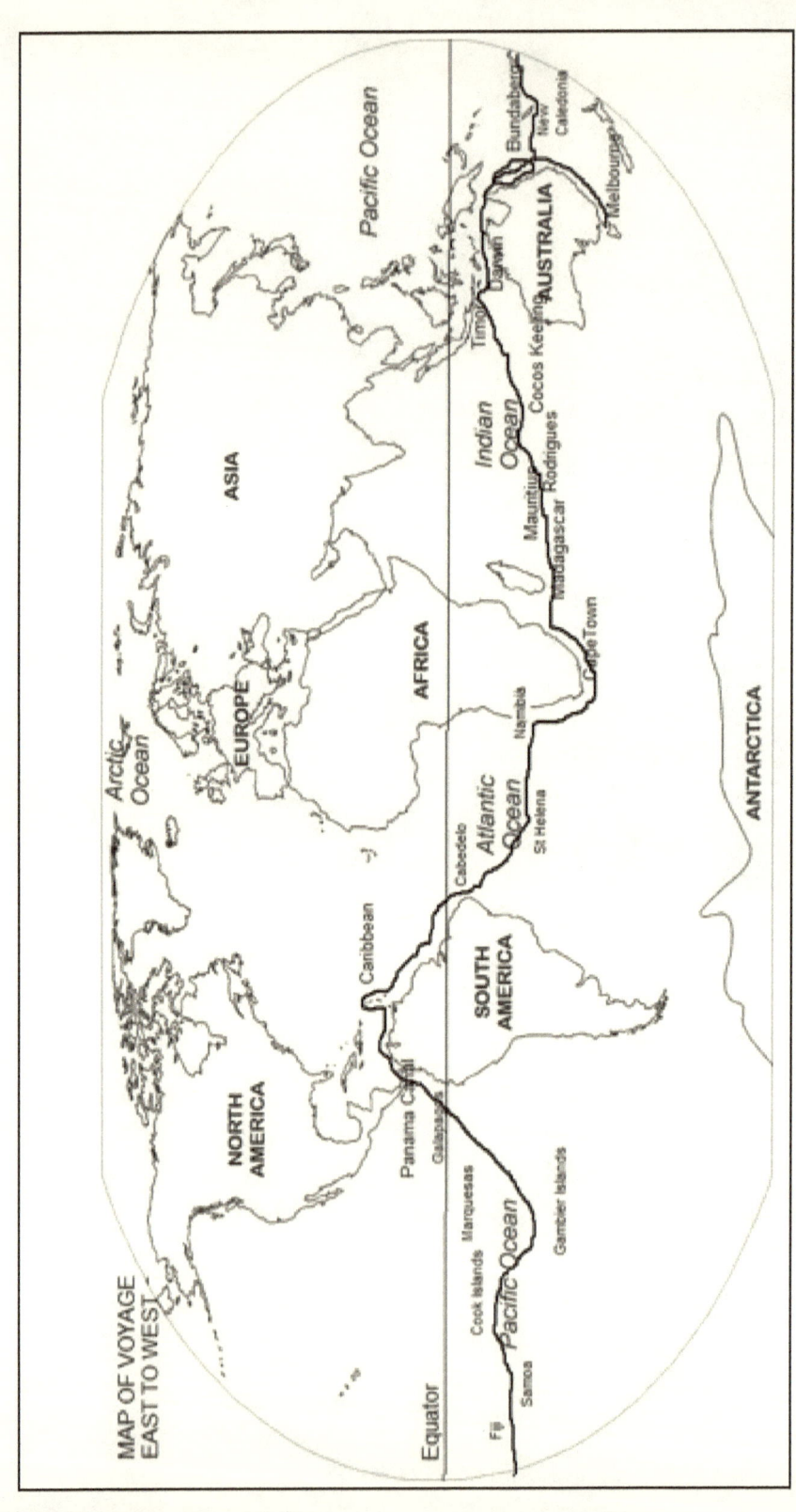

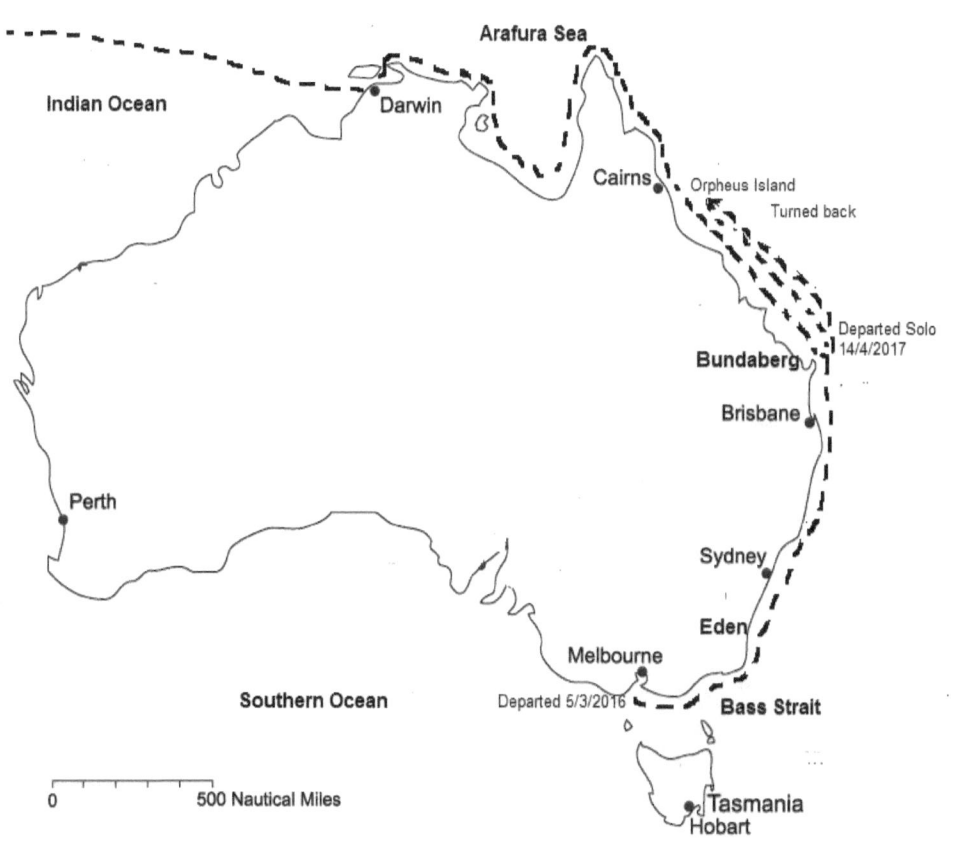

East Coast of Australia

Prologue

"Extreme challenges have the ability, the potential, to push you, or force you into a state of Presence." -Eckhart Tolle.

What madness induces a 65-year-old grandmother to leave the comfort of hearth and home to sail around the world alone? No doubt the same urge that ignites a fire in the belly of any dreamer, the desire to step firmly into the unknown, to stretch beyond the sensible and into the unimaginable.

And for what? For the greatest treasure possible, the gift of selfhood and the opportunity to grow into massively oversized boots.

Dreams are like seeds. Some are planted in fertile soil, perhaps nurtured, perhaps left to lie dormant or to die. Germination requires the confluence of exactly the right conditions.

Having found the exact right conditions, I seized the opportunity to launch this uncertain endeavour. It turned into the adventure of a lifetime, throwing me good and bad, hardship and ecstasy, and the deepest life lessons one could ever desire. Being pushed beyond the edge, I nearly didn't get away with it.

Chapter 1

Pivotal Moments

Legend has it that the Brits and the Greeks were seafaring folks, so some of that nauticality may have seeped down from my ancestors. More likely, my father's decision to relocate us from England to the Land of the Long White Cloud in the 4th year of my life had a hand in it. There is not one place in New Zealand where you are more than 50 miles from the sea, so it is not surprising sailing was such a large part of my early years. In those days not too many girls sailed. Guys would swivel their heads as they sailed by, do a double-take, and make some neonatal exclamation, like, "It's a girl!" The teenage boys I later raced against just wanted me to bare my breasts. Thankfully, half a century later, all that has changed.

When I moved from New Zealand to Australia in my mid-teens, I sought to continue messing about in boats, signing up for a film-making expedition around the world. The film was to be titled "Girl in a Yellow Oilskin", so I guessed it was open to female applicants. In my youthful naivete, I succumbed to the advances of the middle-aged cook, rather than the skipper. Four years later, a daughter was born, and in less than another year I was a single mother. Parenthood and poverty clipped my wings.

Later, in my early twenties, I began building a ferro-cement yacht, alongside a man whom I had sucked into the dream. He would sit writing poetry while I bag-tied a million staples around the weld-mesh, each of us in our own make-believe world. That chapter of the long-suffering dream died of thirst (there was no water on the property to cement the hull), so I went to university instead, with a thirst for knowledge and qualifications.

I'm not a loner and have shared patches of my life with some good men, and some not so good. Along the way, three more children enhanced the journey, demanding the full-time commitment that children do. It's easy for a woman with children to willingly put her own dreams on hold. It's nothing short of a miracle that even the dimmest ember of my dream could have smouldered unquenched through all those years.

As the child-rearing responsibilities dwindled, I found there was new energy available. I started up a small business based on my studies in natural medicine. Its rapid success enabled me to buy an ocean-going yacht (a J-40) and the liberty to sail away. Freedom! The first "shake-down" cruise was to circumnavigate Tasmania, then New Zealand (clearly, I like sailing around things). I took a crew with me, mainly friends from Sandringham Yacht Club in Melbourne.

A trip to Vanuatu in the South Pacific gave me a taste for crossing oceans, and it was there I met the man with whom I was to sail for several years. We did the usual trick of "sell his; sell hers; buy ours" and enjoyed a string of endless summers. Because we had started as a two-boat family, it was easy to buy a second boat in the Mediterranean, where we cruised the Greek Islands, Turkey, Croatia, and Italy during the northern summer. At first, we really were living the dream.

But like all dreams it ended, drowning me in contourless misery. I couldn't even look at a boat without getting teary and truly thought my sailing days were done. Perhaps it was time to put down some roots and settle in one place, where I had family and friends. They wrapped me in a magical sense of belonging and tried to extract me from my depression. I bought a house near my eldest daughter's, where I imagined I would settle comfortably on the land, helping out with her youngsters as a good grandmother should. Infancy is such a precious and fleeting moment. They grow so fast and I wanted to watch that process unfold in all of its hues.

For the next three years, I played that role, happy to be there, living close enough to slip in and out. I could have stayed there forever, in that easy domesticity. But a restlessness wriggled beneath it all, like a worm on a hook. The grandchildren were growing a little like weeds in an overgrown garden, without too much cultivation. It's not the grandparent's role to trim and prune. The younger generations are much more lenient in their parenting, with patient acceptance of behaviours I would have been thrashed for. It's no doubt a better way, but for those of us raised with the belt, there is a disquieting mismatch.

A pivotal moment came during a ten-day Vipassana silent retreat. I am no stranger to meditation but the intensity of this retreat shook me. I clearly saw many things that I had been sublimating; my dysfunctional childhood, my need to please at any cost, how first we harm ourselves before we harm others. How hanging around to rescue my drug-affected son was doing neither of us any good. How life in a house in suburbia was anathema to me.

It was here, on one fog-shrouded morning, watching the colourful hot-air balloons drift over the Yarra Valley, that the fire in my belly resurrected like the proverbial Phoenix from the ashes. Interestingly enough I was sharing a room with an Indian woman named Shanti, who impressed me with her quiet wisdom and serenity. We spoke a little at the end of the retreat when talking was resumed. She was a volunteer for the humanitarian organisation, "Médecins Sans Frontières" (Doctors Without Borders) and she inspired me to rethink my life.

Unless you are switched on enough to get it all figured out while still young, the narrow window of opportunity to pursue your dreams exists briefly between when your children are grown and your own parents are still independent. My aging father was fit and well in New Zealand, with a much younger Thai wife taking good care of him. So the gap opened and I tumbled in.

―――

Having no boat and no vast capital reserves were perhaps a slight hindrance, offset by plenty of skills and a keenness to learn more. Goethe wrote of the whole universe leaning in toward the boldness of a vision begun, lending support and making it happen. And so it began, with amazing synchronicities and fortuitous stumblings over exactly what was needed, when it was needed.

Like the boat.

It is something of an interesting story as to how the boat came to me. I had been scouring the 'Boats for Sale' ads for ages, as well as doing heaps of research into strong, seaworthy vessels capable of blue-water cruising. One evening I came upon the following information:

"Seaworthy enough for offshore voyages in extreme weather conditions, the Contessa 32 was the only yacht in the small boat class to finish the disastrous 1979 Fastnet race, in which 15 lives were lost. A sudden storm of near hurricane strength brought death and destruction to the race, capsizing 25% of the 303 participating boats." (Wikipedia)

"It was inevitable that David Sadler would extend his experience gained in the Contessa 32 into the Sadler range. The Sadler 32 received immediate enthusiastic acclaim and represented an important milestone in cruising yacht design." (Mike Lucas Yachting)

These days cruising yachts are getting bigger each year, with many more creature comforts aboard, such as showers and washing machines. Thirty-two feet is considered on the small side for crossing the oceans of the world but it seemed to me ideal for one small woman to manage alone. So I started looking for this reputable classic.

As a British-designed and built yacht, the majority were to be found over on that side of the world, not in Australia. Then, out of the blue, a yachty friend suggested checking the online market site of Gumtree. This is a low-key alternative to eBay and not a usual place to look for boats for sale. The first boat to jump out at me was a 1989 Sadler 32, just listed that morning, right on my very doorstep at Sandringham Yacht Club. The photos held all the promise they usually do, so it was with great excitement that I dashed down the very next day to meet her.

Standing on the furthest pontoon where I seldom venture, I beheld a sad and sorry specimen of the species. She bore the marks of years of neglect, appearing more like a fibreglass reef, totally encrusted in barnacles with long, thick tendrils of growth hanging down to her knees. Still, I proceeded, with all the naive enthusiasm of optimistic ignorance.

It was all she could do to get around to the lifting bay to be hauled out for a survey, dragging her own ecosystem of mixed flora and fauna along beneath. Friends standing by shook their heads and tried to caution me, but I could already see her potential. And the reduced price reflected her poor condition, which suited my limited budget, now that I had poured most of my capital into real estate. A small balance in my Superannuation fund was all I had left, so with some hard negotiations, I bought the boat for $25,000.

The idea of taking an older, solidly-built hull and restoring it to a well-prepared, seaworthy vessel, capable of making a solo circumnavigation of the world had merit. She would have new sails, rigging, and equipment, and more importantly, I would know her intimately from stem to stern. And so began a year of hard work, which also gave everyone (and me) time to get used to the idea. It would have been too abrupt, had I simply bought something sea-ready enough to sail away immediately.

The first step was heavy-duty sandblasting to strip the keel back to the bone to expose whatever mysteries were lurking beneath all that growth. Once this job was professionally done, most of the rest of the work was mine, along with help from a few good friends. The magical mystery tour had begun. What surprises would each day bring?

There was good luck and bad, perhaps not in equal measure, but all of it an unknown quantity, waiting to relieve or test me. It was to become the first of a long series of lessons in equanimity, taking the good with the bad in their own intrinsic suchness. The lessons were there long before I even got to the "Monastery of the sea". Not knowing what was ahead of me helped me get through the following 350 days, taking them one at a time.

As with everything, there is an interesting story around the renaming. The old name, *Dad's Dream*, was removed with a heat gun, and I was very glad to see it go. I had been brainstorming for days (and often in the middle of the night), trying to come up with a new name, but it was as if, while the old name was still there, it somehow blocked the possibility of anything else.

Friends had been asking me questions about ocean sailing such as "what do you do all day?" They imagine sailing to be a monotonous bubble of everyday sameness, with the skipper simply along for the ride, like a monkey in a sputnik. But the reality is that unlike shore life, which may stay more or less the same for hours or even days, life at sea is constantly changing.

This brought me to consider the name *Constant Change*—a good reminder of the impermanence of everything. This name follows on well from the series of names of earlier boats I had owned: *Quick Fling*, *Sweetheart*, and the last, *Soulmate*—with romantic implications of forever. The name *Constant Change* seemed like a step towards maturity and growth of understanding. All suffering stems from ignorance of this truth, when we try and hang onto what is, under the illusion that tomorrow will be the same as today. But boats, like humans, don't like to be thought of as temporary measures, so that name was rejected.

One day I realised I was missing music in my life. I hadn't been listening to any music while spending all my days down in the boatyard, so I put on a CD given to me by a friend, David Isom. The second song on his album, "Down to the Sea Again" is magnificent, with the haunting chorus, "*Sing me a Shanty*". While listening to it, the word "Shanty" resonated with me, and I thought, that could make a good name for the boat. I looked up its meaning online, and found that a shanty is a "shipboard work song", or "an irregular, low-cost dwelling", which kind of describes a small, low budget cruising yacht, such as mine. I felt quite excited by the thought that this could be it. I liked the sound of the word, and that was an important aspect. When I mentioned it to my youngest daughter Shoni, whose name was also chosen euphonically, she asked why not *Shanti* with an i, instead of a y? So I looked that up and found this definition:

"*Shanti*" – (Sanskrit) "*inner peace; a state of being mentally and spiritually at peace, with enough knowledge and understanding to keep oneself strong in the face of discord or stress.*"

"Peace, calmness, tranquillity, or bliss." T.S Eliot referred to it as *"the peace which passeth understanding."*

Well, that sounded just perfect! A short name that would be easy to say on the radio, fit on the small rear-end of the boat and yet carried an enormous meaning that encapsulated my dreams and aspirations precisely. At that point in time, I made no connection with the Indian woman of the same name, whom I had met on the Vipassana silent retreat. Only later did I remember and offered a smiling thanks.

I looked on the Australian Register of Ships, as I had done with so many other potential names I had thought of, and found *Shanti II* was taken, but not *Shanti*—which meant that there once had been a boat with that name, but its registration had lapsed and the name was now available.

I completed all the reams of paperwork, searched for the previous owners back to the builder, the Builder's Certificate, etc. and coughed up over a thousand dollars for Australian Registration. A week later I was advised that my application had been approved: I could have the name *Shanti*. The next step was new signage on the bow and stern, followed by the appropriate re-naming rituals with libations of bubbly, sacrifices of virgins, penny under the mast, and various other superstitious appeasements. Many sailors consider it bad luck to change a boat's name. Perhaps that thought did occasionally enter my mind; but overall, I had far more good luck than bad, so the appeasements must have worked.

Chapter 2

Never Quite Ready

Seemingly all too soon, the predetermined departure date arrived. Of course, neither boat nor I were ready, but that's the best-ignored common scenario that stalls many an adventure. Certainly, another year of preparations would have helped but there's no sense in waiting for everything to be just so, or you never go. The hoped-for communications via HF radio and Pactor Modem remained mysteriously elusive, as did the untested single-line reefing system. The ancient refrigeration unit gave some slight hint that it might work, but even with two brand new "house" batteries, there was probably not enough power to run it. The Fleming self-steering wind vane bolted on the stern was one of those independently-minded creatures to make friends with. Along with everything else.

It was kind of like starting an exciting new relationship, with an open mind and heart, keen to learn on the go. I can't say it was without some misgivings. Was I too old now to turn this dream into reality? Certainly, the physical hardship would test me more than in my youth. There was also the possibility of illness. My training in natural medicine generally kept me healthy but there were still the risks of accidents, broken bones, wounds, infections, or toothache.

I was scarcely fit to begin. A recent shoulder injury had developed into a painful bursitis, preventing me from sleeping on my left side. The ultrasound showed something like a fluid-filled crater punched into the top of the bone. Cortisone injections were suggested, but I'm not a fan. Add to this, I was hobbling along the dock like a cripple, having twisted my back while loading provisions on board. Onlookers would come to my aid as I doubled over, questioning my imminent departure date. "All good to go," I insisted. "No need for walking about while at sea."

The fact was I didn't really know what lay ahead, either physically or mentally.

How would I cope with the unknown, with the solitude, with having to do everything myself? Many cruising couples divide the work into "blue jobs" and "pink jobs". For me, they would all be purple. I had invested a weekend doing a diesel mechanic course and was on slightly friendly terms with the engine. In the past, I would have stood back and allowed my engineer partner to sort its tantrums. And in doing so, gained no deeper insights into its grey metal mysteries.

But now was the time to step up to the plate, to claim my independence and to accept all problems as mine. It would be my first time completely alone at sea; in actual fact, the first time completely alone in my life. It was hard to imagine going for weeks on end without talking to another human being, not to mention going without physical contact, a hug, a kiss, or the warm intimacy that had always been part of my life. Not knowing when or if I would resume that comfort was a thought I couldn't indulge in, but it was only natural that it should colour my departure day.

On Saturday, March 5, 2016, at 0900 hours, a crowd of family, friends, and other assorted well-wishers bade the good ship *Shanti* farewell from Sandringham Yacht Club, only to have her limp apologetically a few feet to the nearest pontoon, engine alarms screeching. Superheroes Ron and Alex leapt to the rescue and in the blink of an hour, changed the offending water pump impeller. False start! Which one of us didn't want to go? They say that casting off the dock lines is the hardest part. I was later to encounter many temptations to stop, but I made a resolve that only *Shanti* should make that call.

My good friend, Bernadette (Bernie) Moore had graciously offered to join me as far as Eden, to see me safely on my way, as it were. Even though I greatly appreciated this, it seemed as if there were mixed feelings around my going completely solo. People just didn't seem to get it. Perhaps they were afraid for my safety or worried I couldn't really do it alone. Perhaps I hadn't made the point strongly enough, as several others suggested joining me in some of the more pleasant spots up north. After all the help I had been given in preparing the boat, it seemed ungrateful to refuse. It was only later that I dug in deep and learned to say no. I was, after all, on a mission—while not exactly from God, equally sacred to me.

Out on the bay, accompanied by a few other Sandy boats and George Shaw's bugle fanfare, it was time for the neglected sea-trials that there hadn't been time for before. "Time enough for that on the way," was the glib response that I had countered all sensible queries with. A decent offshore breeze revealed a spritely lady, kicking up her heels, riding up and over the choppy seas like a dolphin. She felt well-balanced, as playful as a youngster, as controlled as a ballroom dancer.

Halfway down the bay, I was on my hands and knees bailing out the bilge, regretting not having mopped up the spillage from the impeller change. But there seemed to be a lot more than expected from that little exercise, in fact around 50 litres of it. When I finally remembered to taste it, I found it to be freshwater. The tanks had been filled to the brim and the newly-cut inspection panels were leaking. Stopping at Queenscliff Cruising Yacht Club before going out the Port Phillip Bay Heads gave a good opportunity to sort out these little teething problems.

Bernie was quick to spread the word at QCYC of my intentions to make a solo circumnavigation. The Commodore turned up to interview me and I momentarily became the centre of attention. I felt quite uncomfortable with this as if I was something of a charlatan because after all, I had not done anything remarkable yet, simply said I wanted to. And I had another woman with me.

I don't count that first leg up the east coast of Australia as part of the solo journey as I picked up a few others along the way, for a day here and there, before I got serious. I could say my solo circumnavigation of the globe officially (or perhaps unofficially) began almost a year later on May 14, from Bundaberg, Queensland. Of course, like most journeys, it actually began long before then, along with a few false starts, digressions, breakdowns, and returns. But once committed to my strictly solo attempt, keeping others off the boat became a scrupulous resolve, only bent for the Panama Canal transit, when it is necessary to take on 4 line-handlers and a Pilot, or "Advisor".

Apart from the Panama Canal, I was completely alone for the entire circumnavigation. Whenever I refer to "us" or "we" it is in reference to me and *Shanti*, along with those other electronic or mechanical personifications. (We have an all-girl crew on *Shanti*—the tiller pilot is nicknamed *Tilly*, the Fleming windvane is *Min*). Staying alone became an almost religious piety for me, and indeed, my solo journey became deeply connected to the insights that solitude confers. This was the reward that I couldn't possibly have anticipated in the beginning.

"Why alone?" is an oft-asked question that seems to intrigue. After all, solitary confinement is considered one of the harshest punishments. Many single-handers sail solo by default rather than by choice. For me, it was the fulfilment of a childhood dream. Since the age of 7, when first exposed to things nautical, that seed was sown. I dreamed of sailing around the world alone, wanting to be the first female to do so. For most of my life, I had no means of funding such a venture and had never heard of the concept of sponsorship. I prefer the independence of paying my own way. It is, after all, my dream.

But for the first few days at sea, I was glad to have company. Bernie has sailed with me before on other boats and her ability to whip up a wholesome meal in practically any conditions earned her the nickname "Cookie". We have similar backgrounds in diet and nutrition and both of us have made a living from teaching others how to eat healthily. The need for this has always struck me as being most peculiar. One would think it should be common knowledge, but apparently not. So *Shanti* was sagging under her load of enough healthy victuals to get to Africa. I had no idea how long each of the 2kg gas bottles might last to cook all of this.

As we cast off to make the 0950 slack-water at the infamous Port Phillip Heads Rip, I shuddered silently within, thinking, this is it—all the build-up of being the woman who is going to sail single-handed around the world. Now I have to do it! In many ways, I wished I had simply slipped away quietly, without saying anything to anyone.

Motoring in calm conditions, there was a large, Southern Ocean swell rolling through Bass Strait and I was pleased not to be feeling my usual seasickness. I had taken a couple of Stugeron tablets earlier but felt them wearing off around midday. I took another dose and promptly lost it. Luckily I hadn't yet had lunch so didn't have to have that twice. It's an annoying blight, this weak stomach of mine. Some have said it's largely psychological and it may well be, but I was one of those children who couldn't stomach the swings and roundabouts or read in the back seat of the car. Others have assured me it gets better with "miles under the keel". I certainly hoped so.

The first two nights were spent in rather rolly open roadstead anchorages of Cleeland Bight and Waratah Bay, which further tested my stomach. The next stop was Refuge Cove at Wilson's Promontory where I had my first swim—mainly to free up the log paddle wheel and clean the waterline, but also to test the swim-ladder. The lower rung only just makes it into the water so it's a bit of a contortionist act, with feet around ears, then a big heave-ho to get out.

From Wilson's Prom, it's generally around 48 hours to Eden. It seemed prudent to leave in light airs and motor the entire distance, hoping to avoid the 30-knot winds that were forecast to come in a few days hence. There was an unsettling swell disturbing an otherwise calm sea (stronger winds further south?) but the full mainsail, sheeted in tight, held us steady. Bernie baked some delicious scones which weighted my insides enough to keep them in.

As the sun set and the moonless night closed around us, I suggested we maintain a 4-hours on, 4-hours off watch. Even though an experienced sailor, Bernie expressed some uneasiness about being on watch alone at night on an unknown boat. *Not a worry.* Like a young child allowed to stay up late, I was full of the excitement of beginning my new adventure. It was perfect to spend my first night at sea with *Shanti* as if alone. Staying up on such a night was more of a privilege than hardship, gazing in awe at the arcane infinitude above. I couldn't get enough of the diamond wake of phosphorescence, the dolphins flashing like comets with their fiery trails—all putting on a spectacular show just for me. Even the constant thrum of the engine couldn't pall my delight.

I woke Bernie at dawn, then slept for a couple of hours. Over a healthy breakfast, we discussed her reluctance to stand a night watch. "It's pretty much the same as motoring in the day," I reassured her. "You only need to keep an eye out for lights. Anything else that you might run into you wouldn't see—and you're just as likely to *not* see it in daylight either. You just have to trust."

Trust. That's the thing.

I agree; it is scary when the boat is powering along in pitch blackness and your imagination runs riot. So much of this sailing caper requires an element of trust. You have to trust in your boat, your gear, yourself. If we start thinking of all that might go wrong, well, we'd never take a step.

So at 2100 the next night, Bernie volunteered to let me go down for a couple of hours sleep. I knew she wasn't comfortable but tiredness was luring me to my bunk. "Just for a couple of hours," I agreed, asking her to call me if anything changed.

It's easy to miss noticing as the wind builds gradually and the boat seems to be handling it OK. I woke at 2300 to the sound of waves rushing past the hull and the engine racing. "What's going on up there?" I shouted. "Ease the main!"

By the time I put my wet-weather gear on there was an almighty bang as *Tilly*, the tiller-pilot, let go. *Shanti* rounded up violently into the full force of wind and sea, knocking us off balance. My first thought as I grabbed the tiller was *Shit. Now we're in trouble.* With no chart-plotter mounted in the cockpit, *Tilly* was the only way we had of holding a set course.

Steering by hand at night, it is virtually impossible to see the unlit bulkhead compass from a distance. Without that, there is nothing to steer by. Only the feel of the wind, which now seemed totally at variance with the swell and crisscrossing waves. Who knew which way was up? In the pitch blackness, everything was so much harder to grasp—even more so for me, having just woken from a deep slumber.

The sudden downpour soon had us as saturated as if standing stupidly on the deck of a surfacing submarine. We needed to reduce sail, but everything was so new to me, so untested. God only knew how this single-line reefing system worked? My lack of pre-departure test-sailing was coming back to bite me with a vengeance. What sort of a bathtub toy was this boat?

Shipping traffic and fishing boats all around unnerved us further. Gabo Island lighthouse pierced the darkness with its terrifyingly bright strobe. How close were we to its rocky perch? In the panic and confusion, I even yelled at Bernie, maybe even swore, I don't remember, but I do remember feeling bad about it. I have never had any respect for skippers that shout at the crew, and here I was, doing just that. All in the name of getting this wild animal back under control.

"Can you take the helm?" I shouted to Bernie. The look on her face told me her answer. The prospect of taking just two steps from the relative shelter of the companionway to the totally exposed rear of the cockpit, showered by every second wave, was too much. As the waves crashed and threatened to swamp us, we noticed the depth sounder showing only 1.5 metres below the keel. We both clenched ourselves waiting for the crunch, before realizing it was just bubbles from the turbulence below. We were still afloat, though who knows where.

I heard Bernie's thin voice, scarcely audible above the howling wind: "This stress is no good for my blood pressure. I'm getting palpitations."

Oh no! Please don't have a heart attack now, I silently pleaded.

"Go down below, get yourself dry and hop into your bunk," I told her. At that moment I felt the full weight of a skipper's responsibility for their crew. This was another good reason for wanting to sail solo. I could deal with putting my own life at risk but didn't want to take another down with me.

My mind was racing, all tangled up and unravelled at the same time. *What to do? What to do?* As I sat out there, hanging onto the tiller as if it were a life-ring in a stormy sea, I heard a strange two-pitched sound: *errr, urrr*. Shining my torch, I saw *Tilly* lying in a pool of water on the cockpit floor, still moving back and forth in a feckless spasm, still trying to steer the boat. *Hallelujah! She's still alive!*

All of the possible fatalities that could have happened in that initial failure— from a broken push rod to sheering the metal connecting pin—had gone through my mind. Instead, only the steel ferrule set into a wooden block on the combing had split in two. I lashed *Tilly* more or less in position on the side of the cockpit and attached the other end back onto the tiller. Setting a flimsy course close to the wind, I managed to get a couple of reefs into the mainsail. Gradually *Shanti* settled. It took longer for me to.

The rest of the night was spent sitting out in the rain, trying not to feel too sorry for myself, reflecting on how quickly things can change from heaven to hell.

This mercurialness was something I would have to get used to. With *Tilly* wedged under my arm to stop her from breaking free again, only occasionally could I dash below to check our position on the laptop and call up any threatening fishing boats on the VHF radio. It was helpful to not just see the lights of other vessels in the distance but to know which way they were heading. The AIS (Automatic Identification System) receives the position, course, and name of other boats in the vicinity, as well as sending my information out to them. It is an absolutely vital piece of equipment. Unfortunately, at this moment, it was adding to the stress with the alarm sounding all the time. I made a mental note to change the settings as soon as I figured out how.

Somehow, we survived it all and were very glad to see the familiar port of Twofold Bay in Eden at daybreak. We anchored in Boydtown Bay and slept for a few hours. Later that same day, Bernie discovered that friends of hers were camping nearby and were willing to come and help us refuel at the fishermen's wharf. The next morning, they picked her up and drove her back to Melbourne with them. I can't be so unkind as to say there were "skid-marks" on the dock, but I'm sure that my stalwart Irish companion felt relieved to be back on dry land. We had both learned that *Shanti* is not a particularly comfortable boat in a storm. But she is the only one I have, so I must get to know her better, quickly.

    I spent my first days alone, tied up to the difficultly-tall wooden dock, enjoying the quaint fishing town ambience. I walked up to the library and used the free internet, then shopped for some fresh food. There were other tasks to do, such as replacing the engine raw-water cooling anti-siphon and fixing the broken tiller-pilot attachment. Leaving home port does not mean the end of boat jobs. It's a well-known saying that offshore cruising is all about doing boat jobs in exotic locations. Perhaps I might even work out other postponed mysteries, such as the reefing lines and the self-steering gear. That could have been useful.

    Here in Eden, a weather forecast of strong southerly wind makes it imperative to get off the wharf before it arrives. Many boats have suffered a pounding against the barnacle-encrusted piles while their unsuspecting crews enjoy a drink or ten up at the fishermen's pub on the top of the hill. For me, leaving dockside alone was not without providing local entertainment—this line first or last—and other novice dilemmas. But no harm was done, other than to my pride. How many more hundreds of times would I rue not having another pair of hands at some other part of the boat? Still, my choice, so better get used to it.

    After motoring the short distance across to East Boyd Bay, it was a much easier thing to drop the pick, pull back and appreciate my oversized Manson Supreme anchor. When the 55-knot squalls came through, several others dragged close to shore, getting drenched in the torrential downpours, fighting to re-anchor. Well, this is a taste of some of the trials of this sailing game. Now my true single-handing was about to begin. It was both exhilarating and scary.

Exactly 2 weeks after leaving SYC, I had my first solo sail, from Eden to Bermagui. It was not without some trepidation. The distances ahead of me, the uncertainty of it all played heavily on my mind. Was *I* suitably prepared, even if *Shanti* wasn't? How would I manage sleep deprivation on my own? Would I crack up under the strain of it all?

There were plenty of things to occupy me in quiet moments, learning French, playing guitar and singing, listening to music and audiobooks. My seasickness tendency ruled out the possibility of reading actual books, but I could always find a few words of inspiration from my favourite, Eckhart Tolle's "The Power of Now".

There would be many changes to have to get used to. Not being able to step off the boat to stretch my legs could test me, as I love a daily walk. My pre-departure shoulder and back ailments seemed to have miraculously sorted themselves out, so those physical issues were at least put aside. Probably the greatest unknown factor still haunting me was how I would handle the solitude.

Being alone for the first time created a hollow emptiness and increased my feelings of doubt. I knew that the first few weeks away from family and friends wouldn't be easy. It felt like a strong bungee cord was being stretched out, to either pull me back with a sudden snap of reality or break and set me free to continue. Either seemed equally possible—neither, more nor less probable. Was it the hand of fate? In many ways it seemed so, as if I was a controlled puppet, going through the motions of someone else's play. It would be easy to succumb to a mild pre-panic, but then *Shanti* would throw something that made me feel competent and strong again. Then it was as if my whole life had been leading up to this and I was exactly where I should be.

Min, the Fleming self-steering wind pilot was working beautifully with 15 knots of wind from behind. There was a favourable current assisting and SOG (Speed Over Ground) was up to 7.5 knots, while boat speed was only around 4.5. I made myself a falafel wrap with salad for lunch and felt good for an hour or so until the wind dropped down to 7 knots from dead astern (wallow) and made it necessary to fire up *Yani*, the trusty little Yanmar 3GM30 diesel (for those interested) to be able to make it in before sunset. This temperamental wind is closely linked to my mood, so ecstasy and deflation are never far apart. Another mental note to aspire for "stability regardless." (Maybe next life?)

"Feelings come and go like clouds on a windy day. Consciousness is my anchor." – Thich Nhat Hanh. (What is consciousness? I ask myself.)

In Bermagui Marina, I tied up opposite a 46' yacht owned by a gregarious man who was quick to help me dock, even though I had reversed into the tight berth as if I did it every day. We looked over each other's boats, made the right noises of appreciation, and continued chatting for a few hours, sharing some of our stories. He said I was living his dream, but he was tethered to the land by a large sheep farm and other commitments. He hadn't had his boat for very long and was still feeling intimidated by it (one of the problems of owning a big boat). It was hard to find crew who were able to sail when he wanted to, he told me. This reaffirmed my choice of a smaller yacht that I can handle alone.

It was once said of my adventure that if anything was going to stop me, it would be a man, as in a romantic attachment to a man. Perhaps, more accurately, it would be that very human need to connect with another person on a deeply intimate level. To deliberately turn my back on this possibility for a few years felt strangely unnatural, yet at the same time necessary. There are many prerequisites to being a good partner; becoming free of the need is probably the most important. It had been three years since I had found myself suddenly single, and the shock waves of that loss were still like tight rings around my heart, which I hoped being alone at sea would loosen.

Chapter 3

The Push to Darwin

Single-handing requires many different skills, such as picking up and letting go of a buoy (no reference implied to the human variety). Luckily there's no one else on board to see my mistakes (or my "errors of judgement", as I prefer to think of them.) Little Manly Cove was the second place I almost put my boat on the beach. The first time was approaching a mooring in very shallow water in Jervis Bay, which I luckily aborted at the last minute. I probably should have done likewise with this one.

A small bay in Sydney Harbour, Little Manly, makes an ideal spot from which to row ashore and walk to the shops to buy fresh produce. As with most of Sydney's waterfront, the bay is chock-a-block full of moored boats, all hung very tightly together as if water was scarce. I motored slowly in amongst them until I spotted a vacant mooring. It was the only one left, quite close to the land, where the wash from the ferries was foaming the rocks. A slight breeze from behind nosed me gently up to it.

In hindsight, that wonderful 20:20 hindsight, I should have known better. I think I was afraid to approach in the correct manner, into the wind, as it was already quite shallow. What was I thinking? *Shanti* would hang to the leeward side anyway, in whatever water there was. What I wasn't counting on, was that my forward approach to the mooring buoy left me completely vulnerable if I missed picking it up. I couldn't be in both places at once; at the bow with the boathook and in the cockpit with tiller and throttle.

I realised this as I made my first grab for the mooring and missed. *Shanti* was still moving forward toward the rocks, which were only about three or four boat-lengths away. My second, more desperate lunge, hooked it, but only by the ring on top of the bigger buoy. The smaller one, with the lighter trace line, had disappeared on the other side of the bow.

As the weight took up, the extendable boat hook pulled out to its full length. I was praying it wouldn't break or pull out of my hands. Slowly, *Shanti* swung round behind the mooring to face into the wind. For a second, I wondered about the depth beneath the keel, but mainly I wondered what on earth to do in the predicament I was now in. Thoughts like, "I should have a loose rope up here," flashed through my mind.

I started to use one hand to untie the rope holding the dinghy down. This was completely useless because there was no way I could reach the ring on top of the buoy to thread it through, without being stretched even further than I already was. I realised there was nothing else for it but to free the boathook from the ring and quickly catch the small buoy. I would only get one chance at this.

It took a bit of jiggling to clear the hook from the ring and let it go. By now so much adrenaline was pumping in me I was ready to leap overboard and grab it with my teeth. My first sweep at the floating line missed. I lunged at it again and hooked the small handle on the top of the buoy. Ever so carefully, so as not to lose it, I pulled it up. It jammed around the heavier rope below and clusters of mussels spat their juices out. The mooring had obviously not been used for a while. Eventually, I retrieved two small loops which I hooked over the port bow cleat.

Still shaking, I went back to the cockpit to check the depth sounder. One metre of water beneath the keel. Plenty.

Looking around at the amphitheatre of exclusive homes ringing the cove, I hoped there had not been too many witnesses of that little pantomime. The dinghy was launched in record time and I quickly rowed ashore, trusting that *Shanti* would still be there when I returned. I practically ran to the supermarket and back, with my hard-earned bags of fresh vegetables.

Leaving that mooring was a first in another art-form I had yet to develop. I tried motoring ever so slowly up to it but found that by the time I got to the bow there was already too much weight to release it. So back to the cockpit, put the engine in neutral and start again. This time I took the lines off the cleat but held onto them tightly, trying to pull the boat forward until the mooring buoy was alongside, then throwing them off and dashing back to the throttle, hoping not to tangle the lines in the propeller. It worked and I got away safely; which is to say, I got away with it this time, very aware that I may not always be so lucky. Things are bound to go wrong; there will be other mistakes/errors of judgement before I learn what needs to be learned, and I can only hope they are not terminal for *Shanti* or for me.

The next stop for me was the Pittwater, a serpentine waterway of legendary repute, branching into the Hawkesbury River and Cowan Creek, where many a solitary mariner might find months of mindless meandering. I anchored at the furthest reaches of Cowan Creek for several days, waiting for northerlies to pass, musing on my mission and trying to fathom those incalculable equations of time and distance.

If I am to get to Darwin (the jump-off port to cross the Indian Ocean) by the end of August, I have to keep moving. There are about 3,000 nautical miles between Sydney and Darwin, depending on how many detours off the direct route one takes (for example, sailing directly across the top of the Arafura Sea or following the coastline). From here to Darwin there are approximately 75 overnight stops and approximately 150 days before the end of August, which equates to a stop every 2 days. This makes no allowance for wind in the opposite direction, too much wind, or no wind. Delivery skippers run the engine virtually all the time. Even those cruising at a more leisurely pace turn the key if boat speed drops below 4 or 5 knots. There are only so many hours of daylight, even less as winter approaches. It is not safe to enter an unfamiliar port after dark, especially if there are sandbars to cross. Tides are also important. It's overwhelming to contemplate my limitations.

April 16 is my grandson Michael's 9th birthday, but I have no reception to call from deep in the recesses of Cowan Creek, and this is sad.

I awoke the next morning to the sweet song of local birds and, as often happens, felt brighter. *Shanti* might just as well have been resting on concrete, a rare stillness. I took the opportunity to sit and meditate for a while; not the two-hour Vipassana practice that I had begun in Melbourne, but enough to gather the scattered pieces of myself back to oneness.

Around noon a rower approached in a cockle-shell of a wooden dinghy and called his hello. "So what's your story?" he enquired directly.

"What's yours?" was my rejoinder, to which he countered, "I asked you first."

OK. Fair point.

Unaccustomed to having to respond to such directness, I scratched around amongst a few disused brain cells and came up with a label of identification. But again, it felt spurious to claim to be on a circumnavigation of the world, when I'd scarcely left my home port of Melbourne. But putting words to thoughts is always a good way to knock them into some kind of shape and it helped me to later sit and write them down.

So, this is how it is: I *am* circumnavigating. It doesn't matter how long it takes or at which particular point on the route I currently am. The journey is the thing; not the destination—because that is the same place as the start. I was on my circumnavigation from the day I cast off because that was my intention. I have no intention of finding somewhere nice to stop and settle.

There is no difference between finding somewhere beautiful and interesting to stop overseas as here in Australia. I could just as easily fly home for Christmas from Cairns or Cooktown as from South Africa or Panama. Other people's circumnavigations take as long as they take, according to how often and how long they stop. Some spend years sitting in foreign marinas. That's not for me. Nor am I a floating tourist, much as I enjoy visiting new places.

I love living onboard *Shanti*. I love sailing. I love meeting new and interesting people. Each one is like a talking book. I love the camaraderie of the sailing community. But aside from this, my goal is uppermost. While there is no mad rush, there is still the driving force of my dream to sail solo around the world. This translates into a constant onward motion in accordance with the weather and/or reasons not to.

There are always extenuating circumstances or factors that are unique to one's own situation. For me, my family and friends, my finances, my health, my age, and more importantly my father's age, all bear upon the time available for the fulfilment of this dream. The further away from home I get, the more the weight of these factors becomes. When will they mount up into a gigantic anvil to crush me into submission?

Today is my eldest daughter, Pandora's birthday. I'm sailing from Pittwater to Lake Macquarie, about 40 nautical miles. Pandora's doing a 100 km bike ride. I wonder which one of us will finish first, and which will enjoy it more. It's not one of my more pleasant days; raining and blowy with big seas. *Shanti* got knocked around a lot and I felt quite queasy. Luckily I didn't throw up but didn't eat anything more than a couple of rice cakes. These are the days that I would prefer to be living on the land and a 100 km bike ride almost seems preferable.

I don't know why I bothered motoring through all the shallow, winding passes to get to the Lake, because it wasn't greatly interesting in the pouring rain. Just on dusk, I picked up a blue (police) mooring that I shouldn't have, shut the hatch, and didn't care. It was somewhere to stop for the night. It was a rolly, toss-you-out-of-your-bunk kind of a night but at least the rain had stopped the next morning when I dropped the mooring. I was rewarded by a grand display of dolphins spinning and tail-slapping nearby.

After another uncomfortable night on a mooring in Port Stephens, I lashed out and invested $80 for a night in a marina. It was wonderful to rest fully, shower, do the laundry and shopping. Two nights would have been even better, but such luxuries were not in my very tight budget. As a self-funded retiree, the measly $20,000 left in my Superannuation fund was hopefully enough to get me around the world and back. So at 0700 the following day, I was "on the road again", heading to the twin towns of Forster/Tuncurry.

The tidal river rushes fiercely through the Tuncurry side, where there are only a handful of single-boat docks with barnacle-encrusted wooden piles against which to tie up. A preferable option was to "raft up" alongside another boat. I asked permission of the owner of a handsome American yacht, a Petersen 38. He was a little unsure at first, as he'd never heard the expression before, being relatively new to boating. I assured him "rafting-up" was common practice and completely safe, so he allowed my little limpet to nestle in against something more benign for the night.

The next day he invited me to his house for a meal, where I met his family. They saw in me the perfect opportunity for their father to gain some experience at sea and begged me to take him on the next leg of my journey to Coffs Harbour. It seemed ungrateful to refuse, but it turned out to be a mistake. The poor man suffered terribly, especially when things went wrong, as they do. A strong sou' westerly was blowing up to 30 knots and the sea was a horrible mishmash, all confused about which direction to strike from. This turbulence had the effect of churning up the sediment at the bottom of the diesel tank.

The wind died out overnight and *Yani* chugged along quite happily for several hours before she coughed and spluttered to a halt, having finally sucked up enough gunk to choke on. Naturally, this was in the most inconvenient of places under the dark shadow of nearby cliffs. "No!" I cried. "Not here; not now!" But she wasn't listening. My sleeping crew awoke with the look of someone waking from a bad dream. I explained the situation (not comforting) and pulled out the headsail in an attempt to catch what little puffs of breeze might save us, or at least buy a little time while I changed the fuel filters and bled the lines. The residual sloppy seas made it difficult, but we were soon on our way again, at least until daybreak.

Australia is very fortunate in having the VMR service (Voluntary Marine Rescue) and I was even more fortunate that there was a base a few miles further on around the next headland. A quick "Help!" call from me got an instant response, and half an hour later, a substantial vessel approached to tow us into Trial Bay. Rather than tucking us in under the protection of the headland, they hooked us up to a very large tin can in the middle of the bay, which banged relentlessly against poor *Shanti* no matter how much or how little line I put out. That night we rocked and rolled from side to side with such constancy as to seem worse than Chinese water-torture to my zombie crew.

The following morning it was suggested to try to get us up the river to a mechanic in the town. This meant crossing a sand-bar which had silted up from recent heavy rain and wind; however, I was warned that it might be some time before another high tide allowed return to the sea. This didn't appeal to me at all, so I ran my home-built "fuel polishing" system for a couple of hours. This draws the fuel from the bottom of the tank and pumps it through a separate filter back into the main tank in a continuous cycle. Afterwards, I put in the last of my primary engine filters and bled the lines again.

Following a few half-hearted attempts, *Yani* fired up and at 10 am, I radioed to say we were going to try our luck to continue to Coffs Harbour. There was not a breath of wind so we motored the whole way, full of unnecessary anxiety because the trusty little *Yani*, with her third set of new filters and cleaned fuel, didn't miss a beat.

Once on dry land, it didn't take long for my crew to find the train station; nor,

I later heard, for him to sell his beautiful, scarcely-used yacht.

What is it about synchronicity? Something very strange and inexplicable sees to it that the marina manager wanders up and down the pontoons as if he has lost something; the liveaboards ask his quandary and he says he's looking where to put a yacht that's coming in after hours. And he puts me two berths down from Bruce. The next morning Bruce spots my Melbourne registration on the stern. This would not have happened had I not backed into the berth. He is also from Melbourne and happy to meet someone from his home port. So he stops to chat and after about 15 minutes of standing in the sun, I invite him to sit in the shade of the cockpit.

We don't stop talking for the next four days, alternating mealtimes aboard my boat and his. We have lots in common, having read many of the same authors, such as Stephen Covey and Eckhart Tolle, so there is no shortage of conversation topics. He is highly intelligent and open and we have that kind of instant rapport that seems as if we had always known one other.

We take a long drive in his car, then stop to listen to a group of Celtic musicians jamming with various traditional instruments. The music is wonderfully impromptu as the airy rasp of flutes intertwines seamlessly in a pulsing embrace with guitars, fiddles, and bodhran drums.

We stroll aimlessly for a while, not needing to speak, leaning over a wooden railing to admire distant hills and valleys. It is one of those rare moments in time that somehow stops the clock. We hold hands as if it was the most natural thing in the world.

Driving back to the marina reminded me of that warm, safe feeling I once had. He stopped me in my tracks by asking "could I be interested in someone like him?" The answer was yes, but - BUT! What was I thinking? That soft, innocent, youthful soul that knows no restraint was opening like a flower within me, as if I was a carefree teenager, with no outside world shaping my possibilities.

On the second night, he kissed me, just once, a soft, gentle kiss on the lips. On the third night, we shared a warm, lingering embrace, but it didn't lead to anything. The more pragmatic side held us back, considering practicalities and obstacles. We both are of the same opinion that we don't want to hop into bed with someone unless there is a longer-term relationship in it. Could there be? This is the question that sets my head once again spinning. It is not something I was expecting or prepared for. Of course, there are a great many complications, all of them made by ourselves in deference to the more pragmatic mindset of the not-so-young.

At 4 am, in the predawn heavy darkness, I sailed away from Coffs. Not far away, just another 55 miles up the coast. I needed some distance and quiet time to think this through. The past four days had been so intense. It was a red-flagged danger zone that we were sliding into with "eyes wide closed". As I told him, he had swept me off my feet. It had been over three years since I felt the feelings he was stirring up. And I was afraid, the hurt of the past break-up still not fully healed. Could he be the band-aid I so desperately needed? It would be such an easy warmth to wrap myself in. I must be crazy to choose the lonely, endless sea instead. So, time out to think.

> *"You may think that you need more time to understand the past or become free of it, in other words, that the future will eventually free you of the past. This is a delusion. Only the present can free you of the past. More time cannot free you of time."* – Eckhart Tolle, "Practising the Power of Now".

What am I doing? It seems a cop-out to stop after only two months, having met a man, (as per prediction). So one question to ask myself, is do I want a life partner or do I want to sail around the world alone? These mutually exclusive alternatives bang from side to side inside me like a wasp in a jar.

Why does it have to be so hard? Why do I set myself up to be so tested? Have I created this conundrum myself, sliding into murky waters when I could be sailing freely in the certitude of self-determined crystal clarity? Perhaps this deeper understanding of who I am and what I want will be a gift of the sea, yet to be revealed to me. I sit at the navigation desk, soft-leaded charting pencil in hand, drawing up columns of existing known qualities and propensities, as if that might help.

I love having time to myself. (Irrelevant). I also have a need to love and be loved. (Irrelevant). Bruce made it clear he was not interested in a long-distance relationship, and there's no telling how long I will be gone. For me to stop and wait for him is about as smart as putting a fox down a rabbit hole. Then what? We buddy boat around the world—or we sell both boats and buy one together? Been there, done that. (All irrelevant; or at least peripheral to the immediate dilemma).

As I set sail again, I received a text message: "Go *Shanti*!" as if everyone is watching my tracks, which they are, and urging me onward; because this is my dream and I made the error of judgement to tell everyone. It made me feel sick to the stomach.

When men leave their family and friends to go to war or to sea, it is usually for a finite time and a set purpose, which those left behind can understand. But to just wander off aimlessly is harder to grasp. People ask "when will you be back?" How can I say "never?" Of course, I know this is a temporary reaction to past hurts.

For now, I feel as if I could sit here in this wondrously quiet anchorage where no-one knows me, forever. It is calm and sheltered, with time to write, to think, to meditate, to play music. I am in heaven. Then comes the urge to move on.

That's OK too. This natural rhythm is a rare treasure that the hustle and bustle of civilisation obscure. The gentler pace is soothing. It allows time to tune in to the wonders of creation that spin in the quiet spaces between form and void, time to reconnect the scattered shards of my inner self.

What is my true self? This is. This quiet me, devoid of reflection or pretence, unapologetic, without the weight of various identities, without the need to please or appease. I have decided to be myself. Not to pretend anymore. If people are to like me it must be as I am. I am always afraid that they won't like me. So I put on an act to create a more likeable self, which I don't even know if it is or isn't more likeable, but I know I will get caught out and undone. That fear is slowly shrinking. I know now I can be alone, even though at times an old familiar gnawing creeps back in with a sense of lack.

So this is where things stand right now:

There are two different ways of sailing—for the joy of it and for the destinations. They are not mutually exclusive. Certain things dictate when to move on, the weather being the first. Wind and tide govern the right time for crossing in and out of barred harbours. It is possible to be locked in for weeks waiting for favourable, safe conditions to get going again. Then there is the need to stop near facilities to reprovision, put on more fuel and water and perhaps even have a shower.

It is highly likely that this year will be spent cruising up to the Whitsundays and possibly even back down again. That should give me plenty of time to get to know my boat, my capabilities and to iron out the kinks. It should also give people time to cool their close watch on my "progress". I would be just as happy to "park" *Shanti* in Mackay rather than South Africa while I fly back home for Christmas.

It's interesting the way in which some people regard the actuality of a circumnavigation as if pressing on regardless was the only thing that counts. If a couple set out to sail around the world, then stop for 12 years in Indonesia, are they still circumnavigating? Perhaps it can only be determined at its closure, when finally crossing the outward track. There are many different ways of doing it. Since this is my first attempt, I have no idea how it will unfold for me, other than to be sure it won't take twenty years. I don't have that much time.

But I can see that pausing is necessary to draw breath, to clean up, work on the boat, write. A few years spent moving on, moving on, without any deeper relationship with another person, could lead to a decidedly unbalanced psyche. I like to care and be cared for. This is a basic human need. A person not only needs their story to be heard but by someone who cares. But how can I squeeze such a person into this solitary existence? The two needs are basically incompatible. This adds to the time pressures I already feel. I'm willing to make sacrifices, but not forever.

I have no idea where this dream of sailing around the world alone came from. Most long-distance voyagers cruise in couples. It is by far the most practical arrangement, providing reliable crew and company. I don't think of myself as a single-hander, even though I have chosen to sail alone. A true single-hander (generally male) is a rare breed—someone who would choose to live alone on sea or land, who is more of a hermit, preferring his own company to that of others. Others irritate and drain him. He is not interested in their lives or stories; he actively avoids them.

Most of the other solo sailors I met were not like this. They enjoyed mixing with people and often had others come and sail with them. They might retreat for a while, but then emerge like a hungry hibernator in search of sustenance. I can definitely relate to that need.

On Saturday, May 28, I parked *Shanti* in the marina at Tin Can Bay and flew back to Melbourne to see family and friends and help celebrate my grandson, Felix's 2nd birthday. From there I flew back to Coffs Harbour to help Bruce sail his boat up the coast to Southport, something I had earlier agreed to do.

It was raining heavily when I arrived. One of those nasty East Coast Lows was forming and it quickly developed into the most violent storm. It was like stepping into a war zone. Not long after getting on board Bruce's boat, the police closed off access to the Marina. My timing dropped me right in the thick of it, with no way out.

Huge waves were pounding the northern breakwater, crashing up against it with such fury, as if determined to smash through the man-made barrier. Rearing up and over, they were surging even higher than the tall lamp-posts on top of the wall. Massive concrete blocks were being picked up by the tempest, hurled over the wall like missiles, smashing the ramps and closing off any access to or from the docks. Like it or not, we were trapped. Worse still, knowing that if one of those airborne boulders hit us, we were gone.

The wind was shrieking like a tormented animal, tuning its scream through every stretch of wire. It was almost impossible to stand upright against it. The usually protected waters within the marina were turbulent, surging up and down as each wave flooded in, jerking and snapping dock-lines. A nearby trimaran was impaled on the shards of jagged dock and quickly smashed to pieces. The few owners who stayed aboard their boats were hard-pressed trying to protect others, righting pontoons and tying the dock together. Only the tall piles, driven deep into the seabed, provided some secure points to lash boats and dock to.

It was tough work, everyone bringing all the ropes they could, each ignoring their own safety. The semi-submerged pontoons were jutting out like icebergs, bucking and tugging, breaking free, and taking power posts down with them. As they sank the shore-power leads that were still connected to boats had to be cut.

One man received a nasty shock, fortunately not fatal. Another man jumped from his boat and collapsed on the dock, where he lay in the rain for a long time before a dinghy could transport him to an ambulance. We brought blankets and coats to protect him until help arrived, unsure if he'd had a heart attack or what. His lips were blue, his body quivering like a frightened animal.

For three more days and nights, the storm continued to rage. From the shelter of a tarpaulin over the cockpit, I watched Bruce balancing on the undulating concrete pontoon, struggling to save the small boat next door from sinking. He was soaked through to the skin, feeling wretched, angry at the marina, furious to see the inadequate fittings, the old rusty bolts giving way, upset that I was caught up in this disaster, worried for our lives. His temper was short, worsened by having had no sleep at all for days, his body wrung out like a dishrag. It was certainly not a time for a new romance to bloom. Down below in the main saloon, we stripped our sopping wet clothes off in front of one another without a thought of modesty. Some things override that concern. It was just good to get dry and warm and perhaps later, close our eyes and get some sleep.

Even after the storm had abated, high seas continued to pound the breakwater for several more days, wreaking further havoc. Most of the remaining pontoons broke loose and had to be towed out of harm's way by dinghy. The heaving central walkways sheered into angular tangents, making going to check on the neighbours' boats like walking on a floating log. One brave owner dived underneath the concrete pontoons, passing ropes from one side to the other to tie them back to some semblance of horizontal again. At least the rain was easing.

The only way to get off the marina was by dinghy, which we didn't have. A generous volunteer spent his days and nights ferrying people ashore and back. It was like a parade of shell-shocked boat-people, displaced, disinherited, disheartened. Any support from the marina staff was notably lacking. Even food donations didn't make it out to those stranded on their boats. Tempers flared as documents to indemnify the marina were passed around.

Perhaps those worst off were the local liveaboards who had made Coffs their home and had nowhere else to go. The situation was further exacerbated by the lack of a slipway to haul out damaged boats. A cruising couple from South Australia had only just pulled in to Coffs a few nights earlier, expecting a five-star International Marina. They too were angered by the state of disrepair that rendered the place "a disaster waiting to happen"—one that had happened before and would happen again if allowed. Their lifelong cruising dreams were dampened by unknown damage to their beautifully restored Swanson 36 yacht. At least we were intact and free to go.

A week later the 6-metre swell had subsided and the wind dropped enough for us to leave Coffs Harbour. We were both very glad to be going. Neighbours called by, still holding onto enough humour to pass some wise-cracks about my poor taste in men. Bruce countered this with the usual banter that Australians use to defuse stress, something that I struggle to understand. I smile in agreement, as if I have a clue, while suppressing an inner cringe. I just want to get back to *Shanti*.

It was a warm and clear evening when we dropped anchor in "Bum's Bay", a crowded anchorage on one side of the busy Broadwater. Bruce was unnerved by the stellar skyscrapers, scattering confusing background lights amidst the channel markers. It was familiar territory for me, having lived here with my previous partner on a Southport Yacht Club mooring several years before. Revisiting now as a single woman jiggled my insides in an equally confusing mix of light and dark.

I stayed on board long enough to catch up with a few of my old friends in the area while Bruce caught the bus back to Coffs for his car. After that, he drove me the 300 miles back to *Shanti* in Tin Can Bay, where he helped me service all of the winches which had practically seized. This was a job that had fallen off my job-list before leaving Melbourne. I greatly appreciated his help and his company, but it was clear that we were not suited for anything more than friendship. He himself concluded that he was too brusque while I was too soft. Still, there was that familiar void when he left and I missed him badly. I guess it's only natural, especially after having gone through the traumatic experience together at Coffs.

One of his valuable contributions to my voyage was to introduce me to the blog of his hero, Webb Chiles, a 73-year old sailor with several circumnavigations under his keel. He is currently finishing his sixth in an ultralight Moore 24. His tracks go from Opua in New Zealand to Bundaberg. From there he went outside the Great Barrier Reef to Cairns. This section was done non-stop over 7 days. He then day-sailed from Cairns to Cape York and then non-stop across the top of the Gulf of Carpentaria to Darwin, before preparing to cross the Indian Ocean.

This information, complete with Webb's waypoints gave me one last shot at getting to Darwin before the end of August, which is the latest I can be there to avoid cyclone season. To date, I have wandered slowly up the east coast from Melbourne, taking my time and all but missed my opportunity. Continuing day-hopping up through the Whitsundays would be pleasant enough but that would close the door on this year's attempt to get across to South Africa—which for some strange reason, I am still keen to do.

From Tin Can Bay, I will continue up the inside of Fraser Island through the Great Sandy Straits to Bundaberg, and from there, make the call whether to go for it non-stop outside the reef. It is both an exciting and scary proposition. I think a large part of my prevarications has been around facing my fears of making a longer passage by myself, especially concerning sleep management. But sooner or later that has to be faced if I am to pursue this dream of sailing solo around the world.

Chapter 4

Turning Back

Apart from providing a secure place to leave one's boat for a while, an added bonus is the interesting people one meets in marinas. In Tin Can Bay I encountered a 68-year-old single-hander named "Solo Bob", a self-professed recluse who couldn't stop talking. This is not uncommon with single-handers for whom it is as if they have all these pent-up words waiting to escape.

Solo Bob's tales were long-winded and dramatic, re-enacted with all the gusto of the original event. The longest and most spine-chilling story was of a time, some 30 years earlier, when he had a head-on collision with a coastal cargo ship. He recollected:

> *"It was night time when I first saw it—a small black shape in front of me with its two white lights lined up. It seemed to be a good way off so I went down to check for shipping lanes."* (Perhaps an odd first move I thought).
>
> *"I never knew ships could travel at over 25 knots, like overgrown speed boats. In actual fact, doing such a speed, the ship was only 2 minutes away.*
>
> *When I came back up on deck, all I could see was a massive black cliff-face looming above me. I thought I could see white water behind it.*
>
> *I didn't know what to do. In total panic, I grabbed the helm and turned it one way, but it was directly into the wind. The boat stalled and I tried turning it the other way, but it was too late. Nothing I could have done would have avoided collision.*
>
> *I never thought I was facing death, even though it was almost a certainty. My thoughts were more of curiosity, wondering what's going to happen now.*
>
> *I have no memory of what did happen after the explosive thunder of the crash.*
>
> *In hindsight, I could piece some things together. I was gripping the tiller with an iron grip. Next moment I was inside the cabin. The companionway entrance was very small*

and I usually entered backwards. I must have been thrown through it as the (steel) yacht buckled in half and slid up the square bow of the ship. They suck you in you know; they don't spit you away.

As the yacht was sucked along the side of the ship it filled with water. I must have taken a deep breath just before I found myself underwater, not knowing which way was up. Eventually, I came to a pocket of air in the cabin and drew breath. It all must have only taken a few seconds, but it seemed an eternity. I half expected to be smashed up by the ship's props but somehow escaped that.

Watching its stern recede into the darkness I was astounded by its obliviousness. Surely there would be lights and crew or some slowing or a rescue attempt? But it just continued on its way with no awareness of the collision at all. Of course, it was far from over for me.

I managed to get into my inflatable dinghy before the yacht sank. Thinking I was only about a mile offshore, I was in fact about 8 miles, with wind and current against me.

I rowed for 18 hours. That's beyond Olympic athletes you know. Every so often I would stop in absolute exhaustion, then ask myself "Bob, do you want to live or die?" and straight away I'd start rowing again.

It was winter and I knew about hypothermia. All feeling had gone from the lower part of my body.

Eventually, I closed the shoreline but saw there were 3 big surf breaks. I knew I wouldn't survive long if tipped out into the water. I managed to surf in on the first two, then got tipped out. Luckily a local fisherman had seen me and came to my aid. He gave me dry clothes but I was shaking so much I couldn't put them on, so he had to dress me. Then I was taken to hospital.

My first thought after I'd recovered was 'now I need to get another boat'. Straight back on the horse. I never had any nightmares about it.

They tried to trace the ship that hit me but in those days foreign ships didn't have to report their position in Australian waters. That has since been changed because of what happened to me.

TV crews came and interviewed me and even flew me over the scene of the accident but there was nothing to see. One good thing they possibly influenced was getting the insurance claim paid out on only a cover note, no questions asked. They reckoned I must be the luckiest man alive that day."

He told me that an unexpected legacy of this experience was to become clairvoyant, being able to see his father's undiagnosed illness and other future events. Such stories intrigue me and I generally have a willing suspension of disbelief, but it's probably better to be non-judgemental either way. Perhaps it happened; perhaps not. It doesn't really matter. But his story was one of overcoming the most testing ordeal, which inspired me to push harder against my own resistance.

The time to leave Tin Can Bay finally came. I was beginning to almost regard it as home. It is a place of unspoilt beauty and tranquillity. I was especially enjoying early morning walks along the waterfront, the spectacular sunrises and sunsets from the best ringside seats of *Shanti's* cockpit. There was an almost jellified torpor around that could creep up on one unawares, perhaps spread by the ubiquitous caravan parks on every corner. Such an easy place to sit easy. Heading back out to sea was the perfect remedy.

And what a brilliant welcome back the Great Sandy Straits gave me. It was an unexpected thrill to be able to sail most of the way through the 40 or so nautical miles that I expected to have to motor. Fortunately, a fairly steady 10-15 knot SW was on the beam (side) or from behind. Working the flood and ebb tides gave speeds of 6-7 knots over ground. This could have been very nerve-wracking, flying with committed abandon through the shallow spots.

What boosted my confidence was tailing "Solo Bob" who had been through here 8 times before. If his Swanson 32 touched bottom, I had at least 30 seconds warning before meeting a similar sticky halt. Also, both C-maps and Navionics electronic charts were inaccurate in places, showing us sailing over the land. Where local knowledge came in really handy was crossing the shallows to the anchorage at Big Woody Island.

After dropping the pick and Bob rowing over for an "arrival survival" drink we were joined by Claus from the catamaran anchored nearby. A larger than life, thick accented Swede he entertained us into the twilight with his wry humour. Another verbose single-hander, whose excuse was that these fleeting meetings demand tightly-packed condensed histories. It seems as if sharing histories is de rigueur. I am becoming more of a Cheshire cat listener, thoroughly enjoying all these "talking books" but glad of my own space after.

Continuing on the next day through the turbulent Hervey Bay, the only near mishap was when I went up the bow to check the foot of the furling headsail which has been chafing on the pulpit. I noticed the split ring was missing from the upper lifeline and the barrel was close to falling out. Had this gone it could have meant a WOB (Woman Over Board) disaster. I pulled the boat apart down below looking for spares, broke a nail trying to get the tight split ring through the tiny barrel hole (now there's a girl thing) and then dropped it overboard with a few rare expletives (boy thing?) All sorted out, but a timely reminder to do regular checks of EVERYTHING.

I decided to sail inside the Great Barrier Reef rather than do the 6 or 7 days non-stop to Cairns. There were a few reasons for this, the main one being problems with the solar panels or the alternator. Right from the start, I have suspected them of not charging properly, never seeing more than a few amps going in even when the batteries were low. Hence, I have seldom run the fridge. It's unfortunate that I prefer white wine to red but a good thing that cold beer is not a necessity of life. Sadly, fresh veggies are.

I came close to buying a new alternator at a few ports along the way but fortunately didn't. It turned out there was nothing wrong with this one. It just needed 'exciting'. Apparently, there is this extra little exciter wire that had never been connected, without which the alternator can't get turned on. Hmmm... So it was a relatively simple and (for once) inexpensive fix. White wine and lettuce now chilling nicely!

I have often contemplated what necessities bring a sailor into port. So far, I have listed water, fuel, provisions, repairs, accidents, illness, and loneliness. Hot showers and laundromats are nice but not essential. Power is only a temporary top-up, which was a priority for my hungry batteries. Not now hopefully.

My good friend from SYC, Ron, was flying into Mackay for a few days' cruising the Whitsundays. Other friends, Ray and Di, on *All That Jazz* were already waiting in the marina, just in case I didn't make it. It was good practice for me to have to push on every day regardless of weather or tiredness. I have to get used to this if I am to make it to Darwin this season. From Gladstone, it was a few days of boisterous sailing, mostly with the wind dead behind and lumpy seas (not uncommon up here). The wind was gusting up to 28 knots and I found it necessary to hand steer down the rollers. Boat speed at times was 7 - 8 knots but speed over ground was a lot less with tide against me. The tides up here are phenomenal—up to 6 metres.

None of the anchorages was particularly comfortable, the worst being at Hunter Island in the Duke group. It was perfectly still when I arrived and I was looking forward to a good night's sleep. Just after midnight, an unusual sound woke me, (it's always an unusual sound that seeps through even the most tired skipper's dreams)—rather like a fast-flowing torrent—which is just what it was! Turning on the instruments I saw the depth below keel had gone from 3 metres to 9 and the boat speed was showing over 2 knots through the water. I went up to the bow to check the anchor rope and found it as taut as a steel bar, straining back under the boat. Worrying that it could pluck the anchor out, I let out a few more metres of rope.

I only have 35 metres of chain plus another 50 metres of nylon rope, which I haven't needed to use up to now. A ratio of 4:1 is recommended, so that in 10 metres of water there should be at least 40 metres of rode (chain and rope) out, depending of course on the wind, of which there was none. That changed half an hour later when 20 knots produced a rapid assault of breaking white caps hitting the hull broadside. Not a good angle for an anchor to stay set.

At times like this my mind goes shooting off into "what-ifs" and I start thinking of all possible disastrous outcomes, so sleep is impossible. I inwardly grumble about being alone with no-one else to share the watches and the stress and the decisions. But then I remind myself that this is my choice, so I had best just shut up and deal with it. I am learning that one of the most important things for me to do is to relax. Often easier said than done.

There was more to deal with at day-break when I found the rope jammed in the anchor winch gypsy, which is supposed to deal with both chain and rope. It took a few goes, with short bursts of the engine in forward gear, running from cockpit to bow and back again, tying a rolling hitch on the line to take the strain, free the jam, and get it all running again. I have found that a wonderful sense of elation follows these low points and I sailed away on a bubble of euphoria, my soul singing, YES!

Pulling into any marina berth alone is always stressful so I was glad that Ray was there to take my lines, along with a tall, long-haired stranger, whose bohemian looks caught my eye. Later I spotted him with his dinghy on the dock, bolting beach wheels on the transom. I stopped to chat a while until Ron came and chivvied me away.

It was a very welcome reprieve doing only short day-sails with Ron, in company with *All That Jazz*, enjoying "Sundowners" in some of the top spots of the Whitsundays. Some bad weather was forecast, so Ron opted to fly home from Hamilton Island rather than sit it out for the next few days. For me, it was another opportunity to see how *Shanti* behaves in the rough stuff, so I continued on my way north. I tucked into the top of the Whitsundays in Butterfly Bay, Hook Island, a tranquil spot with public moorings to protect the fringing reef. *All That Jazz* joined me later.

Di is a trained Tarot card reader and that night she offered to do a brief reading for me. I don't lay a lot of store in such things but went along with it. My question naturally centred on the circumnavigation and we were both surprised by the first card drawn—the "Lover". Di went on to elaborate that this person was someone whom I had already met, that he was "the one", a completely faithful man who would wait for me while I was gone, and who would give me a lot of help. I couldn't think for the life of me who it could be. After a few minutes of playing along, I forgot all about it. A lover in my life was the last thing I needed at this stage of the game.

Ron was wise not to join me on this leg. The Bureau of Meteorology website that I normally find reliable let me down. Strong winds, gales, storms, rain (all depicted in vivid red on "Met Eye") were forecast for most of the week. Only Thursday looked like a narrow window of opportunity to squeeze through. The original plan was to sail from Hook Island to an anchorage called Nellie Bay, just before the Gloucester Passage. Then either sit it out there or press on to Bowen, then a couple of nights on the two capes, Cape Upstart and Cape Bowling Green. However, on studying the predicted wind strength and angles it looked like none of these stops would provide good shelter.

The first day's sail from Hook Island was magnificent—a steady 15-knot breeze, clear blue skies, and sunshine, with full main and headsail set, which I boldly carried right through the shallows of Gloucester Passage. I'm getting used to seeing very low figures on the depth sounder. The day was too lovely to stop early so I continued to Queens Bay, an anchorage just past Bowen. The next day's forecast was for winds to abate to 10 – 15 knots before coming back with a vengeance on Friday, so I decided to push on through the night to Townsville.

For most of the day, I carried reduced mainsail and sometimes a full headsail. Having the wind dead behind made that flog, so it got furled in and let out again several times as the wind swung more to the South. I kept expecting it to drop out—but at around 1600 it was gusting up over 30 knots. An accidental gybe (luckily I had a preventer on) encouraged me to drop the main altogether and just set a small amount of headsail. The waves were an annoying washing machine cross pattern and mounting. As it started to bucket down with rain the wind gusted to near 40 knots. Not predicted!!

Winter days are short and it gets dark early, more so it seems in gloomy weather. The combination of complete blackness, strong winds, driving rain (the coldest night on record for these parts), and big confused seas had me shivering. Wise call Ron, not to come along! I was thinking I should have stayed with Ray and Di at Hook Island where it was warm and peaceful and so sheltered that they were able to raft up alongside *Shanti* for the night and share the same mooring. However, this was an opportunity (I kept telling myself) to test boat and captain.

Shanti handled it beautifully, probably much better than the captain did, who, as we all know, is the weakest link in the equation. It was quite a remarkable achievement that I managed to withstand the pounding, bucking, jarring, jerking motion—even down below—without getting seasick. I'm definitely getting better as more miles pass under the keel. In the dark of night, I can't see the size of the rollers that whack into the hull, but I can sure feel their impact as the boat gets stopped in her tracks and slewed off sideways.

Not every wave is a Goliath—perhaps every tenth—but those that crash like hitting a brick wall send torrents cascading over the entire boat and I wonder if the windows will hold and how much water is coming in through unseen leaks. The boat slews over on her side, lockers pop open and everything not tied down becomes a missile. Even the onions from the bottom of the hanging net find their way out. Every hard-edged surface wants to colour in my bruises.

It was one of those endless nights, when my mantra, "this too will pass" was wearing thin. There were moments when I questioned if we would make it through the night, but I just had to keep us on track, avoiding all obstacles, until one of us gave up. How hard this single-handing can be! There are times when wind and tide conspire to slow down progress to almost nothing and it seems like we'll never get to that safe haven. I wrote in my log: "At every step of the way it seems I am tested, questioning why? Why am I doing this?" Tiredness sapped my enthusiasm, like water from a leaking barrel.

At 0200 the lights of an anchored fishing trawler, which I had picked up earlier on AIS, guided me to a shallow patch under the lee of Cape Cleveland, about 10 miles from Townsville harbour. The swell was still very active and the wind howling but I managed to drop anchor and close my eyes for a few hours. At 0600 I got up and punched into waves, wind, tide, and rain for the final leg into Breakwater Marina in Townsville, where I had some old friends to see.

A day later I left the refuge of that calm pitstop, having rushed around like a mad thing doing all those essential chores. I woke at 0300, had plenty of time for engine checks, shower, breakfast, etc. to be ready to leave the marina at first light and continue on another 43 nautical miles to Pioneer Bay, Orpheus Island. In hindsight, it was foolish, as I was still tired from the rough passage up the coast, and it would have been far more sensible to rest for another couple of days.

My spirits were low. It upset me to be leaving the friends whose company I had all-too-briefly enjoyed, declining other invitations and failing to catch up with everyone. This compounded the loneliness I was already suffering, missing my family and other friends left behind. Such emotions gain easy ingress to a weary heart. No, not just a weary heart, but a weary body too. In fact, every cell and atom and molecule were on the verge of falling into the black hole left by a stellar implosion. When I am tired, I make mistakes and I can't afford to make mistakes on my own. At one point, an accidental gybe nearly took me overboard and only a brutal collision of my thigh against the unyielding metal of the winch stopped me.

Heavy rain and a strong NE wind woke me the next morning. I checked the forecast and found it had changed overnight, with much more north in it. That put paid to my plan to sail to the anchorage at the top of Hinchinbrook. An alternative option was to head over to Lucinda to find shelter in the inside passage up through the Hinchinbrook Channel. This is said to be the most scenic, calm waterway on the east coast, offering good cyclone protection in mangrove creeks. The southern entrance has a shoal bar that needs a rising tide to cross. High tide was at 0800 so I set off early to sail the 10 miles in a couple of hours.

The strong northerly wind and waves knocked me about, at one stage putting the cabin windows underwater. This was too much! With hardly a second thought I turned and ran with it. Where to? Back to Townsville seemed appealing, where I could rest up for a few days. This was a very low moment for me. I hate turning around. As I ran south it felt all wrong. For so long I had been heading north that I was making wrong course corrections on the autopilot. I checked the forecast again and found strong SE winds returning further down the coast. Oh no! I really didn't want to be bashing head-on into that, so turned *Shanti* back round to the north and sailed back to Orpheus Island again. Six hours of sailing this morning to be right back where I started. Very demoralizing! I slept for an hour and then ate something, which made me feel a bit better. I can see that this hard push north, moving on every day, takes its toll on me.

Hinchinbrook Channel. July 20.
It's not really surprising, why I'm dragging my heels at this particular point in time. A couple of days rest and more information-gathering helped put things in perspective. It has been rather a relentless push to attain the physical and psychological landmark of Cairns. This is where the solo circumnavigator, Webb Chiles, re-entered the Great Barrier Reef. Sailing outside the reef (which I did consider doing) took him only 6 days non-stop from Bundaberg. For me, going through some of the islands of the Whitsundays, it has taken over twice as long and I am still another 3 or 4 days away from Cairns. I am increasingly aware of the time pressure to be out of Darwin by the end of August at the latest.

I sat down at the navigation station for a few hours yesterday and plotted courses and waypoints to Darwin. It took Webb 14 days, sailing almost every day to reach Cape York. From there he sailed 7 days and nights non-stop to Darwin, which I would also need to do. Cairns is a line of demarcation for other reasons.

Reading Alan Lucas', *"Cruising the Coral Coast"*, he writes about the weather patterns that really do make it a point of no-return:

> *"Balancing probabilities against uncertainties, it can be said that the SE Trade Wind will prevail on this part of the coast for all of winter, much of summer and may or may not give way to northerlies at other times."* Which translates into shutting the door behind you. Facilities further north get scarcer and there is a sense of entering "no-man's land" where one must be totally self-reliant. Step across that line and one is committed to going on.

Oh dear. Am I ready for it? It's time to sit and take stock of my situation, to re-evaluate if this goal is still relevant. The risks of continuing on alone include fatigue, mistakes, discomfort, hardship, possible injury and death. Of course, I dismiss all of these out of hand the moment I start to feel refreshed, but it is important to acknowledge them and to make a rational, rather than emotional or dogmatic decision. It's okay to be dogmatic, but not "pigmatic". A certain amount of pig-headedness must accompany any extreme endeavour, simply to stick with it, but it's also important to maintain some sense of balance. Flexibility has always been important to me. This is where the two sides of oneself conflict, bringing confusion and what they call "analysis paralysis".

Sometimes, it is as if moves are simply made for us, as if guided by some overarching hand of destiny. Sitting quietly by myself in the calm anchorage amongst the mangroves of Hinchinbrook Channel, I picked up my phone and sent a text message to my friend Colin, who lives in Townsville, asking him if he would have time to install a new fridge for me. He instantly replied, "it would be a pleasure". Then I rang the Yacht Club and asked if they had room for me for a couple of weeks, which they did. The SE wind is abating this weekend so I shall head back south and take the time to finish these extra jobs, like the fridge, the HF radio and Pactor modem, the dangerously jamming reef lines.

So just like that, I am back to where I was a few months back, realizing that Darwin, and the world, will have to wait. This decision, which I have been bucking, sits easily with me now.

This is the first morning I have awoken without the pressure to move on. Twelve hours of blissful oblivion vindicated yesterday's decision. I woke up at 0530, as I have become accustomed to, by the sound of someone calling out "Hoy!" (the modern version of "Ahoy there!"). I leapt out of my bunk thinking perhaps *Shanti* had dragged closer to the crocodile-infested mangroves, grabbed the torch (not working), and went out on deck in the rain. (Yes, it's still raining). Not a soul in sight. I must have dreamt it. I slid back into my warm bunk and fell into a really deep stupor of total exhaustion for another 3 hours. Oh, guilty joy!

What will I do with this free day? Perhaps use some of that bucket full of rainwater to have a sweet shower. Hopefully, the midges won't devour me.

All squeaky clean after my first hot shower on board *Shanti*. Thanks to my friend Bruce for the great idea of using a tall rubbish bin and a submersible pump. I bought this rechargeable battery-powered pump from Aldi in Melbourne and just pulled it out today. I love it! It takes surprisingly little water to create a hot shower (all fresh rainwater so there is an abundance of it). Mopping up the head (toilet/shower area) afterwards is the longer part of the process, but it needed a good clean anyway. All I need is a shower curtain and drainable sump in the bilge. Such are the luxuries we appreciate in life aboard a small vessel.

Orpheus Island (again).

Having stayed put these last few days, through rain, mist, sunshine, and moonlight, I have had a delightful taster of the magnificence of Hinchinbrook in all of its moods. The only word that comes to mind is 'Majestic'! The dark peaks rising mysteriously through the mist are draped in silence—a quietude I listen to with my entire being. It's a rare privilege being alone here, immersed in an ancient timelessness.

When I lifted the anchor early the next morning, a thick fog made navigation blind. Following the breadcrumb trail I had left coming in, I hoped no-one else was silly enough to be out. The AIS alarm made my heart jump until I saw the impressive black schooner, *South Passage* emerging through the mist like an old-time pirate ship. The young deck-hands all cheered and waved as they passed close by. It's wonderful to see young people learning the ropes on these tall ships.

Shortly after lining myself up on the leads to avoid the shallowest waters of the channel, *Yani,* my faithful Yanmar engine stopped running. I immediately pulled the headsail out (in only 2 knots of breeze from behind) and hoped I could work my magic quickly to avoid running aground. OK, I thought, it hasn't happened for a while, but I know what to do—just bleed it to get the air out. *Wrong!* This time that didn't work. No fuel was spitting out of any of the usual bleed holes, making me wonder if the lift pump had failed. I opened the secondary fuel filter and found it empty, so topped it up with fresh diesel from my jerry can. Still no good. Thinking it may be a blockage rather than air in the system, I changed the primary fuel filter. This time when I cranked the engine to bleed it, fuel spat out—success!

Luckily we were still on track, drifting slowly over less than 1 metre of water below the keel, but still afloat. What a relief to get motoring again. Once out of the shallow channel, I pulled up the mainsail and lifted into shimmeringly perfect flat-water sailing. The sun was shining and *Shanti* was skimming lightly over what could have been a good day on Port Phillip Bay in Melbourne, without a speed-bump in sight.

Beating into 7 or 8 knots of head-wind in calm waters is a far cry from running with it behind when the "iron spinnaker" is the common recourse. This was fun! Especially so with no great time pressure. It didn't bother me to be only making 4 knots and having to tack back and forth, nor that it took all afternoon to do 10 miles. It was the best sail I have had since leaving Melbourne. They say that the average is one good sail out of every ten. Well so much for statistics.

Back on a public mooring in Little Pioneer Bay on Orpheus Island again, the fuel polishing system is now pumping out the contents of my tank, passing it through a new filter and back into the tank. Hopefully, it will get me back to Townsville tomorrow when time and distance will once again necessitate burning diesel.

I have heard that long-distance voyaging is character building.

> *"Buddha said building character is like making bread—you have to mix it little by little, step by step, and moderate temperature is needed. You know exactly what you need. If you get too excited you will forget how much temperature is good for you and you will lose your own way."* - Shunryu Suzuki

Chapter 5

Better Prepared

Back to the old conundrum, how do you eat an elephant? Answer: one bite at a time.

So here I am in Townsville, chomping away at that old elephant again. This is, after all, a "shake-down" cruise to iron out the glitches and prepare *Shanti* for all that will ever be asked of her, including living aboard in relative comfort. Hence, I'm continuing with tasks that could/should have been done before leaving Melbourne, only here in warmer climes. (Remember that old saying: "cruising is doing boat jobs in exotic locations").

I'm very fortunate to have my old friend from SYC, Colin, here. He's extremely competent in all things electrical (many owners refuse to let anyone else touch their boat) and despite being in high demand, he's willing to squeeze me in between jobs. It was time to bite the bullet on that old, inefficient fridge that many an expert had previously looked at and declared an "anchor". It's fantastic to now be able to cool the ice-box down to around 3 degrees without gobbling up all my battery power.

Other jobs included checking out the misbehaving HF radio which would receive but not transmit. Later, we set up a time to test it out. For some bizarre reason, the moment I pressed the transmit (talk) button, a loud rumbling sound alerted me to the fact that the anchor winch was turning all by itself—causing a potentially disastrous ejection of chain, clanking, coiling, bundling and falling over the deck like a mechanical snake. Luckily the anchor was still tied on so didn't go overboard, but this should not be happening. It took me a while to work out that the winch remote control was on the same frequency as the radio—definitely not something you want happening at sea. I made a note to remember to always switch off the winch circuit breaker to avoid this.

A boat is a microcosm of stand-alone systems—mechanical, electrical, mathematical, navigational, meteorological, aeronautical, and many other mysterious wonders, ending with the suffix "cal"—the running of which involves the mastering of an array of diverse skills before even thinking about the actual sailing. Therein lies its unique challenge and interest, quite unlike anything else. It can be frustrating and rewarding, elating and deflating, a micro roller-coaster of highs and lows, and above all else, lessons in patience. But life is for learning and where else are so many lessons piled up each day, after finishing school?

Shag Islet Cruising Yacht Club Rendezvous.
Everyone who joins this virtual yacht club automatically becomes a Vice Commodore of some self-appointed location, in my case, my childhood home of Bucklands Beach, Auckland—though I'm not sure that the prestigious BBYC that hosted the Louis Vuitton America's Cup series would acknowledge me as their new 2IC. Notwithstanding, the SICYC exists primarily to increase awareness of Prostate Cancer. Having personally known of at least 5 friends and family members with this disease, it seemed like a worthwhile cause to support.

The anchorage was packed. Ray and Di were here on *All That Jazz*, as were Jeff and Leigh, with son and friends on their new catamaran, *Tru Blu*. On the beach, the pirate costume party was in full swing, with many a swashbuckling Blackbeard, stuffed parrots on shoulders, buxom damsels with overflowing breasts pushed up above constricted bodices, golden earrings, tattoos, blacked-out teeth, and three-cornered hats, all mingling amidst the soft sand and hard liquor. Giant speakers boomed out live bands playing Jimmy Buffett style tunes. I was standing next to Ray and Di, aware of the great mass of bodies in front of us, some gyrating, some in small groups attempting conversations over the music.

"I don't know anyone here," I almost shouted, scanning the crowd.

"Yes you do," Ray answered. "There, that tall guy with the long blonde hair."

I looked in the direction he was pointing and recognised the handsome yachty who had helped take my lines at Mackay Marina.

"In you go!"

"No, he's talking to friends. I don't want to interrupt."

"Don't be silly! Shoulders back, chest out," Ray encouraged with a friendly shove.

I practically fell forward, to be rescued by a warm arm and unexpected recognition, "Hello, aren't you supposed to be in Darwin?"

How on earth did he remember that? It was certainly a more effective opening line than many I've heard. One of his friends, who had obviously been tilting the rum bottle heartily all day, wrapped his arm around my shoulders and slurred his recommendation, "Luke's a good bloke. Just do us a favour and let him down gently, will you? We had to pick up the pieces after the last one."

Wow! I thought. We've only just met and we're already at the break-up.

A gorgeous woman, seemingly poured into full-blown pirate wench costume, came and draped herself over Luke. I assumed her to be his partner but later discovered she was with his drunken friend. Shortly after another couple of wenches came for a photo opportunity with the tall, iconic character who stood out in the crowd. I was starting to feel several miles out of my comfort zone.

Still the night progressed. We separated ourselves from the group and sat in the sand talking for a while. Jeff thoughtfully brought me a glass of wine for "social lubrication", grinning salaciously as if in on a secret, but it wasn't necessary. It's never hard for yachties to find a common subject, be it solar power, engines or batteries, as if having an intro to some private club.

After a while, sitting on the beach became uncomfortable and Luke surprised me by saying goodnight with a soft kiss on the lips. "That was nice," I murmured as he was leaving, whereupon he came back for a second kiss, even more delicious than the first. It made me realise how little closeness there was in my life. "*Wait for me*!" I wanted to scream as he walked away.

I shook such emptiness out of me by dancing wildly in the sand for the next few hours. Stimulated to reckless abandon, I dipped and reeled, feet flying, leaping and twirling in an energetic "frog-in-a-sock" impression, until, like a whirling dervish, my soul escaped its physical prison in trancelike ecstasy. Others joined in, kicking up a sand-storm, grinning like fools, letting inhibitions spin off like sparks from a fire.

The following day, Luke invited me to dinner on his boat. We both laughed when I mentioned I didn't eat red meat and he retracted the offer. That could have been the end of that. Rising to the challenge, he managed to put together an impressive vegetarian meal and continued to impress me in other ways. I hadn't inflated my dinghy which was stowed away below the cockpit floor, so relied on others to get ashore. When that failed, Luke went out of his way to come and pick me up and deliver me safely home. He was certainly winning Brownie points.

Over the following days we spent most of our time together in a comfortable companionship and I began to feel the slightest peeling of the edges of my guard. When I cautioned him against any involvement with me, saying, "You know I'm sailing around the world", he answered, "Yes, but not today." It was a perfect response, reminding me of my preferred stance of living in the present. If only we could both remember that.

When the official festivities were over, a mass exodus left me sitting on my lonesome without a dinghy, wondering which way to go. Luke and his friends had headed north to Magnetic Island. I was tempted to join them, but my family was coming up to visit me in the Whitsundays. That's the hard part of this strange life, the meeting and the leaving. We make connections and we move on, sometimes to reconnect, sometimes not. I have to remind myself that this is my choice and it's not forever. I hadn't figured on this interim period of avoiding the cyclone season, expecting I would have been well on my way across the Indian Ocean, but things change and it's best to accept what is.

———

One of the benefits of not pushing north this year was to give me more time to get to know the boat better, to iron out all the glitches, to do more of a "shake-down" cruise. I am still in the "information-gathering/rumination" stage, with no great rush to make a decision as to where to spend the cyclone season. My daughter, Misha, flies into Hamilton Island tomorrow to sail around the Whitsunday Islands with me for the next 10 days. My youngest daughter, Shoni is camping in Airlie for a week with her husband Pierre and son Felix. It will be wonderful to see them all again.

Meanwhile, I see that Webb Chiles has arrived in Durbin. I quote him here on "fear":

"Mostly we are afraid of the unknown. I do not claim to have courage. Courage is doing something you are afraid to do. What I do have is nerve, which is the willingness, after making the best plans and preparations possible within the limits of your resources, to go ahead with an endeavour whose outcome is uncertain and may be fatal."

His advice to others is to *"sail enough so that the confidence in your own ability and your boats to cope with extreme conditions grows and becomes near certainty."*

Webb Chiles had no self-steering wind vane on his Moore 24 and relied on a sheet-to-tiller rig for over 90% of his Indian Ocean crossing. I have watched a few YouTube clips on this system and been interested to try it out. This afternoon I sailed from Airlie Beach to South Molle Island and made a new discovery: *Shanti* sails herself beautifully to weather with only a headsail.

It was blowing around 15 knots from ESE; my heading was as high as I could point into it, doing around 5.5 knots under headsail alone. I haven't done much windward sailing so far, with practically all of the passage north having the wind dead behind or off the aft quarter. Normally I would attach the tiller pilot if I needed to leave the helm for a moment, to go below to check the course or whatever. Today I let it go and was amazed to see the tiller gently moving back and forth by itself. The course fluctuated only slightly, keeping the wind angle around 40 degrees off the bow. *Shanti* felt perfectly balanced. I was thrilled! These are the things I need to play around with more.

———

Ten glorious days of perfect weather were spent cruising the Whitsunday Islands with my musician daughter, Misha.

We went to all the best spots at the best times. We swam, we sang, we danced, we drank, we ate, we laughed a lot, shared some memorable "Happy-hours" with Ray and Di on *All That Jazz*. We climbed to the top of Whitsunday Peak from Cid Harbour, a 5-kilometre trek that took 3 hours and tested our fitness.

Misha had a one day overlap with her younger sister, Shoni and her family. Ray and Di very generously took us all out for a sail on their (much bigger) yacht to snorkel at Langford Reef. It was heart-warming to see the kids leaping fearlessly over the side, swimming ashore and snorkelling in the crystal-clear shallows. There may have been sharks lurking but we didn't see any. Misha and Di knocked off a good deal of red wine on the way back, while the more sober of us snuggled up the tired youngsters. As always, the parting was precursor to that familiar void, which I'm sure contributed to my open sponginess. *Come fill me up.*

There's no denying, it's exciting when a man you think you won't see again pops up. Leaving his friends at Magnetic Island, Luke had sailed back south through some strong headwinds, keen to see me again. I couldn't take the smile off my face, hearing his "Honey I'm ho-ome". Yes, alarm bells were ringing but I chose to ignore them. Every cell of my body longed for his embrace. At that point in time, I would have tossed caution and everything else to the wind. Loneliness had caught up with me.

When two boats cruise in company it's called "buddy-boating", always more fun, with friendly company at the next anchorage. Luke enjoys the feel of the sun on his naked body, so I snapped some calendar-ready shots of him sailing whenever the distance between the two boats closed. He might pretend to object but was quite aware of his appreciative observer. We could hardly wait to launch the dinghy once the two yachts were anchored side by side, to gather up the yearning physicality and fall together again. I never wanted it to end, but as with everything, the good and the bad, nothing lasts forever. Particularly so in this itinerant life at sea, where change is as rapid as the weather, and stopping still for too long grows barnacles.

All too quickly, we were back in Airlie, reprovisioning, refuelling, re-watering in readiness for a suitable weather window to begin the return journey south. Looking out over the anchorage, it was apparent that the itinerant cruising fleet was thinning out as more boats left. Luke was encouraging me to take *Shanti* back to his home port of Bundaberg for repairs. A couple of nasty little leaks have developed. One is finding its exit through the vent above the stove, making cooking impossible during rain.

The other leak is more serious, in that it has the potential to sink the boat. Again, it isn't clear exactly where the seawater is entering the hull, but it is leaking into the stern locker at a rate of around 2 litres a day. I first became aware of this problem while on anchor at Airlie. *Shanti* was not the only boat hobby-horsing violently, at times almost dipping her bow under the cresting waves. The shallow anchorage is renowned for this, making it a very uncomfortable place to be during a strong northerly. The pumping action must have increased the flow of water at the stern, spreading it to other areas below the engine and floorboards. The engine battery was half under water, which could have been a disaster, had it shorted. It's a very good thing that I'm not discovering these problems halfway across the Indian Ocean.

Bundaberg. November 23.
The number one priority is to haul out and fix the leaks as soon as possible, so Bundaberg it is. You can live aboard on the hardstand, do your own work and make as much mess and noise as you want. In fact, the jack-hammering, grinding or sandblasting of nearby steel fishing boats is quite brain-juddering. Earmuffs are the latest fashion accessory. A pleasant luxury is the airline-style stairs available for hire. They make going to the toilet in the middle of the night less challenging than having to climb up and down a vertical ladder.

The task of trying to locate the source of the leak has been a far greater challenge, involving many great minds, much exploratory grinding in confined spaces, great muscle power and ultimately, throwing a few bucket-loads of money at it. It was soon obvious that the rudder needed to be removed, a simple enough sounding job, rather like one of those "just do that ……" type injunctions, where the word "just" implies no more than ten minutes of sweat.

The rudder is hung on the back of a triangular shape of fibreglass, called a "skeg". At the bottom of the skeg is a bronze shoe, or "pintel", which has a bearing which encircles the rudder post (albeit with a rather misshapen and sloppy grip). Before the rudder can be dropped the pintel has to be removed. Theoretically by *just* undoing a couple of bolts, only it's not that simple. It's not just bolted, but glued on with fibreglass resin. The local shipwright, Colin, declares this to be a dodgy 5-pm-Friday-afternoon shortcut that should never have been put together in such a way and was basically an accident waiting to happen. It's nothing to do with the leak, but it's potentially a show-stopper that needs to be fixed. It's always good to find out these things in advance, before losing a rudder mid-ocean.

The fix for this is to *just* grind back a section of the skeg, *just* make up a plug out of solid fibreglass (not just resin) with a protruding tongue to attach the pintel to and *just* fibreglass it all back together. *Just* like that. Back to the leak …

Once the rudder was off, the stainless-steel tube that the rudder stock went through could be cut in half and removed. Then the surrounding area inside the boat ground back. It soon became apparent that the fibreglass had never bonded properly to the stainless steel and was allowing small amounts of water to leak in. A preferable material for the new tube is fibreglass. The tube has bearings top and bottom (new ones will need to be made) which hold the rudder stock snugly in place. It's great to have made all these discoveries and to be getting them fixed now. Just as well I've been living off lettuce and lentils for the past few months, so still have a few dollars in my pocket.

It turned out to be exactly two weeks up on the hardstand, with the usual mad panic and time-compression over the last few days. Each morning I'd write another list of at least a dozen jobs then prioritize them like some crazed project manager. Small things can so easily get overlooked, or get done wrongly, and throw the train off the rails. Assumptions abound (I'm sure you've all heard the saying about making an ass of u and me), like the stainless-steel rudder stock being a stock standard size. *Ba-boom! Wrong!* The boat was built in South Africa where 31.9mm (not 32mm) means the new rudder bearings don't quite fit. So it's take the whole lot back to the local engineering shop for adjustment.

I entertained myself in the meantime by cutting and polishing the hull, a job which I would have liked to have done in Melbourne but never quite had the time. It also seemed like a good idea to raise the waterline again to cope with the extra weight of bulk stores, water and fuel. This had already been done in Melbourne, but it was higher at the back than the front of the boat, and patches of thick black weed were continually creeping up the topsides. With a bit of guesswork, we added an extra 50 millimetres at the bow, which was graduated gently back. I was delighted to find she now floats along a perfectly even line from bow to stern.

There are still about another dozen or so jobs to be done before I leave. It took the best part of the last three days and many trips to the laundromat to clear all the fibreglass dust out of the boat. It's nasty stuff that gets through the tiniest cracks and causes awful itching on the skin. Luckily the shipwright lent me his vacuum cleaner so I could get most of it off the squabs (cushions) and anything else that couldn't be washed. The cockpit locker especially was thick with it, and every single item had to be taken out and hosed off.

Another small job was to re-seal around the chainplates. Keeping water out of boats seems to be a perennial process. I had gooped these down when I re-rigged in Melbourne, but one had started to leak again. I say "small" job because it only took me an hour to scrape the old goop off from underneath, whilst sitting out in the 35-degree heat. Did I mention how hot it is here? Quite consistently so, unlike Melbourne. Generally, around low 30's during the day and mid 20's overnight. Fantastic really, so long as you don't want to do too much work outdoors.

Shanti will stay in Bundaberg while I fly back down to Melbourne for the Christmas/New Year period, then over to New Zealand for my father's 99th birthday in January. Meanwhile, a comfortable routine was forming with Luke, walking up to the local pub once or twice a week. Walking is a great pleasure for me and I love getting off *Shanti* to stretch my legs whenever I can, revelling in the variegated hues of greens and browns on the land. A trek alongside the Burnett River goes past a solitary windswept tree, which could be a fir or a she-oak, or any other riverside genus (I'm not much of a flora or fauna identifier). I call it the whispering tree. The wind sets up a constant whooshing sound through its foliage, something like the magical sound you hear when you put a conch shell to your ear—the sound of the sea. I appreciate the fact that I have time to stop and listen.

Further on, there's a bridge across the creek with a metal grated fence, which also sets up its own chorus of harmonic vibrations. Next, there are a few towering Acacia trees (perhaps) with flame red flowers in full bloom. The iridescent green and crimson parrots hide amongst the colours. Less pleasing are the birds that dive-bomb me as I walk; ("Plovers", I've been told), making a strident, chattering screech of warning to stay away from their hatchlings. They swoop up close to my face, then veer away at the last minute, before coming in again from the rear. I've been told they have barbs on their wings and could do some damage if they make contact, so my heart skips a few beats on each attack. A suggestion is to wear sunglasses on the back of my hat, but I doubt the effectiveness of this, given that the forward-facing sunglasses don't seem to deter them.

Returning to *Shanti* at the beginning of February, I was keen to get out for a sail, partly to test everything and partly to escape that other insidious trap, the long-term attachment to the dock. So, early one morning I cast off, very pleased to find the engine fired enthusiastically into life at first key-turn.

A minor job still on the to-do list was to take the near new headsail to a sailmaker to have a protective strip of leather sewn along the foot, which had been chafing on the life-lines. I decided to lower the sail, (for the first time since it was made) which ordinarily would be a simple, quick and easy thing. Not so! The sail jammed halfway and would go neither up nor down. Fortunately, there was very little breeze, so I was able to half furl it in and return to my marina berth without creating too much of a spectacle.

One of the great things about the cruising community is the willingness to help one another. We each have our strengths and weaknesses. I'm useful on the other end of nuts or bolts but no good with heights. I realise that one day I may have to overcome this fear. I have made a plywood mast-climber which allows someone (other than me) to "walk" their way up the mast while I merely take up the slack on the supporting halyards. This could be used by a single-hander in an emergency, using mountain-climbing equipment to grip the ropes, slide up and lock. Or, a simple friction hitch, like a Prusik knot.

On this occasion, someone with less fear of heights kindly volunteered to try my new mast climber. Once at the top of the mast, he swung out and attached himself to the forestay, then slowly slid down the hypotenuse of the fore-triangle. He discovered that practically every single grub-screw securing the sections of the foil was loose. Hence the foil had been able to shift slightly out of alignment, preventing the sail from sliding freely on its track. It appeared as if the grub screws had not been bonded with "Loctite", so each was removed, (taking care not to drop any), treated and tightened. Then the sail tracks were washed out with detergent and rinsed by hoisting a hose aloft.

If you stop too long in one place, boat jobs catch up with you. A boat that you might have thought completely seaworthy and ready to set off around the world, begins to demand further attention. This was one of the objections I presented to those who argued the irrelevance of delay. The longer you delay, the more the peak of preparedness slides toward the slippery realm of entropy. Of course, some delays, like some boat jobs, are necessary, some perhaps less so. It was important to get the leaky rudder post repaired, the pintel bearing restructured, the alternator and solar panels charging. And who could resist the luxury of a working fridge? It seems that turning back last year from just south of Cairns to the cyclone-proof haven of Bundaberg was a wise move.

My current job-list has 14 items on it, including things like sand and paint the aluminium hull of the dinghy, bolt wheels on it, affix a clever lifting harness for ease of launch and retrieval. I'm also working on making fly screens, rearranging and inventorying stores and provisions, securing extra jerry cans of drinking water down below. The battery charger that was installed in Townsville died, so a replacement needs wiring in. It's only really needed in a marina on rainy overcast days, of which we have had one so far this year.

An ongoing concern is what food I need, how much to take and in what form. I have looked into freeze-dried meals but they are expensive and most seem to have flavour enhancing nasties added. One of the more time-consuming necessary/unnecessary jobs has been playing with the freshwater plumbing, which seemed to be leaking. A largish puddle appeared in the bottom of the tight little space that is home to most of the water inlets and outlets. Of course, it's always a very tight, scarcely accessible space.

It took several extremely hot and humid days to pull it all apart, remove defunct hoses to a non-existent hot water system, etc. All accompanied by blood, sweat, tears, bruises and a few well-chosen words of encouragement; then to install a new foot pump, new hoses, joiners, reducers, T intersections, clamps, etc. I guess you might call it ironic, or just plain annoying, but the water in the bilge turned out to be condensation from under the fridge. What can I say? Not much, other than it's a far neater layout now than it was before, with all those superfluous hoses gone.

One more trip to Melbourne in April for the imminent birth of my youngest daughter's second child, then cyclone season should be over and the great migration north resumes.

Chapter 6

Solo Departure

May the 4th, (or as someone so wittily observed, Star Wars Day) was to be departure day, in an ideal world without weather. However, words of wisdom from my son in law, Dr Andrew Watkins, a senior meteorologist at the Bureau of Meteorology suggested the cyclone season may not fit so neatly within its usual parameters of November to April this year, and patience could be the more sensible course.

Clearly, Mother Nature doesn't watch the calendar as closely as we sailors do. After three weeks of living in the protected environment of a house in Melbourne, it is easy to forget the weather. Mostly it was sunny, quite mild for autumn, occasionally rained and blew a little. Nothing of any great concern. So it seemed perfectly reasonable to come back to *Shanti* with a departure date in mind. Wrong!

Looking at the forecast for the coming week—gales of over 40 knots and 2-3 metre seas, with potential for another low forming within the monsoon trough that could develop into another Tropical Cyclone—staying tied up in the marina seemed somewhat more appealing than going sailing. TC Debbie left a trail of devastation through the Whitsundays last month. After tracking inland she re-emerged at the coast near Bundaberg, bringing torrential rain and winds up to 55 knots. During this deluge my life raft self-inflated. It was stored in the well under the cockpit floor, which ordinarily is reasonably watertight but I had omitted to lock it down securely.

Luke and I were sheltering near the marina office, waiting for a lull in the rain to return to our boats. Palm trees were bowing to the ground in a humble genuflexion. There was no avoiding it so we too bowed low and ran. Scrambling back aboard *Shanti* I found the cockpit floor lifted to a 45-degree angle, as if some subterranean iceberg was surfacing! It took me a while to realise what it was. A few days later, the two of us dragged it out and repacked it with a new gas cylinder (after evicting a resident cane toad) and a memo to store it in a drier spot henceforth.

While in Melbourne, I bought myself a second-hand sextant, just for fun really, but you never know when those satellites that we take so much for granted might be shut down. I'm looking forward to learning how to use it, kind of like learning a foreign language. I also bought some Bluetooth wireless headphones and scraped together a collection of audiobooks, plus a few French language courses, which should keep me amused for months out on the ocean. Till then, it's a waiting game...

Finally, the weather settled, all imminent cyclone threats headed off to New Zealand, and there were no other excuses not to leave. Well, there's always at least a dozen, but sometimes prevarication is the mother of perversity. Saying goodbye to Luke was harder than expected but we could stay in touch as long as I was in phone range.

Sunday, May 14 (Mother's Day in the land of the land) seemed an auspicious day to leave, it not being a Friday. Non-land dwellers consider leaving port on a Friday to be tempting fate to overturn everything. Along with most sailors, I have perhaps a thimble-full of superstition in seeking to appease and avoid calamity.

This time I opted for an overnight sail directly to Great Keppel Island. The reasons behind this were partly to cover some distance, in case I changed my mind, and also to test the possibility of being able to cat nap for 20 minutes at a time, without the usual nervousness that something was about to run me down, or I was about to bump into something hard.

It's a common occurrence that there's either too much wind or not enough. It seemed like a good idea to start the journey without getting hammered too much at first. Later on, fine, if it has to be that way, but not right at the outset after months of quiet marina life. The old mal-de-mer is still lurking not far away on those first few days before I get my sea legs.

My plan was to actually sail all the way, meaning to use those white bits of cloth hanging off the big white stick, without running the engine if possible. I was really over "driving up the coast", which seems to be a necessary evil in order to enter the desired anchorage in daylight hours. Well, so what if I slop about doing only one or two knots? So what if it takes 90 hours to go 130 nautical miles? Others have done it. Surely I can too?

After half an hour of motoring out of the river, I puristically cut the engine and commenced a few miles of glorious sailing, before the wind dropped to 6 knots. I persevered for a few more hours. It was quite pleasant and nice and quiet. I was contentedly bobbing along at 3 knots of boat speed. Later, only 2. The night grew darker and colder, and longer.

I'm not sure what exactly it was that seduced me into turning the key. Perhaps the thought of another couple of nights without sleep. Perhaps the slight queasiness. Perhaps the desire to be going somewhere. Perhaps the fact that on a long-distance ocean passage, time is less important because you're going to be out there for months anyway, and making a daylight landfall is a distant nicety, and you can sleep all night long if you want; but it's different on the busy coast. I ended up motoring for 19 out of 28 hours and just made it into the southernmost anchorage on Great Keppel Island as total blackness obliterated it from sight. Then I gratefully slept like the dead.

This morning, I once again turned the key and drove around to a more sheltered anchorage on the northern side of the island. The water is crystal clear, so I dove on the hull with scrubber in hand to clean off the rest of the Bundaberg slime. For lunch, I ate a salad with the Morton Bay Bugs that one of the local fishermen at Bundaberg had given me. They are funny looking critters, but taste delicious, rather like baby lobster or crayfish.

A strong wind warning with heavy rain was forecast for the rest of the week, so I opted to make the break while it was still fine and sail north to shelter in the inner reaches of Port Clinton, a distance of 44 nautical miles. If no one else is leaving, it's questionable whether to follow the herd mentality and stay put, or sail one's own course. Of course, there are often other reasons for staying, such as engine problems, fear of leaving the flock, or simply plain inertia. Many of those clinging to their anchors have no other places to be or any time constraints. I have both, and a fine day in which to put another 40 miles behind me is not to be lost.

So at 0600, I weighed anchor and continued north. It turned out to be one of those glorious day's sailing that is so few and far between. The wind never went above 16 knots and stayed comfortably just aft of the beam. Only later when it backed further to threaten a gybe did I take over hand-steering. Then I really got into the zone.

I can understand why many sailors have written of the great advantages of tiller steering, not the least being the direct feel of the boat and its responsiveness. Also, it's possible to sit side-on with the tiller in hand for hour after hour without the fatigue that those standing behind a wheel suffer.

So what does it mean for me, to be in the "zone"? When I sit for a few hours hand-steering it does have an interesting effect, almost mesmerising. It's a feeling of eternal now, an immediacy and connection to the wind, the waves, the motion, without the distraction of mind. There is a sense of being completely alert and tuned in to the present moment with no strain; being at one with everything, being here and now. An endless now. This is what I love most about being out here.

In Port Clinton, I anchored near a sleek, magnificent looking sloop of 60 plus feet. We chatted a little on the VHF radio, it being far too wet and windy to cross the distance between us by dinghy. They were leaving soon, heading to Mackay to sort out a dental problem. Strong wind and rain were no deterrent to them in that fully enclosed yacht. It occurred to me how we all are having such different experiences out here on the same water. Some are very much more protected from the elements than others, some have water-makers and washing machines. I might envy those creature comforts for a minute, but then I think of the richness of my proximity to the environment, so much so that I am almost a part of it. At times it stings and bites me, but I would not trade that for a hot shower. Perhaps in another ten years.

I woke at 0700 to a rainy, windless day. The batteries were low. I had turned the fridge off overnight to defrost it and save power but needed to run the engine if turning it back on again on such an overcast, no-solar-power day. I decided to motor out of Port Clinton to the next stop, following my track in from last year. This is proving to be such a great help to me, relieving a lot of the anxiety and stress I felt last year when approaching unknown territory. Having traversed this section of the coast before, up and down, gives me a lot more confidence, knowing what's ahead. I noticed a big difference in myself.

The entrance to Island Head Creek is a fairly narrow channel, with breakers washing over the rocky outcrops and shallow shoals on either side. Add a heavy broadside roll and it's not easy to hold a straight course in. I hoped that the thin yellow line on the Navionics chart showing last year's track was accurate.

It's only been one week since leaving Bundaberg but it feels like a lot longer. I departed Island Head Creek at first light (0600 these short days of winter) and made my way to Hunter Island in the Dukes. I hadn't originally planned on anchoring off Hunter Island after my awful experience there last year with the strong tidal race, but I followed the herd instinct and joined three other yachts, which appeared peaceful enough. Big mistake! The new moon tidal race was just as ferocious and I got into all kinds of strife with my inadequate chain/rope situation. A restless night of dragging and re-setting rope that kept kinking, knotting and jamming in the gypsy was followed by a dismal dawn, with nearly an hour of fighting to get the anchor up. The circuit breaker kept tripping out against a howling cross-wind and tide that had us riding forward with the rope back under the keel. It took several goes with rolling hitches led back to a primary winch to take the load off, and lots of running back and forth between cockpit and foredeck before I was finally off. I again envisaged myself being stranded on Hunter Island forever.

Last year, Curlew was a relatively quiet stopover, with an encircling reef and shoal water breaking the swell. Perhaps due to the bigger tides, this year it was one of the rollier anchorages and I was glad to only have to endure one night of it. En-route from Curlew to Mackay, I was speaking to my youngest daughter, telling her how fortunate I was to be having positive tidal influence with me all the way, enabling an average speed of 5 knots. Shoni was rather bemused by this, commenting that it seemed slow, in fact, even slower than walking. Yes, I am travelling at a slow walking pace up the coast! I have 2000 nautical miles to go to get to Darwin. It's like walking 2000 miles over the next two months. I never really thought of it like that before. Shoni asked if I don't get very bored and frustrated by going so slowly. Not at all; it's necessary to slow down in oneself. But yes, part of the frustration is in having to "walk" 2000 miles up the coast before I even kick off to begin crossing an ocean. I guess this coastal passage is part of it, but not too many long-distance cruisers begin their journey in such a manner.

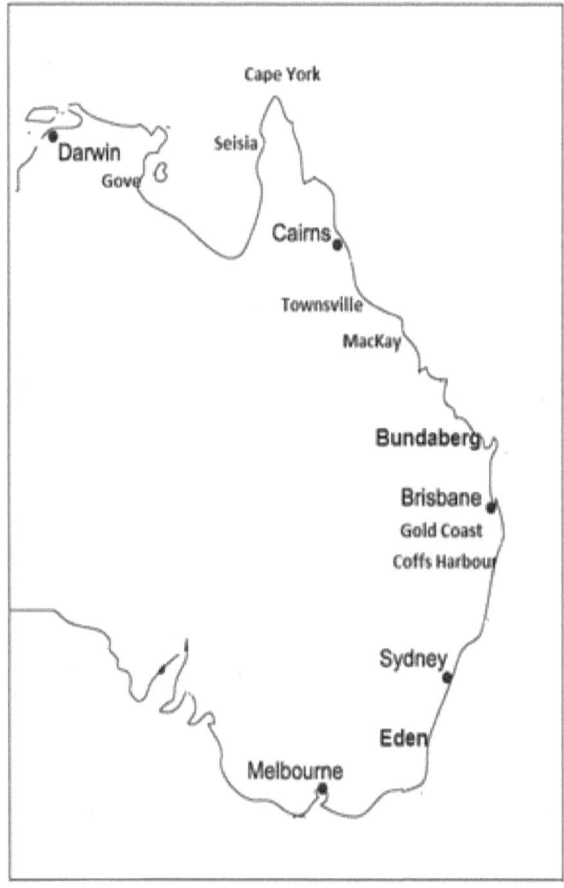

Some of the stops from Melbourne to Darwin.

I paused long enough in Mackay to do all the usual marina stopover chores: refuelling, refilling gas bottles, taking the bus to town for provisions, doing the laundry, putting on a new fan belt and topping up the fresh water tanks. And most enjoyably, taking a few hot and cold running water showers. I allowed myself two days instead of the one that I usually try to cram it all into, which made it much less hectic. In some other lifetime, it might be interesting to stay longer and explore the area.

I departed at the respectable hour of 0900, considering I only had a short run of 20 miles to Brampton Island at the beginning of the Whitsundays. As it turned out, the ebb tide was so helpful I decided to continue on to Goldsmith, an island I haven't been to before. I anchored rather too close to exposed rocks which looked like crocodile's eyes peering at me as the tide dropped and more emerged. It was another rolly night and the chain was growling, telling me it was more rock than sand on the seabed.

Day-hopping up the coast like this is full of little anxieties when my mind often runs down the "what-if" trail. So far, that important element of luck has been with me. I do my best with the knowledge and skills I have, but never fail to appreciate the hand of fate that guides the uncontrollable. Every time I leave a potentially tricky situation in one piece, I take a moment to give thanks. Thanks!

As I approached Whitsunday Passage, boat speed was less than 3 knots, but Speed Over Ground was up to 7.2 knots. I anchored in my favourite spot at Sawmill Bay in Cid Harbour. The water is a bit milky but still a beautiful pale jade with sunshine shimmering over the ripples. There are signs of Tropical Cyclone Debbie's visit. The treetops are bare, looking as if a bush fire had denuded them. The general feeling is of recent carnage, but the charter boats are still aplenty, so it's business as usual. I wanted to hike to the top of Whitsunday Peak again, but the trail had too many obstacles with fallen trees and branches. One of the loose rocks, slippery with recent rain, toppled me and I landed heavily on my left hip, which is now very sore, despite Arnica. I have noticed I am not as sure-footed yet as I should be, but it's early days, so hopefully soon I'll stop knocking myself about so much.

I had a brilliant sail from Airlie to Gloucester Passage, the scene of the annual Shaggers Rendezvous in August, which was such fun last year. Of course, passing through in May this year was a much quieter, solitary affair; basically, just another overnight stop. My mind naturally re-lived the good times with Luke and I felt a desire to see him again. The weather forecast was for strong winds for the following week and I really didn't fancy a repeat of the beating I took last year sailing up to Townsville. Instead, I opted to park *Shanti* in Bowen Marina for the duration of the blow and catch a bus back to Roslyn Bay, where Luke was staying on his boat, in need of some help.

The entrance into Bowen is narrow and shallow and a strong crosswind was blowing when I arrived at 0930. The berth I had been allocated could scarcely be given the illustrious title of Marina berth, being more like a narrow gap between the rock breakwater and the floating plastic walkway. Half a dozen people were standing on the end of the dock, yelling instructions at me. The trick was to turn immediately toward the shallower mangroves (0.2 metres below keel), then reverse back toward the rock wall, then do a last-minute pirouette to parallel the pontoon, all the while avoiding the barnacle-encrusted piles and moored boats. I had three quite respectable goes at it, after which it was obvious *Shanti* just didn't want to go in there. I can't say I blame her. The helpers agreed and yelled out a change of plan. Apparently, there was a proper berth available, a lot easier to get into. It was the spare berth belonging to a man called Kerry, who perceived that my need for it was greater than the others who had said they were (possibly) coming. I was soooo grateful! He even told the club not to charge me for the larger size, just for the 10-metre berth I had requested.

I took the Greyhound bus back south for a few days and hired a car to take the semi-immobile Luke with his mysteriously inflated knee out for dinner for his birthday. I sometimes wonder at why I run after men in this way because it often leaves me feeling disappointed and vowing never to do it again. Of course, that is entirely due to the expectations I set up in my head, which are laid bare and ignored. How could I possibly expect that today would be the same as yesterday? Or that my lover would be as devotedly attentive as he was in the beginning? Yet again, the same lesson is drilled into me: drop my expectations. It is always those unrealistic expectations that cause problems, and at the end of the day, all of my problems are within me. I am seeing this more and more clearly out at sea. Staying by myself on board *Shanti* is not so bad; undoubtedly made easier by a less heart-wrenching parting.

Cape Upstart found me laid up with some kind of tummy bug. At first, I thought the nausea was due to having lost my sea legs after the Bowen interlude, but when it developed throughout the night into some serious evacuation of my insides to the outside, I knew it was different. So another lay-day was necessary, feeling quite wretched, with thoughts of the perils of life at sea.

I have been giving some consideration to contingency planning concerning possible vulnerabilities from breakdown, loss or damage. Last year, it was the inverter, which converts 12V battery power to 240V. Its failure would mean there would be no way of charging the laptop, on which I run my main electronic navigation system, using Open CPN with C-maps charts. I thought about buying a spare inverter but chose instead to get a 12V DC charger, the kind that plugs into a cigarette lighter. This uses a lot less power than the inverter. I also bought a second, larger iPad that runs Navionics. And in case all that fails, I had the sextant and paper charts. I think all bases are covered there.

Vulnerability # 2: *Tilly*, the autopilot. The Fleming windvane, *Min*, is the main hand for long-distance passages but doesn't work so well up the coast with the wind directly behind. So *Tilly* gets to have most of the fun, whenever I let her have it. We have a kind of co-dependency and I rely heavily on her unerring support when I am otherwise occupied. Solution: a back-up tiller pilot, an oversized Simrad TP32, *Tilly 2*.

Vulnerability # 3: reading glasses. It suddenly occurred to me that if lost, I would literally be lost without them. An easy fix to that one.

Vulnerability # 4: Me. Hmmm. Stay safe, stay well, STAY ON THE BOAT.

A new motto occurred to me recently: *"Everything is fine until it isn't."*

I am learning to stay more in the present moment, not letting my mind run so freely down those "what-if" tracks, trusting that I will deal with things as they arise.

The passage from Upstart to Magnetic Island, near Townsville, is a long one, around 70 nautical miles. It requires an early morning start, and even though I didn't really feel like getting up at 0330, it needed to be done. The full moon was very welcome in helping me avoid the few other boats anchored nearby. On my "lay-day" I had set up the "whisker pole" (a lighter and shorter pole than the spinnaker pole), ready to pole out the headsail on the opposite side to the main if need be. This goosewing effect (butterfly) allows both sails to fill, instead of the mainsail blanketing the headsail.

I am more than a month ahead, which gives me a better chance of getting to Darwin by the end of July. I have been reflecting on how different things are this year. *Shanti* is far sounder, with her rudder post leak and other things fixed. The Yanmar diesel engine (*Yani*) is less of an unknown quantity and *Min*, the Fleming self-steering wind pilot can generally be trusted to relieve me from the helm.

After a year's "shake-down" I have much more confidence in both boat and self and can relax a bit. Last year I was constantly vigilant, feeling that if I wasn't standing in the cockpit watching everything, every second, things could go horribly wrong. Every wave that rolled us beyond the point of a gybe, every slat of the sail that thwanged so violently it seemed as if the mast might come down; all required me to be at the ready. There never seemed to be a point at which I could leave *Shanti* to her own devices for a moment and trust that she would be OK. Initially, I couldn't even force myself to lie down and rest for 10 minutes. Of course, such vigilance is sometimes required, for example in a storm, but cannot be sustained constantly, without burnout. So I am learning to pace myself and not suffer unnecessarily. There will be time enough for that.

"A voyage is a problem to be solved with your mind and body." (Webb Chiles, on his 6th circumnavigation).

It's interesting the way things can change, from absolutely perfect to all messed up. The morning sail from Mourilyan was glorious, flat seas, beam reach, light SW winds up to 12 knots. The coastline was spectacular with layers of gentle hills fading to a backdrop of steep mountain ranges. One forecast was for nothing over 15 knots; another had it getting up to 25. Always confusing that! As the wind increased and the seas mounted, *Tilly* decided it was all too much for her and let out a long, plaintive squeal, meaning either "I've had enough" or "I need a rest". So I gave her a rest for a couple of hours. Then I needed a rest. But the waves were getting bigger, lifting the stern and throwing it off at wild angles, requiring a strong grip on the tiller. I started wondering what to do. Reduce sail was an obvious thing, but I was hoping we could just hang on for another hour and we'd be in the lee of Fitzroy Island, which would make it much easier to deal with.

As invariably is the case, the time for me to act was overpassed and it was taken out of my hands. One of those infamous "double the average height" waves hit us hard, slewing us sideways down its face. The force on the tiller was uncontrollable. The boom dipped in the water as we broached, the side canvasses were ripped off and water poured into the cockpit. Down below, the cutlery drawer flew open, spilling its contents; everything that could move from the starboard to port side of the cabin did so. OK, a big hint that the time to slow down was overdue—much as surfing down the backs of waves at over 8 knots was thrilling. I let us round up into the on-coming waves, lashed the helm and dropped the main. Luckily I had furled most of the jib in earlier so there was not too much flogging. It surprised me how well she sat in that semi hove-to position while I started the engine. It would have made so much more sense to do it an hour before. Still more learning required.

Sailing from Fitzroy the next day, the wind was again over 30 knots, but I was prepared for it with hardly any sail up. *Shanti* jiggled and danced up and over the choppy assault, giving me more confidence in this solidly-built little boat. I am seeing how much her ability to handle it is in my hands.

If I thought the entrance to Bowen was scary, coming into Yorkeys Knob was terrifyingly heart-stopping. Entering the marked channel an hour before low tide, the depths below keel went rapidly from 0.6 metres, through 0.5,4,3,2,1 to 0.00! With a strong crosswind, had I grounded, *Shanti* would soon have been on the rocks. It's hard to believe they don't have a warning attached to this place. When friends of mine enquired about depth at the entrance later that same day they were told there was no problem. Nonetheless, I enjoyed a 4-day respite in the muddy, croc-infested shallows of Yorkeys and am preparing to depart tomorrow morning.

From here on up, some things get a bit tighter, like easy access to shops and fuel stations and water taps. So it's been number-crunching time, trying to calculate how much of everything vital is necessary over the next few weeks of relative unavailability. Water is probably the biggest concern. The Trade Winds should blow consistently strongly from the SE, obviating the need for too much diesel (of which I carry around 150 litres in the tank and jerry cans). I have been experimenting with water rationing, seeing if I can manage on 2 litres per day. My water tanks hold 200 litres, theoretically enough for 100 days. I decant 2 litres into an old vinegar bottle each day, only to find I'm short by about a cup in the evening when I feel like a cup of tea. This is partly because things like rice, pasta and lentils are also thirsty and shouldn't be rehydrated entirely in saltwater. Gas for cooking is supplied by a 2 kg gas bottle, fitted in a small dedicated locker in the cockpit. I carry two extra spares and each one lasts around a month.

Newfound friends on a catamaran called *Hard Yakka* have been very kind and supplied some scrumptious, freshly caught fillets of Mackerel. Ric is sailing up and over the top and on to the Kimberleys with his all-girl crew, one of whom happens to be an ex-work colleague of my daughter, Pandora's. Small world!

From here on up, outside contact with the world becomes a bit more rarefied. There are two more possible stopovers, Port Douglas and Cooktown, but I will most probably by-pass those. I have reprovisioned with enough food for Africa, (as the saying goes) filled up with water and diesel, done the laundry, scrubbed myself clean, and am as ready as I'm ever going to be. From here to the tip of Australia at Cape York should take about two weeks, with nightly rests in some apparently stunning anchorages. The town of Gove is the next civilization if I choose to go there. Otherwise, it's a non-stop run of around a week across the top of the Arafura Sea to Darwin.

As suspected, there are some stunning anchorages north of Cairns, many of which are little more than a coral reef with a smudge of yellow sand on top but boast crystal clear water, birds, and plenty of black-tipped reef sharks. From Low Islets, my latest stalker, son Baillie, picked it right; yes, Hope Islands. How could I not go there, being my name-sake?

The pass between the Hope Islands may be fine for boats with more than one person on board, but for me on my own, it was a potential hit or miss. The tricky part is spotting the "bommies"— underwater coral uprisings ready to take the bottom out of your boat if you unsuspectingly go over one—which I did, luckily with a couple of inches to spare. They're hard enough to spot from the bow or halfway up the mast—impossible for me from the cockpit. Again, luck was on my side. (Occasionally my more superstitious side thinks about cats and their nine lives.) I even managed to pick up a mooring that was only a couple of boat-lengths from the reef without needing too many goes at it. The exit out the eastern side was far clearer and I had an easy sail to Lizard the next day.

Lizard Island is a northern cruising destination in itself, a wonderland with magnificent scenery and best of all, a sheltered, swell-free anchorage. It was here that I first began to encounter the international fleet, the hardcore, long-distance cruisers who were also heading offshore. I spent six days relaxing, hiking, and snorkelling over the subterranean paradise of colourful coral gardens. Giant 100-year-old clams seem like rocky, immobile shells, but can close around an unsuspecting foot should you be silly enough to test them. Transient friendships were made over bonfires on the beach and I savoured the cruising lifestyle at its best.

At the next stop, Flinders Island, a rescue helicopter airlifted a French single-hander off his boat with suspected bowel haemorrhage. He was totally distraught at having to leave his yacht on anchor in this remote spot. We heard later that his insurance arranged for a boat from Cooktown to return him to his boat, so it ended better than it might have. It made me realise just how vulnerable we are out here. What was interesting was that another French couple alerted the rescue mission via France.

For me, the sailing inside the reef has been excellent, with mostly flat water and tailwinds up to 20 knots. It requires constant vigilance to dodge the myriad of islands and reefs and the odd container ship but has been mostly enjoyable. There seemed to be a favourable current assisting me in doing the 75-mile leg from Morris Island to Escape River in 12 hours, quite a record for little *Shanti*.

Over the top end, Cape York was a significant milestone. Of course, the final hoorah of self-congratulation wasn't going to pass unchallenged, so from Escape River on, the wind increased and I ended up in a difficult predicament. Sailing back south on the other side of the Cape, the seas were high, the wind gusting up to 40 knots, and when it came time to turn into the approach to Seisia, my little "egg-beater" of a propeller was unable to drive the boat into wind and waves. I couldn't even make one knot of boat speed and it wasn't possible to try to tack, the channel being very shallow on either side of the leads. I gave up and ran with the wind until the next island, which was little more than a large rock. Dropping anchor there at least gave me some time to take stock of the situation. I knew I couldn't stay there, so plotted a few possible courses out. I finally managed to up anchor and claw my way back to windward, sailing across some very shallow waters, trying to stay in close to the shelter of Red Island and entering the leads about halfway down the channel. The wind was so strong it took nearly two hours to cover the short distance into the anchorage. I felt so, so relieved to make it safely in. (Another cat's life?) Thanks!

I realised yesterday that I may have just had my last day sail up this reef strewn Coral Coast. From here across the Arafura sea to Darwin is about 750 miles of virtually open water. No more day-hopping, pushing to reach the next anchorage before dark. Of course, this also means no more sleeping through the night. I'm not sure yet which is harder. I guess I'll find out.

I was wrong when I thought day-hops were over. This was because instead of sailing non-stop over the top of the Arafura Sea for a week, I chose to go via Gove. Seisia to Gove is only three days and nights, and I discovered how tough sleeplessness can be. The first day was virtually windless, so it was a reluctant key-turning, diesel-burning time. (I was very conscious of my limited diesel capacity, but thought at least I could top up in Gove if need be.) The next two days and nights were a battle-ground, with confused seas throwing *Shanti* about like a cork. Sleep in that? Forget it. I was hanging on by the skin of my teeth (and had already broken one of those). Everything down below was getting thrown about as if by some petulant giant sick of his toys. Attempting to put a reef in the mainsail at midnight as gusts topped 30 knots I wrenched my shoulder—quite disarming (if you'll excuse the pun).

Friends on *Hard Yakka* received only half of my VHF transmission and were unsure whether to turn back to look for me (to windward into 3-metre waves—don't think so!) They were greatly relieved when I eventually came sneaking in, threading my way through the other boats to find a welcome rest. Ric convinced us to stay until Thursday when the Gove Yacht Club opened and I have to say the meals were extraordinary. None of this nouveau cuisine, fancily decorated half-empty plate for them; rather a mountainous serve of simple, unadulterated fodder, enough for two or more hungry bears. And the free shower facilities were beyond luxury, so it was well worth the stop.

Hitch-hiking into town, we were picked up by an expat resident, who shared insights into the local culture, which I found fascinating. I have never seen such a predominantly indigenous population, no doubt the reason behind the need for a liquor permit to buy alcohol and then only after 2 pm. And the crew is only allowed to drink in the presence of Ric, the permit holder. But the Gove detour really digs you into a bit of a hole. Looking at a chart of the area, you can see that a string of lumpy bits—the Wessels—bars the way west. So back to day hopping, threading my way through them all, at times through some narrow and shallow slices in the terrain. The so-called "Hole in the Wall" is another such adrenaline surge. With currents running up to 12 knots it's important to time the tide right. The only trouble is opinions on when exactly is "right" differ. *Dream Catcher* and *Mikado* were given information by a local fisherman, which surely should be right. One would think. I fell into line and tagged along behind them for the 1630 tide, only to get a last-minute VHF radio call from the leader warning me their powerful engine could scarcely give them 1 knot of boat speed against the flood tide. There's no way known my little egg-beater would make any impression there. I didn't want to risk having to wait until dark for slack water, so peeled away and sailed another 10 nautical miles down the coast to join *Hard Yakka* in the nearest shelter for the night, arriving just on dusk. Early the next morning, *Hard Yakka* and *Shanti* punched back to windward to make the 0800 tide. This time it was right. No turbulence, just a smooth, very rapid transit, with a top speed of 10.5 knots. Very exciting!

Once on the other side of the island chain, there were more day sails; in fact, potentially dozens if one chose to meander and explore at a more leisurely pace. But I was keen to push on to Darwin, so left our little fleet, to set out for another couple of overnighters. I figured these were like mini tests for me, seeing if I could indeed sleep at sea. This one was only 256 miles to Cape Don, the final stepping stone before the last 100 miles down into Darwin. But again, the wind was fickle, at first stranding me with not enough to stop the sails from slatting, later slamming me with the same force as before, making me question if I'd made the right decision. Not just on this interim passage, but on the whole thing. I'm always on the lookout for reasons, or rather excuses, to give up, while there is still that option. Soon it will be gone.

By choosing to go out to sea, I was the recipient of a real gift. Lying down below, listening to Eva Cassidy singing about happy little bluebirds flying, I noticed a shrill chirping sound. How clever, I thought; I never noticed that before. But when it continued after the song finished I thought some real birds had come to roost, as they often like to rest (and poop) on my solar panels out at sea. Emerging from the cabin, an unbelievable sight met my eyes. *Shanti* was surrounded by dozens of the biggest Minke whales that I have ever seen. Some were almost as big as *Shanti*, and some were close enough for me to touch. I wasn't sure whether to be thrilled or freaked.

More and more joined in from afar, slipping alongside effortlessly, diving, surfacing with huge spouts, splashing the water with their tails and breaching right in front of the boat. They stayed and played for well over an hour, an unusual length of time for a pod not to lose interest in a slow-moving boat. Down below, the hull reverberated with their chittering song. What a privilege! One of the things I love about *Shanti* is her proximity to the elements. Of course, all boons also have their banes. The bane is she is so close to the elements as to almost be a part of them, at times rather too much so!

At last, Darwin! The Holy Grail.

Sitting on anchor in Fannie Bay, the city skyline in the background, I reflect on this journey so far and all that I have learned. For the most part, *Shanti* has been brilliant. There have been some issues around self-steering gear (quite critical for single-handing) and at times I question her diminutive proportions. I know that lots of people sail across oceans in even smaller boats (often they are younger with something to prove, or older, with a death wish). I am neither, and have to admit that single-handing is damn hard—and a tad unsafe. This small boat bites. It throws me about like a rag doll; it brings out old symptoms, such as shoulder bursitis, backaches and, more scarily, debilitating attacks of vertigo (not a good thing on a boat). I'm sure my system is overflowing with adrenaline, cortisol, norepinephrine, glucagon and enough other stress hormones to sink a ship.

    I don't feel like continuing on alone. This sad acknowledgement is one that I scarcely want to admit. But it may just be time to put my childhood dream back into the toybox. Or at very least to take some time out to consider practicalities, such as water/fuel supply, safety, comfort vs hardship. There's no argument there. Or am I simply suffering from a crisis of confidence and looking for a way out? At this point, the best solution seems for me to crew on other people's boats, keeping *Shanti* as a home base.

    So what now?

Serendipity! Ric, off *Hard Yakka*, gave me a contact in Darwin for a marina berth for $100 per week, so there is somewhere to safely leave *Shanti* parked behind the lock gates that Darwin's 8-metre tides require. Luke has signed on for delivery of a 39' Leopard catamaran from the Seychelles to Australia, skippered by a mutual friend of ours. At the last minute the third crew member pulled out, and they asked me to replace her. I list the pros and cons of this—4,500 nautical miles, against wind and current—not an easy decision. Airfare, marina berth, all food and drink covered. Is this jumping out of the frying pan into the fire? But once again I am drawn to see Luke.

Chapter 7

Confidence Restored

I made the leap.

Leaving *Shanti* safely locked up in Bayview Marina in Darwin, I flew to the Seychelles. What a tranquil oasis, the crystal-clear waters reflecting a sumptuous slice of paradise. How lovely would it be to linger in the languid ambience of charter-boat holidays? But that was not our mission.

As I was the last crewmember to arrive, it was expected that we would depart within a day or two, for the long beat to windward to Australia. It didn't turn out that way. Whilst waiting for the paperwork to be done, we left the marina for a short sail to a nearby anchorage. There were four of us on board, Luke, myself, a young Swiss woman named Patricia, and Marten, the Dutch skipper.

Put a handful of people together in a confined space and there is a great opportunity to observe human nature. Also many opportunities for self-discovery, for practising being like a duck, letting water flow off its back. Perhaps the biggest lesson is in letting things go, completely and absolutely, with no lingering residue upon which to stack a pile of minor quibbles.

What tickles one person may topple another. Like the dinghy ride back from the beach. I couldn't stop laughing; Patricia couldn't stop fuming. There was quite an active surge rolling in against the steeply shelving shoreline, which can easily swamp a dinghy if it goes broadside. We landed without too much drama, we two women leaping over the bow with the rope to pull the dinghy in, not quite quickly enough to stop the next breaker dumping over the stern and soaking Luke. "So much for changing into clean clothes," he grumbled.

When it came time to return to the catamaran, we worked out a strategy: we girls would get in the bow to paddle. Luke, who was already wet, would push us out from waist-deep. This sounded good in theory and I had a clear picture of it in my mind. But like many clear pictures, it didn't go anything like that. Within one or two seconds, the others pushed from either side and leapt aboard. Patricia began paddling while Luke lowered the outboard to start it. Patricia was paddling away, Luke swearing loudly at her to keep the dinghy from going broadside on to the surf. "No need to talk to me like that!" she shouted. Neither seemed to notice that I wasn't aboard.

"Hey, wait for me!" I called, but of course, they were loath to return. "You'll just have to get wet," Luke said. I pondered for a second if there was anything in my pockets that might object to a salt-water bath, then waded out, chest-deep. The lifting straps of the dinghy were broken so it wasn't easy getting aboard. My two travelling companions were not seeing the funny side of it. Luke was still stressed over the possibility of capsizing and Patricia was still mad at him for swearing at her. Back on board the catamaran, she found the most distant spot up at the bow to sulk. A grown woman of 38 years old acting like a 2-year-old child. After a while, I went up and sat next to her. "Are you OK girl?" I asked.

"It's not the first time," she replied, with a melodramatic flourish. "This morning, when we were leaving the dock, he ordered me about, also with bad language. There's no need for that. It gets my back up." She heaved a loud sigh before continuing. "I have this problem with authority, with people telling me what to do. It's gotten me into trouble before."

I made some sympathetic noises, not wanting to derail her train of thought, despite questions being flagged. She was on a roll, eyes glistening, emotions welling.

"And there's a big lack of communication with the skipper. He has changed in the last week, become more withdrawn. I'm having trouble reading him." She paused to look straight at me.

I had to agree with that. We were all feeling it. I cast my mind back to the morning, hoisting the sails. The reef lines were tight, preventing the sail from going up. I called this information out, but was told to "relax". A strange response, I thought.

But this was her time to vent, so I stroked her shoulder gently and let her spit it all out until finally, she drew her own conclusions. I never got the chance to ask her if she had been in this situation before or to pick up any of the other breadcrumb trails she had tossed out, or to offer ameliorative viewpoints. It takes a certain largesse to step aside, allow, understand and accept others, whose rough edges may be skinning your shins. Much more so, in the confined spaces of a boat. But you know you just have to accept it when you sign on. It's quite rare for deal-breakers to crop up so early in the piece.

A couple of days later, I wasn't too surprised when she had a quiet talk with the skipper, telling him she couldn't sail with Luke, who was, in her opinion, foul-mouthed and rude and would never change. Perhaps the suddenness of this conclusion seemed like an easy way out but there was no negotiating; her mind was made up. She flew back to Switzerland the next day, leaving a slightly bad taste, and an excessive collection of exotic tea-bags. Luke took a more cynical view, believing she simply had a fully-paid holiday in the Seychelles and never intended going sailing in the first place. Marten seemed sad to see her go.

The morning after she left, we took all the sheets and towels to the big commercial laundry, where they charged by the item, a total of $120! I wouldn't have put my knickers in had I known. The expense account that the owners had supplied would have been like a cash-register on steroids, practically on fire. I was starting to feel ashamed by all the free meals and drinks that Marten so generously splashed out on. But who could have guessed we would be dock-bound for so long?

There is a cushion in the cockpit, embroidered with the motto: "Enjoy the simple things of life". Living on a boat there are simple things which others on land take for granted, like the ease of getting supplies, and showers with hot and cold running water. Perhaps the blue sky and sunshine are the simple things to enjoy, when they are there and when we notice them. What the cushion is really telling us is to take the time to notice these things. Thank you cushion, for the reminder.

Walking around the Seychelles by myself each day is another time to notice things. I notice the contrast of the opulent marina precinct and the slums just across the bridge. The apartments are small, stacked 2 – 3 stories high, built of prefabricated concrete, painted in pastels, pale green, blue, yellow, ochre; or, more drearily, not painted at all. The guttering is often rusted out and broken; the footpaths are uneven concrete slabs laid over open culverts. There is a strong smell of raw sewage.

The main street is narrow and busy, lined with derelict buildings, uneven rock walking tracks, tiny convenience stores with barred entrance and windows, skinny dogs, and fat Creoles. A continuous stream of cars, trucks and old Leyland buses look like they've been badly panel-beaten too many times. There are no motor scooters, pushbikes, or impatient horn-blowing. Oddly enough, no smiles, something I have seen in the South Pacific islands, amongst the poorest of peoples, who are clearly enjoying the simple things of life. Possibly because there, they are free to wander, sit, chat, laugh, sing, dance, play music, whereas here there is zero unemployment. Everyone has a job, even if sweeping the street with a straw broom, or sitting in one of the ubiquitous sentry posts, guarding who-knows-what. The shifts are short, perhaps only a couple of hours a day, giving everyone a go. The high school is completely encircled with a razor-wire-topped concrete wall, like a prison, with a guard at the gate. Are they keeping the students in, or others out? The crime rate is supposedly low. Not surprising, with so many guards everywhere.

Across the border in the marina, everything is beautiful, the manicured gardens, the vibrant tropical flowers, the boutique shops and cafes, and everything is expensive. Most things are imported, and cold or frozen goods have an additional premium, like cheddar cheese at $15 a kilo, or plain yoghurt for $12. It makes my pockets squint. The Australian purchasers of the catamaran have given Marten an open cheque book, which is rapidly ballooning out of all proportion. Just sitting here at the marina, waiting, day after day is not cheap. Nor the hire car, which Patricia mainly used as if it was her own, much to Luke's chagrin. That at least was given up after she left.

Most evenings Luke goes up to the local boutique brewery on his own, saying he needs time out. He likes to sit and drink beer alone. His justification is, "You have your time out when you take a walk." But he has misread that. I would happily have him accompany me if he wanted to, but he doesn't enjoy walking. In fact, he doesn't seem to enjoy many of the things I do. This is not a good basis to build upon, and the fact that we don't really know whether or not we are even drawing up plans doesn't help. It is an empty landscape, miles broader than a blank canvas with no brushes or paints, never mind a rough idea. And yet in some weird way, I feel as if my future hangs on it.

Tentatively broaching the subject of our relationship, albeit long-distance and to-date undefined, prompted an angry response in him, saying it was not something we could discuss.

"Other people seem to," I answered, to which he snapped, "And see where that gets them!"

OK, fair point; one can't really argue with that. It's true, most people do seem to revolve around one another like distant satellites in unguided orbits. I guess I was holding onto hopes for better, my expectations once again setting me up for disappointment, dissolving like a pillar of salt in the rain. And so he continues to drink up at the pub each evening and then drink more back on the boat, coming to bed several hours later. He seems to be avoiding me, even though he claims to be glad I'm here. I feel hurt and confused and wonder why I came.

The days drag on and we seem to have reached some kind of impasse, with nothing resolved. Nothing really can be. I don't want to ask him to change his behaviour for me. It is not my place to do so when there's no sense of commitment or 'coupledom' between us. I feel I have no rights, but this is not something new or unexamined.

It seems to me that there is a hierarchy of position, one which is very much based on perception, and, like most perceptions, tacitly agreed upon. Having some degree of close connection provides the possibility of being heard, understood, and conciliated. Without that sense of closeness, we might just as well be like strangers who couldn't care less what the other does, so long as it doesn't disrupt our own world too much. With degrees of caring and sharing come stages of influence. Least significant of all are strangers, who generally care very little for the faceless masses (although in some instances show more respect than those who do have some familiarity). But in general, people outside one's immediate circle are of no consequence— we don't know them and spare no thought to their personal problems.

Then there are friends, (from casual acquaintances to bosom buddies) who can be more involved in each other's lives, trying to help out whenever they can, often sharing their opinions and advice. This group tends to tread lightly, with a readiness to listen openly, to respect differences and not be judgemental. While even the closest friend is replaceable, it would not be without some pain. Rights to influence are limited; they care, but not to the point of jeopardy and are more willing to back down for the sake of preserving a valued friendship.

Lovers can be quite passionate in their caring and sharing, though retain a degree of separation to live their own uncompromised lives. I believed Luke and I to be at this level. A lover status is one of greater intensity, though usually has less longevity than that of a friend. Their rights, as I was feeling, are practically non-existent, unless there is some deeper neediness, which the potential loss of the other would threaten. Partners are often symbiotically entwined. What hurts one hurts the other; they have a deeper self-interest in seeking to influence and request compromises. Their union is almost a oneness of being. There are promises and expectations (even if only implied), ideally followed up on with mutual respect.

Perhaps it is a wife's role to act as the brakes to her man's throttle, but it was never something I could do, believing that as adults, we are each responsible for our own behaviour. Perhaps that made me a bad wife in the past and I should just accept it's a role I'm not cut out for. So here I sit, trying to extract some relevant guidelines as to how to function in an adult world that seems as far beyond my comprehension as the life of an amoeba. How many lifetimes does it take to get the hang of this game?

———

After interminable waiting on bureaucracy's buckled wheels to grind, we were all feeling a bit like caged animals. Each day Marten would visit the Port Captain to check if the boat's clearance papers had arrived, only to be further frustrated. The owners back in Australia were also losing patience.

Finally, on Monday, August 21, we were let loose. The following Monday, we were back where we started. Things didn't go at all according to plan. Everyone who knows anything of the proposed route back to Brisbane, against the prevailing SE Trade Winds and counter-currents, said it was not a sensible idea. Well, they were right.

Afterwards, the skipper wrote to the owners, outlining some of the issues that caused us to turn back, followed by his conclusions and recommendations:

> "Another reason to turn around is the way the boat behaves on an upwind course. We were really banging into the waves at a speed of 3-5 knots and the current was setting us more to a northerly drift. To set a course for Cocos Keeling was out of the question. You could say this was an extended sea trial of about 600 nautical miles.
> The big plus of this catamaran is the downwind sailing, the comfort and space on board and complete layout. I would take the boat on a world circumnavigation any time! But sailing 'the right way' of course.
> So, my intention of sailing to Australia more or less directly via Cocos Keeling Islands may have been a bit too optimistic. The alternative route, more north via the Maldives and then to Indonesia is a better option. In my opinion, the best sailing option would be to go 'the long way around', via Africa".

———

So …… "*the long way around*" eh? What a thought—that we might change course and head down toward South Africa—the way that I myself had originally been heading on *Shanti*. That thought for some strange reason rattled me. The past few weeks have reminded me of some of the challenges of crewing. It's interesting how others can so strongly affect one's notion of self. Lately, I have been seeing myself as if I was looking through others' eyes, and in their eyes, it really does seem as if I am an ignoramus. This is making me feel a bit like a constantly beaten dog, one that will automatically act cowed. It is easy to undermine confidence in those who have worn that black cloak before.

One uncomfortable night in that futile first attempt to tackle the Indian

Ocean, I noticed a discrepancy between the chart-plotter track and that on my iPad. When I made mention of this to the skipper, he said, "Ignore that. All that matters is the waypoint and the heading to it." Later, when he came up to relieve me, the first thing he said was, "We're way off course." I said I had been doing what he told me, and that the waypoint and heading matched. He changed screens, made a few entries that I couldn't see, and moved the track and the waypoint. Nothing said.

For a paid delivery-skipper, I would have expected slightly better communication. On another occasion, he mentioned, "We are just crossing the Mascarene Ridge."

Me: "Where it goes suddenly shallow from very deep?"

He: "Look at the sea."

Me: "It's all lumpy."

He: "No-o." (no further explanation).

He has an interesting way of saying "No-o"—almost polysyllabic, that carries so much more meaning than just the word itself. It seems also to say, "What kind of stupid question is that?" And "Why do you need to know?" And "It's none of your business."

I have definitely detected a chauvinistic trait, one that downplays my boating experience, most likely because I am female. Luke is spoken to quite differently, though they clash at times. But clashing is at least mutually respectful, not belittling. I miss being master of my own ship, to have my errors of judgement serve only as lessons to learn from.

So, here we are, back in port again, awaiting spares and repairs, not sure which way to go.

The potential for further delays seems highly likely, causing all of us to doubt the sense of staying on. I am reluctant to go the "long way round" on someone else's boat when I have my own boat, patiently awaiting my return in Darwin. To head to South Africa was the next step of my dream and it was shouting at me loudly, beating like a war drum against my fears, tearing them up into tiny pieces of confetti. This was my personal battle, not something I could verbalise to Luke, or anyone else.

I realise that I came to the Seychelles in search of a new dream to replace the one I had abandoned, hoping that this man could fill that void with pretty promises—something to give me hope again. My confidence had been challenged and crumpled. Who was I fooling, imagining that I could sail around the world alone? It seemed way too big an ask. And yet ….

What satisfaction could there be in doing it as crew on someone else's boat, easier as that may be than going it alone? But in the past week, I had sampled the big Indian Ocean rollers and didn't think they looked that scary (admittedly we were in the north Indian Ocean, which is reputably more benign than the south). But I felt I could handle it. At least I wanted to try. A few of those motivational mantras were playing in my head, rekindling my dreams, making me question my decision to give up on my quest, right at the start-line, as it were. The idea that dreams choose us, rather than we choose our dreams, especially resonated with me. And the aphorism:

"Win if you can,
Fail if you must,
But never quit".

And my own notion: "It is one thing to try and fail, but to *fail to try* is true failure."

I feel that I had failed to try. I had gotten to the start-line in Darwin, was assailed by doubt and fear, and was too afraid to step off into the great unknown. I know that my body may not take the strain of the Indian Ocean, but the challenge still calls me. When you quit, you fail. That's it; end of story. If you persist, you may just succeed.

I took a long walk, sat on a grassy embankment on the poor side of town, thought about all the poor people in their downtrodden lives, lifted my closed eyes and sought guidance. If ever I needed help it was now.

The embrace and kiss that Luke gave me by the open door of the waiting taxi really felt sincere, momentarily bending my knees and tearing my heart. I have no idea when, or if, I will see him again. We have not talked about it at all, as per usual. I know he feels annoyed by my seemingly sudden decision to go.

Chapter 8

This Is It

Today, September 5, is my birthday. It seemed an auspicious date to call Customs and arrange clearance. Tomorrow I will clear out of Australia, buy a courtesy flag for Mauritius, and stock up on fresh fruit and veg. Then at the first opening of the lock gates on Thursday morning, *Shanti* will creep out of her captivity and resume her voyage. The route will take me across the Indian Ocean (the right way), to Cocos Keeling Islands, then Mauritius, then South Africa. All going well I should be there by mid-December. For some strange reason, my crisis of confidence had dissolved, being replaced by a strong sense of independence and a powerful passion of purpose. This was exactly where I was meant to be. I pre-cooked a couple of hearty meals, drank a toast to courage, freedom, and new beginnings, played some rousing music and danced wildly. Life is good when you think you know where you are going.

With my first real ocean crossing ahead of me, I was pumped with excitement. It felt great to be heading to sea, leaving the land behind, with no pressure to get anywhere before dark. No more day-hopping up the coast. No more surf-strewn bars to cross. Just the big wide blue out there for days on end. *And just me!* That thought was both exhilarating and terrifying. I wasn't sure how I'd go with sleep management or any of the other unknown challenges yet to test me. Leaving *Shanti* to her own devices for very long during either the day or the night still eluded me. The thought of going to sleep for an entire night, as I had heard other single-handers report doing, was inconceivable to me. I was far too nervous for that, despite having the AIS alarm to warn me of shipping. Nevertheless, it seemed essential to at least try and establish some kind of routine. Initially, getting up every 20 minutes, then lying back down to rest, if not to sleep, became my "proximity to land" routine. Eventually, nights and days would become indifferent to my normal biorhythms and I would learn to grab sleep whenever I could.

The Bureau of Meteorology showed light winds for the next few days. This was to be my last weather forecast until I made landfall in another country. VHF radio only has a very short range, and I hadn't yet figured out how to get forecasts by the more global HF radio. I wasn't too fussed by this. From experience, I know that forecasts are often inexact, providing a broad generalisation that doesn't cover local variations. And things can change unexpectedly.

The first day out was glorious sailing, doing an easy 6 knots across smooth seas. By 1800, the wind had dropped to only 2 knots—time to fire up *Yani*, being very conscious of my scarce fuel supplies and the many miles ahead. Still, I was prepared to sacrifice half a tank of diesel if necessary to get clear of Australia and motored through most of the night. I took advantage of the lull to change the Dyneema lines and pulley arrangement on *Min*, the Fleming self-steering, because I had noticed the rear lines were over-riding the front ones and getting jammed.

At 0730 the following morning, the wind was up to 6 knots, so I optimistically shut down *Yani*, but that was short-lived. Then at 0930, 12 knots of breeze filled in from the east and we could sail wing and wing, with a poled out headsail. The sea-state was very rolly, making it difficult to work on the foredeck, a confined and dangerous enough place at the best of times. Even though everyone knows it's advisable to be tethered to the boat, it's an unfortunate fact that tethers just get in the way, adding a tripping hazard and limiting the range of movement. They are of dubious value to the solo sailor who is just as likely to be drowned while being dragged along behind the boat, like a fish that's given up the fight. So my edict was simply, "STAY ON THE BOAT".

At 1030 an Australian Border Force plane flew overhead and called me on the VHF radio, asking my details and destination—Cocos Keeling Islands. They then called another yacht, *Troll*, which was heading for Christmas Island. That little bit of human contact was somehow reassuring, knowing I was not completely alone out here. But the cold hard reality of it was that for the first time in my life, here I was, facing a boundless blue completely alone with only a few centimetres of fibreglass between me and death. Definitely not a good thought to entertain.

At least 9 or 10 ships passed nearby. *The Pacific Centurion*, bound for Darwin appeared right on my Rhumb line when I awoke from a half-hour nap and passed by very close. My AIS wasn't on, conserving battery power, which still seemed quite low, despite the motoring I had done. As I'll be passing through oil wells and shipping lanes for the next few days, I really do need to have the AIS on all the time and run the engine for a couple of hours each day to top up the batteries.

On day 3, the wind was up to 25 knots with big, lumpy seas. The course was 240° Magnetic, the furthest west I could sail without gybing. There were large rollers, some breaking, hitting us broadside and slewing us off course. *Tilly* couldn't handle it, quit working and threw an accidental gybe in protest, which threw me across the cabin, injuring my wrist. I wasn't sure if it was broken but the pain was intense when I moved it. Great, I thought; now I'm truly single-handing.

I dropped the mainsail completely, glad of the full moon and gave the helm to *Min*, who still needed more attention than I cared to give. It's not an ideal "self-steering" system that requires me to sit out in the cockpit all the time. I was feeling disheartened, knowing that I absolutely must have reliable self-steering or cannot continue. Thoughts of escape invaded my mind once again, with desperate ponderings on how to get off this tiny boat: Australian Border Force plane? Passing ships? Christmas Island? It's only day 3—and some pitiful tiny voice whispered within me: "At least I tried". Defeatist excuses. Lame!!

I cooked a healthy meal of steamed vegetables: carrot, celery, potato, broccoli, and red capsicum, mixed with a spoon of olive dip and camembert cheese. A full stomach always helps revive the spirits. I furled the headsail to reduce the load on the tiller and reminded myself of something I learned at University: *all that is required is to stick with it and you'll get there in the end, no matter how long it takes*. Students that drop out have no chance of getting their degrees. Those that simply hang in there generally reach the goalpost, unless their grades are abysmal, and even then, they are often given second and third chances. So here I was, counting on obstinacy and beneficence.

I had a saltwater shower in the cockpit. Feeling clean is as uplifting as a good meal. I'm not tired, despite having had very little sleep. These first few days have gone by surprisingly quickly. I find myself calculating time and distance to the next port, as if that was important. Then I pull myself up by the ears and say, *Stop!* Stop and look around at where you are, at this most rare, deep blue animation, ever-changing constancy, perpetual motion, each froth-lipped crest its own unique display of perfection; a profound parallel of our own lives, each uniquely different, yet all entirely the same; a transient flash in time, yet an ongoing part of the whole; a reminder that nothing, absolutely nothing stays the same, and yet, within that transience is constancy. Lives come and go; *life* continues.

What can we make of this philosophical musing? The reality of the sea is harsh and unforgiving. It can squish me like an insect if I am inattentive. I have a part to play. My task is to work with the elements of nature, not against them. Am I equal to it? I have so much to learn. And it is only by being out here alone that I can.

By midnight there was nothing, not a breath of wind to shake the velvety carpet of the sea to even a ripple. The next day was more of the same, though with a large ocean swell rolling *Shanti* from ear to ear. And it was so hot!—around 45 degrees in the cabin; even harder to handle than in Darwin because there, at least I could run a fan. Here, it wouldn't stay on its feet with the rocking and rolling. I decided to stabilize the base by screwing it to the wooden breadboard.

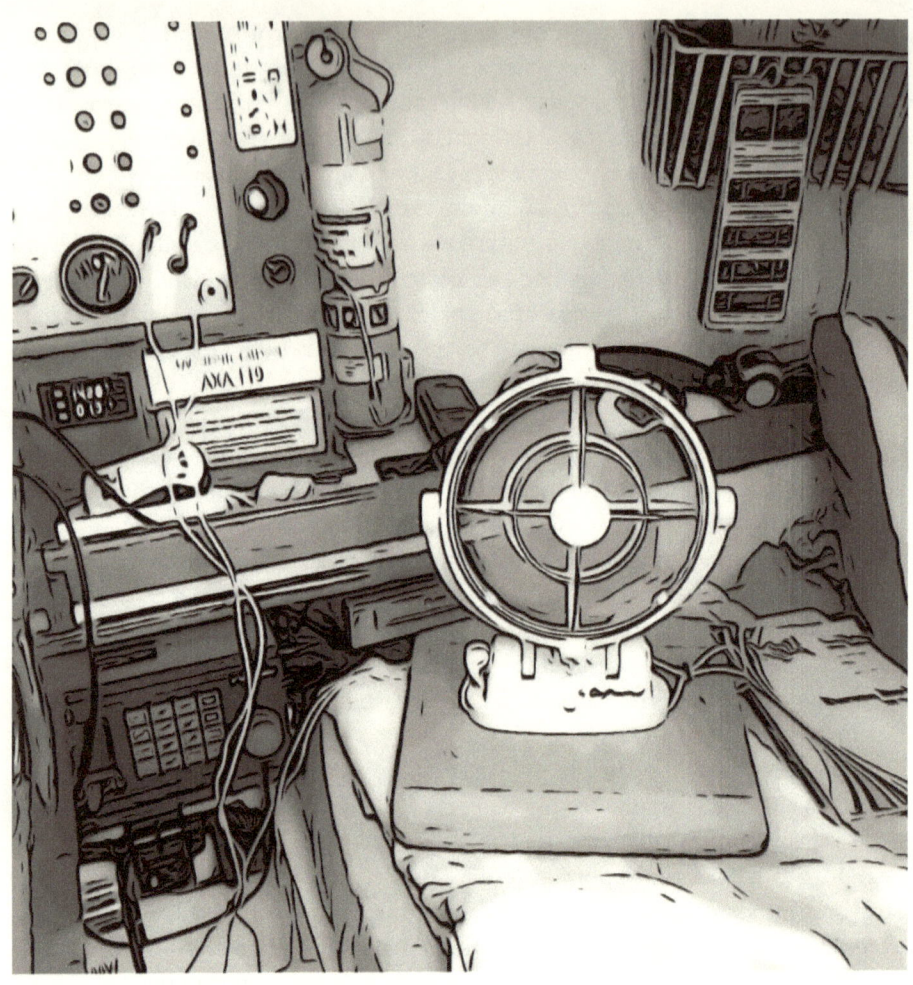

How long was this going to last? A Satellite phone text to the outside world confirmed my fears—no wind below 11 deg south—almost as far north as Indonesia, which was 200 miles away. I stood in the cockpit staring at a mercury sea with an unbroken meniscus. Not another week of this, please! Oh dear—impatience, so early in the game.

After much deliberation and calculation, I decided that the best option was to burn the rest of my diesel and head for somewhere it could be replenished—Timor, even though I had made no notes of preparation for this landfall. I'd just have to wing it. There were several compelling reasons for making this call. I knew there were some serious issues with power. It seemed as if my batteries weren't charging or holding a charge. This was confirmed when after 16 hours of motoring, within a short time, *Tilly*, the autopilot, was squawking, the voltage down to 10.7V.

The second issue is diesel. *Shanti* carries 75 litres in her fuel tank plus another 80 in jerry cans. I have used nearly half a tank in the few days since leaving Darwin.

Running the engine for 2 hours a day to power the batteries, I will use around 60 litres in the estimated 20 days to Cocos Keeling, and that doesn't include any light wind motoring. I now have about 120 litres in total remaining. Averaging around 4 – 5 knots, burning 1.5 litres per hour should give me a range of approximately 350 nautical miles. Not enough to get to Cocos Keeling.

The third thing is the self-steering. Despite changing all lines and blocks, *Min's* control lines keep slipping off the pendulum pulleys and getting jammed in between. I don't feel that I can trust her enough to go to sleep for long. Running *Tilly* all the time uses too much power, so I have been trying to use her as little as possible. It is an absolutely one hundred per cent game-ender for me not to have reliable self-steering. My experiments with sheet-to-tiller steering have had some success, but now there is my injured wrist limiting what I can do.

How can so many things conspire to trip me up so early in the piece? I survey my undulating surroundings, which are at once both miraculously stupendous and spirit-crushingly endless, spreading like a desert through aeons of nothingness. *What am I doing here?*

Motoring over a glassy sea to Kupang, Timor, was not a planned detour, so Australian Border Force had to be advised of the change of destination. Thank goodness for the Inmarsat Satellite phone, albeit the most basic, second-hand, cheapest to run, with only 160 characters of text available, including spaces and the recipient's address.

I wrote abbreviatedly: "Australian reg yacht, Shanti, dep Darwin 7/9 for Cocos Keeling. Becalmed 300 miles W of Darwin. Suspected broken wrist. Only enough diesel to motor to Kupang." I wasn't sure if that constituted any kind of emergency or one deserving of special dispensation, but I felt vindicated in at least letting them know. Truth be known, they probably didn't care either way. I had left their jurisdiction and was now in no-man's land. So I just kept on driving like a crippled bird across the contourless ocean until I got there.

Entering a foreign country with no idea how is interesting. I found an old cruising guide with advice to report to the Harbourmaster at the commercial port, so I motored up and down in the suddenly strong headwinds, calling constantly on Channel 16, but got no reply. I gave up and returned to the most obvious anchorage opposite the main town. Three other boats were anchored there, including a small, decrepit-looking yacht with two men on board. They later went by in a semi-deflated, half-sunk inflatable dinghy (too long in the tropics?) and I asked them how to clear in.

"Just take your dinghy ashore and ask for Michael," they informed me. That easy!

Even though I only want to be here a couple of days I know this is going to cost me. An entry visa is $US35; the agent's fee $US250. It seems exorbitant. Everything was put on Michael's "tab", as I didn't yet have any Indonesian Rupiah. I shall have to keep an eye on this tab. Everyone seems to work for the agent; his "dinghy boys" will carry your dinghy up the stony beach for a fee of 70 Rupe, and possibly even guard it for a bit more. They will collect and deliver water of dubious quality.

At 0700 the next morning, my wrist was feeling better; it was probably just a bad sprain rather than a break and rubbing it with Arnica cream made it usable. I was able to row ashore and found a slightly less rocky landing that wasn't quite so surge affected, so avoided a dousing. Michael's taxi driver, William, drove us firstly to Immigration, a long drive out to near the airport, amidst crazy peak-hour traffic. It seems to always be peak-hour here; mainly mopeds and motor scooters, weaving wildly in an out, with common courtesies rather than road rules reducing the still high road toll. I was glad to be within the more protected metal shell of a car.

Next, we headed to the opposite side of town to Customs, a fairly modern building overlooking the sea. A broad sweep of marble stairs led to a large, open foyer skirted by a rabbit-warren of offices where no one seemed to be working. After several trees worth of paperwork and many hours of practising patience, a most unlikely-looking young man in a denim jacket, presumably the I.T. expert, was called in. He was needed to create an online dossier which would become my permanent record for all future visits—rather overkill I thought for a two-day stopover. I had to sit at the computer and fill in my details, before being stood against a blank wall for mug shots, like some suspected criminal.

Unfortunately, they wouldn't do the check-in and check-out at the same time. Young denim jacket would need to come and view the boat at 0700 next morning after which we would have to come back to get the clearance papers to leave. This was my first introduction to the bureaucracies of clearing in and out of different countries, some taking hardly any time at all, others the best part of a day, all of them showing curiosity about me and my single female status. I never encountered any chauvinism or lack of respect.

The next stop was Quarantine, which I expected to be quicker, but no, still more paperwork and rubber stamping. They must have used half a rubber plant in official stamps. I was supposed to have a boat stamp for *Shanti* and did make some attempt to get one, without success. Despite this, Michael said things went well in Quarantine because I didn't speak. It's a bit hard to say anything when I don't know any of the language at all. I kept hearing Michael use the expression *"force majeure"*, which I thought meant that my stopover in this country was forced by maritime emergency, though it didn't seem to be helping.

The final step in this process was to visit the Port Captain, where more explaining by Michael, with me mute, lots of smiling and nodding supposedly greased the wheels. Four young women sat around, not appearing to be doing anything other than to look beautiful, cast sideways glances at me, and giggle shyly.

When they took out their boxes of local food and began eating lunch, I realised how hungry I was, regretting not having had breakfast. For some stupid reason I didn't imagine this would take so long. Five hours so far! I got some unexpected kudos as a solo female sailor and various officials came to shake my hand and have their photos taken with me. Very disconcerting!

Meanwhile, the Port Captain is watching music videos on his computer, playing music loudly, "*Send me the pillow that you dream on*", and occasionally dancing. Always smoking. Now there are eight people in the small office, all of whom share the same disregard for doing any work. Apparently, there's been an accident down at the port. A worker inadvertently straddled a sling and was lifted by the crane, then dropped. He didn't die, but one leg is badly broken. This has created a big diversion and roads may be blocked for a while.

Is anybody working here? Ah, the girls have just been presented with an old ice-cream carton full of stamps to do some rubber-stamping. But then a man in an impossibly crisp blue uniform with many important-looking badges came and took over. The girls giggle and slap one another playfully. Later they fall asleep on their desks. Overall, a fascinating experience, so long as there's no time-frame or first-world expectations of efficiency. One of many more lessons for me in patience.

Getting the diesel was easier—a longboat and Michael's boys to deliver it to *Shanti*. The batteries were a bit harder—no deep cycle batteries are available here, so I had to make do with lead-acid car batteries. Not ideal, but a temporary measure which hopefully will get me to South Africa. The heavy batteries were also delivered to the boat and left for me to deal with, wondering how and where to fit them. I finally found a spot in an adjacent compartment which only required a few holes drilling and a hefty plank of wood to keep them off the bottom of the hull.

Michael obliged in sourcing new battery cables and a suitable length of wood, cut to size by a local timber yard. I rode on the back of his moped, my unwieldy plank held widthways across my lap. Carrying all this amongst hundreds of other motorcycles in heavy traffic was an exhilarating experience. You see many a family zooming about, always with the youngest perched up front as the sacrificial lamb. The women pillion riders often sit side-saddle, with never a helmet to be seen. Whenever we parked outside a store, even for a minute, someone's palm had to be crossed with a few coins for the privilege. I guess this in some way controls the general chaos and drip-feeds the economy at the community level.

Friends on *Dream Catcher* arrived and we explored the town, wandering aimlessly, eating and drinking whatever seemed safest. We visited the night market in search of someone to repair a flag and discovered a great many sewing machines buzzing away in the tiny booths that flank the narrow paths. Everywhere was a bombardment of the senses. Masses of movement, the smoky smells of outdoor cooking, the vivid colours of slushy drinks, made to order with your choice of ice, liquor and tropical fruits.

Kupang is a fascinating blend of old and new world. Going from the grubby outdoor market to the huge shopping mall, all shiny and immaculate was a bit of a culture shock. The rows of stock on supermarket shelves were displayed with military precision and the checkout chicks wore smart uniforms like airline hostesses. I wondered who shopped here, as the prices were much higher than in the markets and the wide aisles were spacious enough to drive a tank down them. Who was it all for? The well-to-do minority no doubt, who preferred not to be crammed cheek to jowl with the great unwashed.

I spent two nights fitting my new batteries in after the wind had died off and the boat stopped pitching. After consulting many "experts", near and afar, I took the easy path and connected them in parallel to the existing bank. There was a great attraction in this—for the first time, having double the capacity. Optimistically I bolted my new 6" x 4" plank in place, screwed the plastic trays on and lashed them all down. They just fitted perfectly lengthwise. The first time I cranked the engine it was exciting to see 44 Amps going in, the first positive charge I had seen in ages.

On Sunday, September 17, exactly 10 days after leaving Darwin, I'm ready to go again. Unfortunately, after it has been blowing the crabs off the rocks for the past few days, we are lolling listlessly in a breathless, mist-enshrouded morning. I shall row ashore with my rubbish and see what develops …

I was expecting the leg to Cocos Keeling to be uneventful, with light winds, at times not enough to sail—but that's far from what I got. That evening the wind was gusting up to 30 knots from the east as *Shanti* valiantly rode it. Whilst preparing dinner, a bigger than usual wave slammed us over to a bigger than usual angle. The cutting board and its contents, plus my favourite paring knife flew south, the knife to completely disappear. Later, when I went upstairs to eat, shrinking myself as small as possible into "coward's corner" (the tiny, semi-protected space behind the dodger), that same wave's brother dumped itself all over the cockpit. And me! Luckily my bowl of vegetables was spared the addition of too much salt.

The wind died out completely the next day, so we motored for an hour. I noticed this was NOT charging the batteries! The solar panels were putting in 4 Amps, the engine alternator only 1.2. Aaaah! Turn everything off, including the recently-stocked fridge. It was depressing to think that the only way I'm going to make this passage is with zero power consumption, no autopilot, no computer, no instruments, *no fridge!* So much for the new batteries! It's funny how I used to imagine that I would run the engine once a week, just to make sure it still works. Now, here I am thinking of running it for at least three hours a day just to keep the batteries charged.

I've been experimenting a lot with sheet-to-tiller steering, which I first read of in Webb Chiles' blog, and have been fascinated by the concept. It requires a lot of tweaking, setting up a couple of snap-blocks (pulleys) through which to run the jib sheet back to the stern then across to the windward side of the tiller. This force is counteracted by a few strands of shock cord which allow some give, as well as variable adjustment. It's important to adjust the sails first to get the boat as balanced as possible. Once it was steering a reasonably straight course, I said to *Min*, the Fleming windvane, "you may just have been made redundant."

Now was that tempting fate or what?

Life at sea is a much more condensed and accelerated series of highs and lows than life on the land. Almost from one moment to the next, elation can turn to misery, success to disappointment. The great challenge is not to get too caught up in this, with moods attached to the roller coaster. The lesson isn't easy. We are so accustomed to being reactive rather than responsive, to being driven by external forces, giving over our inner peace to whatever is going on outside of us, rather than to rest in that elusive foundation of equanimity. As human beings, we are designed to feel emotions and to think thoughts, but our freedom comes from being the witness to this drama, like the director of a play; to stand back a little, with a certain amount of detachment. In other words, not to get swept up and lose ourselves in the storyline. A helpful analogy is to consider one's thoughts like a screen onto which scenes are being projected. A blazing inferno doesn't burn the screen, any more than a violent storm wets it. The screen of life is neutral to the drama unfolding upon it. I try to be more like an impartial investigator, approaching things with an attitude of curiosity.

The batteries aren't charging ….. that's curious. It's also curious how many things happen in the middle of the night. So whilst standing back ever so slightly from the blazing inferno of the screen, I pondered what was going on. I soon realised that connecting the old and new batteries together was definitely NOT the way to go, exciting as it was to think I had 400 Ampere hours, which is a minimum requirement for long-distance self-sufficiency. Nigel Calder's boating "Bible" states, "*Never connect different types of batteries together, wet cell and AGM, or old and new, which will result in quick death.*"

Durrrhh!! Even a small child knows not to put new toy batteries with old ones. The voltage was down to 10.7V in the old bank and rapidly dragging the new ones down to the same level of depletion. Even though I too was sharing the same exhaustion, and longed to crawl back into my bunk, I knew I had to change them over. Everything had to be removed from the compartment that the new batteries were in; a large canister of safety flares, hot knife, cordless drill, extension lead, spare computer, etc. In a last gasp of self-preservation, the old battery voltage increased to 12.8V, but it hasn't got me fooled. They're coming out! I have been resisting this task, with the tangled web of heavy cables spread like an octopus over them, but now there's no choice.

Each battery weighs about 20 kg. Their L-shaped, dedicated space is about halfway down the quarter berth, where there's not even sitting headroom, so no way to get your back into it. How to lift them? Here's a clue: there's a small window in the side of the cockpit that more or less lines up with the battery bank. Passing a rope through the window, round the old batteries and back to a winch, I could winch the heavy load up and out of the way before sliding the new batteries into their place; all without breaking my back! Another minor win and grin.

With the power back on, the batteries are maintaining good voltage, so *Tilly* took over the helm while I got some sleep. I'm learning stuff in this classroom of the sea. (Some would say I should have known it all before setting out, but most of it can only be learnt on the job).

I woke to find us sailing beautifully in 12 knots of steady breeze. The seas are a bit lumpier and there are white, puffy, Trade Wind clouds in the sky for the first time. The barometer is 1013.8 and steady apart from its usual diurnal fluctuations. Thank God for the SE Monsoon current. We are doing 7.5 knots SOG, have covered 120 nautical miles since the last waypoint, and still have another four hours to go until noon when I will record our progress. Time is losing one hour for every 15 degrees of longitude; it is as if I'm sailing slowly backwards in time to yesterday. Time at sea has a whole different reality, completely abstract and only measured by sunrise and sunset. I could so easily lose track of it, were it not for keeping the daily log.

Chapter 9

Stay on the Boat

Unexpected tripping hazards in the open sea include FADs (Fish Aggregating Devices), which are large conglomerations of flotsam (logs, bamboo, nowadays even concrete) that are used to attract ocean going pelagic fish. They are rather like a man-made micro-island, tethered to the ocean bed, which local fishing fleets then "anchor" themselves to. Often these are unmarked and unlit, but in this instance, I did spot the "loom" of the lights on the horizon at dusk and set my alarm to wake me in an hour. I'm not sure if my usually trusty kitchen timer (*Tammy-timer*) ran out of batteries or I knocked her with my arm, but two hours later, I woke up in hell.

The first indication of trouble was a low rumbling noise, like a ship's engine, and I fully expected I was about to be run over by a tanker. A pungent odour filled my nostrils, and bright lights were flooding through *Shanti's* cabin windows. Leaping up, I found myself right in the middle of an Indonesian fishing fleet, with perhaps half a dozen boats all around me. There wasn't a lot of wind, so I must have been ghosting quietly through their midst under full sail, receiving no warning from them, not by radio, horn, yelling or beating on pots or pans. Perhaps they didn't want to disturb me.

It's feasible that I could have continued on obliviously in my sleep, with no harm done. I spotted a long-boat, not more than a few metres away. "*Hey! Watch out!*", I called at the top of my voice. With a loud, sickening thud the heavy wooden boat smashed into the back of *Shanti*. My only thought was to get away from it as quickly as possible. I dashed below to turn on the engine, which produced a loud squealing sound just before it died.

Back in the cockpit, I saw a small, dark-skinned man crouching on the bow of his boat, rather like a monkey. He kept repeating, "*What to do, what to do?*" I could see his dark animal eyes, flashing in confusion and panic.

"*Are we stuck?*" I cried, thinking some part of his boat was entangled in the metal frame of my wind vane. I could see the rope from the front of his boat disappearing into the dark depths beneath my stern, as taut as a steel cable. His heavy boat repeatedly smashed and smashed and smashed against the stern of poor *Shanti*. She must surely be holed!

Grabbing the sharp cockpit knife, I leaned over the stern and sliced through the thick rope that bound us together. I could see the fisherman wasn't too happy to lose it, but it wasn't the moment for being considerate. Released from her bondage, *Shanti* pulled quickly away. My heart was pounding as I kept berating myself, *You silly, silly girl!* But there was no time for that. What was the extent of the damage? Was any water coming in?

I noticed the lights of one of the larger vessels following me for a while, perhaps to check if I was all right, perhaps to retrieve their rope, perhaps to shoot me or slice me up into small pieces for my intrusion in their night. But after another half an hour they turned and left me to my own fate. My heart didn't resume its normal rhythm until dawn.

Fortunately, there didn't appear to be any major structural damage to the hull. *Min* had acted heroically in the thick of the assault, staving off the battering ram as self-sacrificially as any Kamikaze fighter. Somewhat like a roll-bar in a Formula One racing car, she saved the stern from being holed and *Shanti* from sinking. Unfortunately, she died in the process. I wrote in my log: "*Min* is dead, set in some weird rigor mortis contortion." Her heavy-duty stainless-steel frame was completely misshapen, rendering that form of wind-driven self-steering henceforth useless. It saddened me greatly to see her like that, almost like losing a fellow crew member. Other damage immediately obvious was the bent stainless-steel tubing of the rear Pushpit and the smashed up outboard motor. Petrol was leaking from the cracked fuel line. The wooden mounting board was broken so it was hanging on by one screw. Later I noticed the life-ring, immersion light and danbuoy were missing.

Gradually, as the night ebbed and my agitation settled, I extracted the broken pieces of my confusion to try and understand more fully what had happened. The wooden long-boat must have had a line tied either to the larger mother ship or to the FAD. I must have gone between and hooked up on that line. It may have been just the keel at first, luckily not the rudder, but then it wrapped around the propeller when I started the engine.

I lifted the heavy cockpit floor to check the shaft which seemed not to be leaking. But the gear stick was jammed, making it impossible to run the engine. With a wind of over 20 knots and very lumpy seas I'm not going overboard today; maybe tomorrow. It's another 330 nautical miles to Christmas Island, the closest possible stop where I might get help. I changed course to head there instead of Cocos Keeling.

I contemplate all those before me who have circumnavigated without having an engine at all. Out on the ocean, a small auxiliary engine is more for charging batteries than for distance making. Now I have to get sheet-to-tiller steering working. I have sat and studied it closely for hours because I need to understand it fully. It's all a matter of balance and even a small adjustment can change everything. For some strange reason it seems to work perfectly while I'm sitting in the cockpit watching it; the minute I go and lie down it goes awry, running off toward the gybe.

I set my alarm for every thirty minutes but couldn't sleep. It occurred to me that there must be another end to the rope that I cut between *Shanti* and the fishing boat. There's a good chance that I am dragging a lot of rope, perhaps even with an anchor on the end of it. I wish I could hop over the side and have a look but it's still blowing over 25 knots with big seas and the thought of going for a swim is not appealing. It's the first night that I have entrusted the steering to anything other than *Tilly*. We have made a lot of North, which is good if we want to go to Christmas Island. I have visions of the freeloading anchor snagging land just as soon as it can.

I listed some lessons from this misadventure—ridiculous as they later seemed.

1. Don't go to sleep.
2. If you do go to sleep, don't rely on a kitchen timer to wake you up.
3. Don't expect others to get out of your way, or to let you know they are there.
4. Don't expect plans to remain the same.

Unable to run the engine to charge the batteries, I shut down the fridge and all other unnecessary power drains. I still have three solar panels, putting in around 6 or 7 Amps per sunny hour of daylight, but of course, nothing at night. For the next three days, I felt like a crippled bird, knowing something had to be done but unsure exactly what. I read whatever information I could find on Christmas Island, learning it was rather an exposed anchorage; sailing in without an engine could be tricky. I could possibly radio someone (who?) for a tow.

It all seemed rather fraught. The only way to find out the extent of the entanglement was to heave-to and go over the side for a look. This was something I didn't relish the thought of, knowing there might be sharks, and the number one rule is STAY ON THE BOAT.

The more I thought about it, the less I wanted to do it. Best not to think about it. The wind didn't seem to be abating any time soon, and waiting for the ideal conditions, I could become petrified, in every sense of the word. So after summoning all angels, dismissing all sharks, visualising the best outcome and digging deep to unearth some buried courage, I backwinded the jib and lashed the tiller. This virtually stalled the boat, though she was still jogging on the spot, making perhaps one knot of headway. With my small boarding ladder fixed in its brackets on the deck, I sat for a while, staring over the side, feeling immense resistance. The water looked so deeply blue, so bottomless. I really DID NOT want to step over the safety lines onto that ladder.

Wearing face mask and snorkel, fins for propulsion to dive deeper under the boat, I tied a couple of long ropes around my waist and stepped gingerly over the side. At least the water wasn't cold, but I felt extremely vulnerable being immersed in it, seeing *Shanti* from the outside. Gripping the cockpit knife as if it might save me from a shark attack, I took a deep breath and dove.

There it was, a thick, yellowish rope wrapped several times around the propeller. The first slash at it was completely ineffective and I quickly pushed myself back up for air. My lungs felt constricted, only capable of holding my breath for less than a minute. The second and third attempts saw some result, with frayed strands of fibre trailing like tangled ringlets. They looked strangely beautiful in the refracted light. Surfacing again, I took a rest, clinging to the lowest rung of the ladder, being dragged slowly through the water.

There is an underwater cave in Tonga that has a rock ledge barrier to swim under. The test for this is if you can dive from one side of your boat to the other, passing beneath the keel. I can do it easily. Fear is the enemy. Fear that you won't make it from the ocean to the air inside the cavern, that your lungs will burst, that you will need to surface half way through, with the merciless rock ceiling stopping you.

But here, mid-ocean, completely alone, the fear was harder to control. Thoughts of sharks or whatever other life-forms were sharing this unnatural habitat with me made me not want to linger. Pushing such thoughts aside, I dove again, three or four more times, my breathing becoming tighter each time, panting like an overheated dog. My pulse was throbbing loudly in my ears, my limbs as limp as a rag doll. Clutching my lifeline to the boat I pulled myself closer, trying not to get tangled, trying to avoid *Shanti* knocking me out.

Again I dove, knowing there was no choice but to continue until it was finally cleared. It shouldn't be so hard. I seemed weaker than I have ever known before. It was hard to fight off the self-pity that can undermine me when I'm feeling hard done by, wondering why me? Who am I to be doing such things at my age? What am I thinking? This is beyond me. It's too much to ask. It's unfair! These are the thoughts of self-doubt and victim-hood that are my nemesis. They make me want to stamp my feet, give up and cry. They can sap my strength quicker than any exertion. They can make me feel like I don't belong here, that I have no right to exist. Back to those old "no-rights" tapes in my head. Now is not the time for them. Push on!

At last, it was done. There was no great sense of elation or anything. I hung off the ladder, being jostled up and down by the waves, towed like a fish on a hook that has lost the fight. There was not an ounce of strength left in me. Climbing back up that ladder seemed impossible. The curve of *Shanti's* hull, which should have meant home and comfort and life and somewhere that I really ought to be returning to, was replaced by a blank canvas of meaninglessness. The boat, the sea, the rope, the ladder, myself, all were strangely unreal. Their only meaning was in the fact of their being. They were, that's all, just what they were. Existing in a void.

I felt nothing, neither fear nor urgency, just a numbness of body and mind, where nothing had any meaning. No thoughts called me. I simply was, just holding on by the merest thread. Without meaning there is no call to action, there is nothing to do. I don't know how long I hung there, until I finally found the missing connection to survival, hearing a voice in my head that asked if I wanted to die, and somehow, like Solo Bob had done, answering No.

It is still a mystery to me as to how I did it, how I summoned the determination to climb back up that ladder. Finding strength when all strength is gone—that is the unfathomable mystery. Where does it come from, when I am an empty vessel? I collapsed onto the cockpit floor and watched stars circling like fireflies inside my hollow skull. Too spent to even give thanks, gradually the enormity of that gift seeped in.

With the engine once again operational and batteries rechargeable, *Tilly* resumed duties for a while, enabling me to sleep a little more trustingly. She is power-hungry and makes this incessant two-pitched noise as she goes back and forth, errr, urrr, just to let me know she is working and that I should be ever so grateful, which of course I am. I never take her for granted. I'm learning not to take anything for granted.

The wind was up around 32 knots for the next week, and the seas were massive, knocking poor little *Shanti* off her perch, dousing her in cascades of water and covering me in bruises. I was disappointed to find that the newly-installed centre hatch aimed a jet of water directly at me on the leeward bunk, as if to say, "get up and bail out, lazybones." I can hear water sloshing in the bilges, but it's not over the floorboards yet and it's too bouncy for me to get down on hands and knees with a bucket and sponge. All I'm really good for is lying down. Any more than that results in too many bruises. There always seems to be an extra huge lurch every time I try to prepare a meal.

Right now, the seas are mountainous, with yet another sea on top, all going at cross-purposes. I didn't expect this. It is up over 30 knots every day, sometimes touching 40. This leg, going to Cocos Keeling, was supposed to be the easy bit. What will the next leg be like? So much for comfortable, down-wind 15-knot Trade Wind sailing that they promise in the cruising guides. I have never seen anything quite like the Indian Ocean. The sea is a great boiling cauldron as far as the eye can see, all froth and bubble, toil and trouble, with billions of dancing wavelets scalloping the surface. It is overcast and raining so there's no solar power input. I should set up sheet-to-tiller steering, but I don't want to sit out there in the rain. There are three reefs in the mainsail and the headsail is heavily furled. I'm thinking of dropping the main, but it seems to be managing OK.

At 0830 *Shanti* was knocked down, which is to say put on her side, with the mast in the water. An especially big wave hit us broadside just as I was preparing my breakfast. Everything flew across the cabin, including me. I clutched frantically at anything that might stop me, not knowing if we were going to keep rolling through a full circle or come back up. Within seconds *Shanti* bounced back and the world was upright again. I scarcely had time to register what had happened, other than to see the unbelievable mess of things strewn all over the place. Water was halfway up my legs and the floorboards afloat. I sat for a long while, processing it all in some kind of delayed shock. The aftermath weakened me most.

Under the cockpit floor is what I call the "bathtub", a removable fibreglass well, where I keep jerry cans of water and diesel. The knockdown had half-filled it with water. It's a bucket job to empty it, but first, the heavy cockpit floor, which is about 4' long and 2' wide has to be lifted and secured on the leeward seat. Once emptied, I need to lift out the unwieldy bathtub, balancing myself at one end and lifting it by the two lengths of string that I fitted to enable one person to do the job. It's backbreaking work manhandling this. Once it's out, I rest it on top of the upturned flooring and lash it to a winch so it won't fall back in on me while I'm down in the hole, bailing the water that has found its way inside the boat. This all needs to be done in haste, lest a nasty roller breaks over and sinks the boat through this huge open cavity. I'm like a drowned rat in a hole, with only my head peering out at floor level.

I slowed *Shanti* down a bit to possibly take less water over the boat and started timing the interim between the really huge waves. It's not *all the time* that a bigger than usual wave slams like a freight train against the hull and cascades gallons of water over the deck and into the bilges. So far today, it's pretty much hourly. But, words of wisdom from Keith, in Darwin, who has sailed hundreds of thousands of miles with his beautiful wife, Marion: "You get used to it." I wonder if I ever will.

I had a weird dream last night, about giving up. A Master or Lord of something or other was talking to me, telling me the debt had been paid, the evil withdrawn, and it was going to improve now. He asked me a question: "Was I good for it?" I said, "I think so", to which he replied, "*No – say I'm good for it.*" I repeated his words and just then Tammy-timer went off and woke me up. What was that about? Some kind of subconscious affirmation of a tenacity I don't feel. Maybe if I repeat it often enough, with heartfelt conviction: *YES, I'm good for it…. I've got this.*

———

I managed to cook the last of my vegetables before they went off, even things like pumpkin and potatoes that keep well without refrigeration. At 2030, I saw the lights of a ship that wasn't transmitting anything on AIS. I'm about 245 nautical miles from Cocos Keeling.

The wind has dropped to the mid-twenties, though the waves are still big. It's interesting how relative things are; gales seem pleasantly comfortable after storms have abated. "The beatings will continue until morale improves!" Crew morale is improving, possibly because landfall is imminent. I noticed last night that the pin that *Tilly* connects to on the tiller is loose. I have bandaged it with double-sided Velcro. I love that stuff. And non-slip grip mat, which is excellent at keeping things where they should be—to a point of course.

The sun has come out and things seem to be settling down a bit. There haven't been any big slams or dousing for a few hours now. The seas are still quite big, but pleasantly going with us, lifting the stern and rolling easily under. I can't imagine sailing back to the east, from Cocos Keeling to Australia. It really is a one-way trip. Probably just as well, or I might be looking for more excuses to give up and go home. But I know it is forward and onward so I had better make the best of it. For dinner, I ate couscous with onion, canned peas, corn and carrots with a boiled egg. Standing in the companionway watching the sunset and clouds and sea, I felt the sudden exhilaration that follows a reprieve and began singing "Gaudete", an old Steeleye Span favourite.

The wind is dropping slowly, around 12 – 22 knots. There are some big dark clouds ahead and masses of puffy ones all around the horizon. I'm not sure what to expect. I should make landfall in Cocos Keeling Islands tomorrow morning if I go slowly enough through the night. Time to clean myself and *Shanti* in readiness for human contact. I had a salt-water shower in the cockpit and followed it with a one-cup freshwater rinse. Going about stark naked makes me realise the shame of my body that was instilled in me in childhood. I wonder if I can ever get over that? The rationale for always covering myself is to hide my imperfections as if I expect my body to be as perfect as a supermodel. I have always had a critical eye, judging this one too fat or too thin, or in some other way imperfect. We are all imperfect people. I have a new saying about this: "it doesn't matter if you're a little bit fatter or a little bit thinner, a little bit older or a little bit younger, a little bit smarter or a little bit dumber, because very soon, you're going to be a little bit deader, and none of this will matter one little bit."

On October 1, as the sun rose, I beheld before me—GREEN! A canopy of coconut palms rising unexpectedly from the low-lying coral atolls, like vibrant green icing on a yellow cupcake. After navigating the circuitous passes over shallow reefs, I dropped anchor in the turquoise waters of the uninhabited Direction Island. I had been wondering if there would be any other boats there, only to discover the anchorage full with about twenty or so yachts from the World ARC rally. Fortunately, they all left the next day, leaving only a respectable three or four long-distance cruisers.

The white sand is warm and grainy beneath my feet, softly solid in an unmoving kind of way. It takes a while to adjust to being on the land. There is the blueness of sky and sea, but the shallow waters caress the shore in limpid transparency. Tall palm trees bring verticality to my otherwise horizontal world —and *colours*— yellow, beige, amber and greens, all in variegated subtlety. Textures are also a novelty; firm roundness, frayed leaves, and crisply desiccated fallen fronds. Movement is ever-present, but dancing to a different tune, swaying a warm "Aloha" in the gentle morning air. There are new scents too, the smell of land, which is strangely unique to each place. Breathe it in; this quintessential island Paradise! How thankful I am to receive this wondrous reward for my efforts. I decide that Cocos Keeling is my all-time favourite place on earth and I would like to stay here forever.

Two German men have sailed here in two separate boats. Klaus is 80 years old, an inspiration in so many ways, including his bronzed physique, his lean muscularity and agility. He built his boat himself in East Germany before the Wall came down when getting materials was nigh impossible and the sea inaccessible. It is a pale-yellow colour with a top-heavy coach-house and resembles a lifeboat from the *Titanic*. At only 10 metres long, (still bigger than *Shanti*), it is rather like the *Tardis* in its storage capacity and has the unpronounceable name of *Tiedverdriew*. I just couldn't get my tongue around it.

Wolfgang is about my age, more solid, with a round, openly friendly face. His first question to me seemed bizarre in this setting: "What are you doing tomorrow?"

"Hmmm, no particular plans".

It turned out to be an invitation to share a meal of freshly caught Mahi Mahi with them. Unbelievably, Klaus carries a large metal drum on his small boat, which he uses for smoking fish. I admired him darting about, gathering coconut husks and fallen twigs for the fire, while Wolfgang sat at the wooden table talking to me. He told me the two of them were "buddy boating" around the world and helped each other keep watch at night. One would sleep for four hours until the other called on the VHF radio to wake him, just as any couple on the same boat might share watches.

Their two boats were quite evenly matched and they adjusted sails to stay close to one another. Only once had they accidentally nudged in the night. Seeing how I was a single-hander on a similar-sized boat, Wolfgang proposed that I join their little flotilla. That way, we could each potentially get 8 hours' sleep. It sounded good in theory, so I agreed.

There is a palm tree on the foreshore, where cruisers have attached signs, engraved or painted with the names of their boats. This is a very select club, which few ever get to join. I feel very privileged to be amongst them. Most yachts are much larger than *Shanti*, at 9.6 metres, and have more than one person aboard. Tony on *Tangled Up*, is an electrician by trade and happy to look over my battery problems. We walked around the island together, scuffling through mounds of loose coral, chatting easily. Nearing the metal frame of the lighthouse out on the point we were astonished to find huge piles of washed-up rubbish. I have read since that there are an estimated 414 million pieces, mainly of single-use items like drink bottles, straws and plastic cutlery, on this atoll. Over 90% is buried under the sand, but it is tragic to consider the impact on this seemingly pristine environment and the surrounding marine life.

Still, I found it a wonderful place to rest and relax after my first challenging passage. I felt as if I could stay here indefinitely. There is a small yacht in the middle of the bay, about the same size as *Shanti*, well-equipped for the open sea. But it is abandoned. Story has it that a solo sailor, like myself, took a pounding on the ocean, like myself, and felt overwhelmed by it. But then, unlike myself, he somehow managed to get himself off the boat and catch a plane off the island. Again, I count my blessings and my short-term memory, which seems to forget the hard times, in the light of a glorious present. In fact, I love my life all the more, for it has brought me here.

Wolfgang delivered two 20 litre jerry cans of diesel to *Shanti* from the main centre of Home Island. Like most, his dinghy is much bigger than mine, and his arms much stronger. There is a woman here who laments the attention I seem to be receiving, having given up her independence for an older partner and late-life child. Their young son is handsomely curly-headed and articulates in a refined accent, with the precocious maturity of all cruising children. He is nonetheless thrilled to share his sixth birthday celebration with some other youngsters who have just arrived. They swim and play together as if they are best friends since birth; something we adults could learn from.

Both Klaus and Wolfgang love to bake all kinds of delicious treats which are a rare delight at afternoon tea time. Sitting together on the aft deck of *Tiedverdriew*, listening to them chatter incomprehensibly in German, a colourful selection tempts the eyes before the taste-buds. Wolfgang's speciality is cheesecake, sometimes topped with juicy morello cherries or other fruits. Klaus presents individually crafted cupcakes, decoratively layered bars, creamy pastries, coconut squares—each as precise as would not look out of place in any of the world's finest bakeries. They both give me bread-making lessons, which will expand my limited culinary repertoire.

And so the days pass in blissful, blue-sky indulgence. This must truly be Paradise, with all its sensual delights. Were it not for my loyalty to Luke I could easily have been tempted by Wolfgang, who made it obvious that he liked me. My daughter, Misha, would chide me for this old-fashioned attitude, but for now, that tenuous connection keeps me bound, free only to enjoy new friendships at arm's length.

Chapter 10

Calling All Angels

As with any of life's sybaritic indulgences, be they food, drink or frivolity, there seems to be some kind of inbuilt clock that flicks past the hour when the cuckoo pops out and chimes, *"enough"*. So at 0730 on Sunday, three small yachts lift anchor and bid farewell to this utopian sojourn in the Cocos Keeling Islands. *Shanti* is a bit hobbled with a reefed main and furled headsail in 20 knots of wind, a breeze which the other two heavier boats can easily handle. At midday, my guts are threatening to evacuate, as per usual after having rested in sheltered waters for a while.

Darkness falls heavily and I don't manage to sleep at all, being nervous as to where the others are. I'm constantly going up and down the three high steps over the engine box in the companionway, peering about for their lights. Occasionally Wolfgang calls me on the radio, letting me know I'm too close or I'm too far away. I turn on my engine to move to a better position and notice the tachometer isn't working and there's no charge going into the batteries. I pull the engine box off and fiddle with some wires. Yay! Success!

From 0200 to 0600 is my watch. I take this responsibility more seriously than if I was on my own, never leaving the cockpit for the four hours, standing up and looking around a full 360 degrees every ten or fifteen minutes. I try to maintain a good distance and not to disturb the others at all. It's nearly impossible for me to pronounce the name of Klaus' boat over the radio. I notice he has pulled away from us and is sliding well off course. When I query this, he says it's of no importance when there's another 2,000 miles ahead. He may be right, but personally, I prefer to stay as close to the Rhumb line as possible. I say nothing and follow.

On Tuesday afternoon, I couldn't believe my eyes. I looked up and saw a couple of curly "pig's tails" starting to unravel at the top of the windward lower, the wire stay that begins just below the spreaders. The wind was gusting up to 30 knots. The following day, four more wires had broken and unravelled about 30 cm down from the top. This was definitely not good. If these stays fail, the whole rig, mast and sails and everything would fall down. When that happens, there is a possibility of the broken mast holing the boat and sinking it. Then what? Abandon ship?

The rigging was relatively new, having all been replaced prior to my leaving Melbourne. I sent off a brief text message via Sat phone to the rigger, asking his advice and prognosis. The response was not encouraging: "*The stays will fail and the mast will fall down*". This is rather like being given a diagnosis of a terminal illness and wondering *When? How much longer have I got?*

Another rigger wrote this: "Generally it's not the wire rope that's the issue but the swaged terminals. I used to repair a lot of these in the shop and the swaging pressure used is critical to ensuring wire fibres are not crushed in the process." This didn't really help. Whatever the cause of it, there was no point in asking why, for anything other than academic curiosity. The fact of the matter was the rig was failing.

I called Wolfgang and suggested they go on without me. I would need to slow down so as not to stress the rig, and didn't want to hold them up. He told me to "stand by", which is marine radio parlance for "hang on a bit", while he discussed this with Klaus. A few minutes later he came back with their decision. They had friends coming to meet them in La Reunion on a certain date and really needed to be there. So they would go on without me. Sorry.

It was a wistful gaze at the diminishing white dots on the horizon that left me feeling very alone in this great big ocean with a mast that may soon be coming down around my ears. The AIS showed them doing over 7 knots of boat speed and I thought they must be glad to be free of me. In light winds I am faster, but once the wind gets over 20 knots, they are the ones hobbled for me. Being so much heavier they can carry much more sail in stronger winds. I don't often envy faster boats, but at that moment, they seemed far better suited to the conditions. However, there's no point in entertaining thoughts that *Shanti* might not be the best boat for the job; she is the boat I am on.

Then it was back to setting my own watch-keeping timer, either for 30- or 60-minute intervals. It was tiring, but in a way I felt a certain relief, to be dancing to my own tune again, unconstrained by others. And I didn't have to try and pronounce the unpronounceable name of *Tiedverdriew* over the radio. Well, that surely had to be a good trade-off? Hmmm, eight hours' sleep a night, or that? It's interesting to observe the machinations of a stressed mind.

My attempts at supporting the mast involved using every halyard, wire, rope, winch, jammer and cleat available. Luckily *Shanti* has a toe-rail with holes spread along its length at about 6" intervals. These made good anchoring points to attach spare halyards to. I also lashed the baby-stay to a windward chainplate with Dyneema and tightened the rigging screw. The angle wasn't ideal, but it was the best I could do. Apart from pray. I have been told that there's nothing quite like a ship in peril on the open sea to shift the most hardened agnostic towards faith in some higher power that might intervene benevolently. Me, I'm more likely to call upon extra-terrestrially powerful, mast-supporting angels.

On Thursday, the mast was still standing. Following the two Germans had put me a long way south of my course, so gybing, to put the wind on the other side of the boat would be necessary. This wasn't such a bad thing, taking the stress off the damaged stay. It reminded me of when I was a young girl, sailing my Moth in the Hauraki Gulf of Auckland. The leeward stay let go, and I knew that as soon as I changed course, which I would eventually have to, the mast would fall—which it did. I sat quietly waiting to be picked up by the local fishermen, who knew me well. But there were no such rescuers here. Other than perhaps one of those giant cargo ships, which look far less user-friendly.

After having braced the port stay as well as possible, I discovered the starboard stay was playing the same game, also unravelling from the top. I took two halyards off the port side and attached them to the starboard side. Then I made a small loop out of double-sided Velcro, wrapped it around the stay, attached it to the twine that was used as a "trace" for a spare spinnaker halyard, and pulled it up. This applied some pressure to the broken strands of wire, preventing them from unravelling further. Of the original 19 strands in a healthy stay, five or six were now broken.

Worry was wearing me down. My tired mind ran freely down "what-if" tracks, imagining worst-case scenarios. Some people may think this helpful, being prepared for what might come, but in fact, it is totally enervating. It is enough to think it through once or twice, to work out logical plans of action, but then let it go, allowing some repose to a wound-up mind that is more in danger of cracking than the mast. For three nights, I hadn't had more than a few hours of sleep, listening for any slight change in anything. Whenever the timer beeped, I had to force myself to get up to look around, check the sails and everything. Some serious pep-talk was needed in the wee hours: *Come on now, this is your job, it's not forever, make the most of the off-watch times and go quickly back to sleep, please.* There were at least two ships I saw close by each night. I wondered how many more I didn't see.

I spent more time looking up than at the horizon. Why do those small white birds, with an elegant long whip of a tail, always try and land on top of the mast, threatening to break the antenna and wind anemometer, when there are so many flat surfaces they could choose instead? Why can't they be more like the big-footed Boobies, who always rest on the solar panels? That would be preferable, were it not for the load of thick cement-like guano that they dump before taking off. Maybe the white ones flitting at the top of the mast are my angels in disguise, keeping an eye on things for me. That's a comforting thought.

We're sailing very square, only under reefed mainsail, trying to gain some slight westing, rather than sailing south-west. This is the legacy of the German armada; 200 miles off course in only a few short days. Klaus's theory that it doesn't matter in the long run may be so, but I can see the errors compounding unless corrected. If one makes a very long tack off to one side of the course, the wind may change against its opposite correction. So smaller zig-zags across the Rhumb line suit me better. And now I am alone again, I am master of my own course.

I cooked some pumpkin and lentil soup in the pressure cooker, and listened to an audiobook of Jane Austen's "Emma". In the chapter where Mr Knightly confesses his "attachment" (love) for Emma, the language is so thick and rich, like the grand finale of a fireworks display. The book could have ended there, but no, there is more. I love the old English style of writing and could easily slip into that mode of speech, had I someone to speak to. That would be amusing. It's good to find small things to smile at. The Michel Thomas French language course is another source of amusement. I notice that these tiny up-turnings of the mouth echo deeply, suffusing my whole being with an unusual gladness. There are moments when I can almost forget the imminent threat above me and bathe in profound silence.

Just when I thought I was getting used to the constant motion and not knocking myself about as much, I took an unexpected tumble backwards against the stove and the little T-shaped screws that lock the fiddles in place stabbed me hard on the spine. Personal injury is an ever-present concern, knowing how from one moment to the next, I could be rendered incapable of sailing the boat. I move cautiously, like a cat about to pounce on its unsuspecting prey, and always follow the well-known rule of "one hand for me; one for the boat". I try to time my moves in cadence with the waves, but there are still those odd out-of-synch bursts that spring from nowhere as a not-so-gentle reminder that I can never be sure of anything.

Saturday, October 14.
The mast is still standing, bless it. I have started writing an abandon-ship list—well, two actually, one of the bare essentials, like Epirb and passport; the second of "if-possibles", such as phone, laptop and photos. This is rather dependent on who comes to my rescue, and whether it's blowing a gale and pouring with rain. It's interesting to consider one's belongings in this way, what is essential, and how deeply the loss would be felt. At the end of the day, it is really only my life that is worth saving. Living in the tiny space of a 9.6-metre yacht, there's not a lot of room for things. Minimalism is the current trend, said to increase happiness in inverse proportion to our belongings, but to lose everything sanguinely must take some great inner reserve.

Cocos Keeling Islands are now about 700 miles behind. With 1600 miles still to go, it is certainly too far to motor, possibly even too far to sail under jury rig or to be towed. If the mast falls, there isn't a lot of choice other than to scuttle the boat, though I hate the thought of losing her for the sake of a few strands of wire. I also hate the thought of having to climb a multi-storied rope ladder up the sheer face of a passing tanker. I try not to worry my family, but ask my eldest daughter, Pandora, to check with my insurance company—am I covered if I intentionally sink my boat, to prevent leaving a shipping hazard afloat? They side-step politically, saying that they would need to consider this. My four children are naturally concerned.

A Korean tanker passed too close for comfort just on dusk. At less than half a mile away, I watched him ploughing headlong into the waves, throwing a wall of white spume up as far as the anchors on the bow. I shrank into myself, imagining if I was sitting here, disabled. NO! I inwardly yelled. *Go away!*

At 2220 I lay down to rest, but immediately my mind shifted into gear, trying to come up with anything else I could do to further reduce risks. It occurred to me that when (not "if") the windward shroud breaks, there's a high chance that one of those razor-sharp curly pig's tails might puncture the dinghy on the foredeck. And I might need that dinghy as a life raft. So hop up again, and do more—this time, attach another "sky-hook" to the top of the stay to control its fall to the deck. Now I can lie back down again and rest for another half hour. Ten minutes later I felt *Shanti* setting up a more boisterous motion. The wind was back up to over 30 knots; time to put that reef back in the sail that I shook out two hours ago. Such is the way of it. Now to try and fix the broken handle on the toilet's inlet seacock, which renders the toilet unusable. Hardly great weather for the "bucket-and-chuck-it" method.

Sunday 0700. The wind has been up closer to 40 knots all night long. The ocean is tumultuous, undulating like an Alpine ski field, wielding Thor's hammer against the hull every second wave. It's as if the little boat is an unwelcome obstacle, giving pitiful resistance to its mighty march. Here I am reduced to a storm jib, while the Germans would just be getting into their stride, if not already in port. I mustn't entertain such thoughts.

At 1330 we were knocked down again, splintering the "barge board" that was lashed on the side of the deck. The jerry cans of water and diesel that were tied to it washed overboard, just hanging on by a thread. It took over an hour to retrieve them, completely sapping my strength. The cockpit filled with water, and again found its way into the bilges. I hove-to, going through the same trying procedures, lifting the floor and bathtub and climbing into the hole to bail out. Without the strength to do otherwise, I stayed parked until it became ridiculous, and then resumed "sailing" in 2 knots of wind from the north.

A Sat-phone message to Luke prompted him to notify the Australian Search and Rescue of my situation. Friends on *Dream Catcher* were a few days behind me. If worse came to worst, there was a chance they could possibly pick me up. That was comforting to know. I would much rather them than a cargo ship. I replayed the rescue attempt over and over in my mind, wondering if they would want my supplies, how we would do the transfer in high seas, if we could launch a dinghy or if I would have to swim. At what point would I sink *Shanti*? Horrible thoughts.

On Tuesday, it was blowing strongly again with huge rollers breaking like surf. The canvas bimini (awning) ripped along its front stitching and was flogging wildly, so I took it down. Hanging on to the wobbly frame I asked myself, *what am I doing?* Risking going overboard just to save a bit of canvas? I lay down after, feeling very weak and tired and cried. I thought I should pack in readiness to leave the boat, just in case, rather than wait until the last minute. The toilet seacock is leaking more; water is sloshing round in the bilges. *Shanti* is sailing on, slowly, despite everything, despite me.

My noon position is 16° 21'S; 80° 17'E. I have somehow done 103 nautical miles in 24 hours. It's astounding that the mast is still in place. I realised how much I was placing my hopes of rescue on *Dream Catcher*, by how disappointed I was to learn they have not yet left Cocos Keeling. They are waiting for this front to pass through. I ask myself silly questions like, "Do I want to leave the boat or continue trying to make it?" The fact is I don't have a choice. I'm still about 1300 miles from land. Doing some calculations, based on all kinds of unknown quantities and assumptions, I figure that by the time *Dream Catcher* catches up, if the mast is still standing, I will be only another 3 or 4 days from Mauritius.

On Thursday, October 19, I did all the washing, just in case. As a child, my stepmother counselled, "One should always be wearing clean underwear in case of accident". I had visions of the paramedics checking. Today is my youngest's birthday. I sent him a text: "Happy Birthday Son. You must be about 32. I hear you are doing well and in a good space. Wonderful! Please send your strong angels to hold up mast." An immediate response came: "Thanks Mum. Strongest are on their way. Love you." It had me in tears all morning. Feeling as if my life is hanging by a thread makes me more sentimental.

Each night the wind goes more to the east, which pushes me more to the south of my course. *Dream Catcher* left Cocos Keeling this morning, on their way to Rodrigues. If my mast stays in place, we should both be there around the same time. I certainly hope I don't need them. I have run 20 miles south of my course, even with only the mainsail up. I gybed back onto a course of 310°, which has too much north in it, but there's no choice. I need to get back on the Rhumb line, so I can be more easily intercepted. Hopefully not by too much shipping traffic.

Having a stand-alone, dedicated AIS removes a lot of stress for the single-hander. Mostly I see the ships visually first. Then I fly downstairs, turn everything on to check what it is, which way it's going and how soon before it runs me over. This can take up to ten minutes. I can't afford the power to leave the computer on all the time. So it's all a bit hit and miss and more cat's lives get used up every night. Lady luck dances above the clouds, holding hands with the watchful angels.

At 2130, I was thrown out of my bunk. That's it! Definitely time to put a third reef in the main. Coming back up to the cockpit I discovered we were sailing by the lee due to the nocturnal wind shifts. *Min*, the Fleming wind vane, would have followed these shifts; but not so *Tilly*, who doggedly holds her compass course, no matter what. In true "after the horse has bolted" fashion, I tied the lee cloth on the starboard bunk, the somewhat claustrophobic sheet of canvas that renders the narrow bench where I sleep more coffin-like.

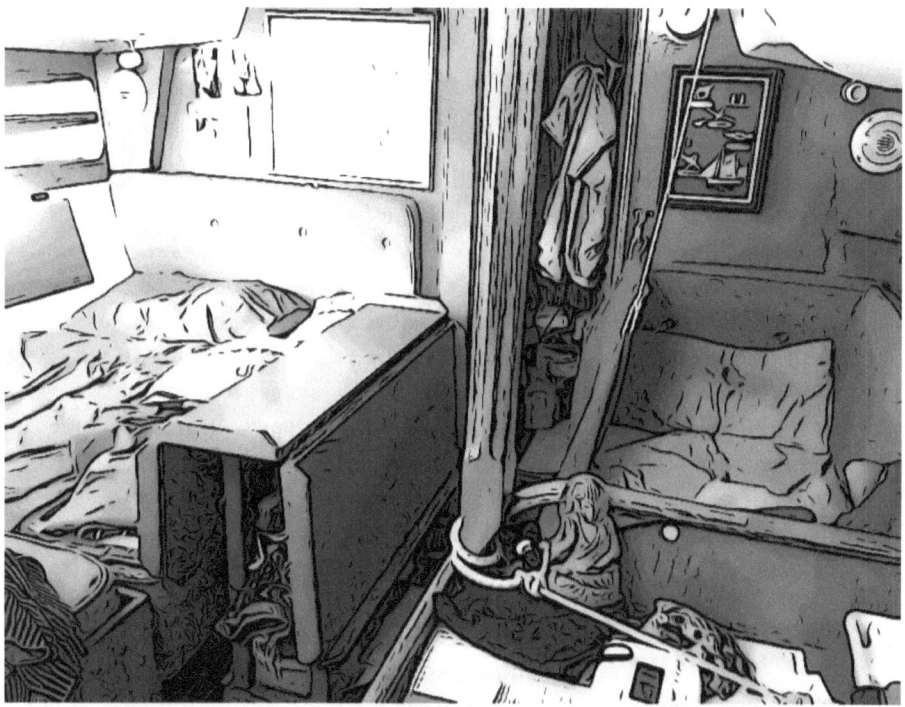

Saturday 1500 hours. I'm starting to feel quietly confident that we'll make it, so spent two hours cleaning a very mouldy fridge. Norm wrote from *Dream Catcher*, saying if I at all suspect imminent rig failure I should get off the ocean as soon as possible. He recommended stopping at the next closest port, Rodrigues, and using galvanised wire or whatever to jury rig it to get to Mauritius. I feel as if I'm about as jury-rigged as I can be, but other brighter minds than mine may have better ideas. It's another 5 days to Port Mathurin in Rodrigues and 3 more after that to Mauritius.

It was a very long and trying night, with rain squalls and calms. Each time I went out and turned the engine on, the wind came back in at 25 knots. During the calms, the boom was swinging violently from side to side. I tied a "preventer" to one side, which bent a stanchion while attempting one of its wild sweeps. I could say I'm tired of this constant motion, I'm tired of being thrown about constantly and lots of other things I'm tired of. But then I work on my attitude and try to accept, not resist. If I drop the word "of….", then I am simply tired and needn't ascribe it to anything in particular. I'm just tired—and that's OK. It's been two weeks at sea. Another 730 nautical miles to Mauritius, 403 to Rodrigues.

I made pizza for lunch with onions, tomato paste, canned capsicum and champignons, olives, cheese, and oregano. Sitting outside in the cockpit, I followed up with a cup of lemongrass tea and some sweet treats—cashews, dates, ginger biscuits and one Mocha Macchiato bliss ball. Yummy! This is food for the mouth, the spirit and the senses, not the stomach. It's not something to eat when hungry, but when almost replete, only wanting that *aaahhh* contentment. So I savour it slowly in the mouth, rolling its subtle nuances around the taste buds.

More contentment—it has stopped raining and turned into a glorious day. The wind is 15 – 20 knots from the SE. The big rollers are still chasing from behind, or slanting askew and slapping the quarter. The colour is deep, dark blue, like Indian ink—perhaps which was named for its similarity. Someone must have noticed it, long, long ago. It feels a huge privilege to be here. I'm standing at my favourite place, legs wide, straddling the cockpit seats, gripping the bar at the back of the dodger. Looking forward, I see a great chasm before me, like the edge of a waterfall that we are about to go over. I can see the other side beyond that, the crest 4 – 5 metres high. It is like spanning a broad, fluid canyon. Awe-inspiring!

Everything is done legs spread wide like an unbalanced tripod, hanging on, one hand for the boat, one for me. It's always the unexpected broadside whack that knocks me off balance. I notice that I have improved a little, getting fewer scrapes and bruises. At times, I can even dance. At times, I can forget.

Monday, October 23. At 0820, I heard a loud *"pop"* sound, as the baby-stay unravelled and snapped. It curled considerably before dropping to the deck so didn't pierce me through an eye. *Dammit!* That's my main support gone. Position 18° 52'S; 68° 50'E; 305 miles to Rodrigues. Now I'm forced to remember the overarching threat that is hanging over me like the sword of Damocles. Will we make it?

I had been feeling equivocal about stopping at Rodrigues for several reasons, primarily time. November is the start of the cyclone season and all boats should be gone from the Indian Ocean by then. Mauritius has a rigger and the services I need to make my repairs quickly. Who knows what I will find in Rodrigues? Norm is encouraging me to stop there. They are now only about 3 or 4 days behind me, so may be able to help with some further jury rig. This makes sense because while the mast is still standing, there is some chance of saving it. Once it falls, it's all over. I wasn't sure which way to go. But when my 'mainstay', the windward baby-stay snapped, it was decided. I set course for Rodrigues.

Two ships passed close by in the night, one with the interesting name of *Landbridgeprosperity*, registered Hong Kong, 335 metres long, doing 12.2 knots, bound for Singapore. The closest point of approach, 1.2 miles in 12 minutes. I saw the lights of another at 0100 hours, but it didn't show up on the AIS. Made me wonder how many more I don't see. Thankfully they all seem to alter course if necessary to go around me. That's assuming they see me.

At 1400 hours I gybed again to cover the 12 miles to get back on course. I have to take my chances with the starboard lower shroud breaking. They are both pretty much the same now. The wind is fluctuating between 12 and 18 knots. The main is doing its horrible snatch and grab and partial gybe when the wind drops. It's a huge stress on the rig, jarring my whole body in sympathy. I try not to clench my teeth. It's tempting to drop the sails and motor but we may need what little fuel is left for later. At 1700, I gybed back onto the port side, willing that shroud to ease gently back into its strain. It's amazing how much of my body is involved in this, as if it was me, my body, mind and spirit, unravelling, weakened, scarcely holding it together. Like the rig, I have to be strong.

The jerry cans from the broken barge board have ended up in the cockpit, all lashed together, sliding to and fro and banging into one another. Even more annoying than that is the lack of foot room, so my acrobatics exiting the cabin are mainly aloft, standing on the cockpit seats. There are not many handholds for getting across to *Tilly* to change course, so there are quite a few inelegant crash landings. Which I am getting used to.

The fenders may be needed for going alongside the wharf at Port Mathurin, so I went through the tiresome process of lifting and securing the cockpit floor, securing the fenders somewhere while I hopped in and bailed out. Before doing this, of course, the jerry cans had to be off the floor and secured somewhere else. I'm running out of somewhere elses. Finally, all clean and dry. The fenders have found a new home tied on the outside of the Targa bar, so they are not intruding into my living space in the cockpit. I don't know why I didn't think of this before. It's the perfect spot for them.

Wednesday, October 25. 0930. I dropped the main and unfurled a small amount of headsail on the starboard tack, heading 290°. It's so annoying that I can't sail a direct line. It makes the division of the remaining 98 miles into 3 legs somewhat irrelevant. I had thought it might be necessary to slow down a little to arrive in daylight tomorrow. Hmmm, *tomorrow* —yikes! I'd better get a move on.

Thursday, October 27. 0800, "Land Ho!!" Distance to go 25 miles. Almost there! Don't let go now, angels.

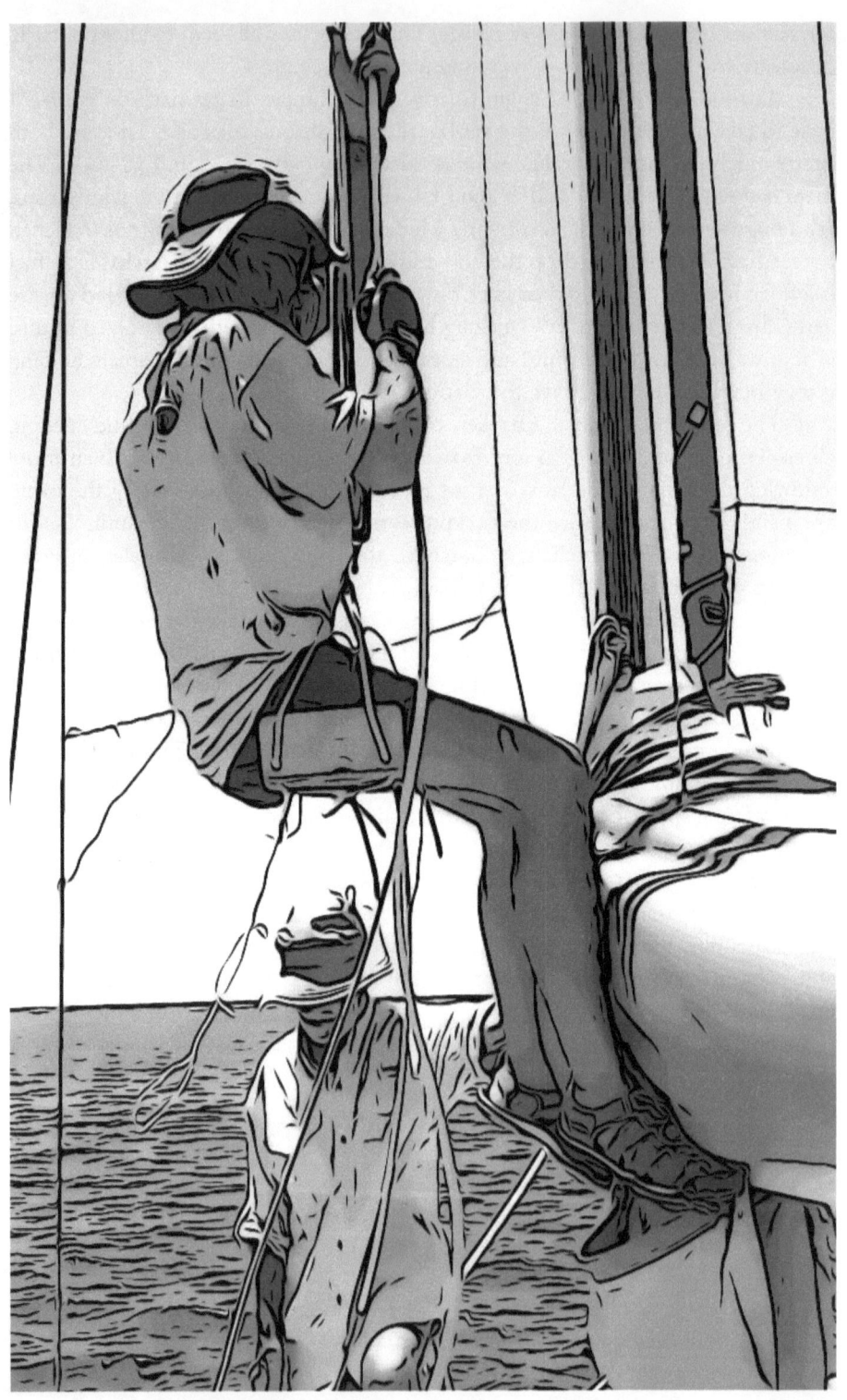

Chapter 11

Digging Deeper

Finally.

I am tied up alongside the main commercial wharf in Port Mathurin. What a great relief!! I have almost finished the clearing-in process, gotten internet and made enquiries as to a rigger, though, as suspected, drawn a blank here, but confirmed that one does exist in Mauritius.

Whenever a ship comes in, it's necessary to leave the port to free up the turning basin, so it will be back out to sea for a bit this coming Sunday, the day *Dream Catcher* is due to arrive. I sure hope Norm has something clever up his sleeve, or at least a mast rat capable of going up and reinforcing things aloft. Then I suspect it will be a further limp to Mauritius. Time is against me, because of cyclone season starting mid-November, so I mustn't dilly dally.

On a positive note, my power situation seems sorted. With the solar panels charging the new batteries each day, I have hardly had to run the engine at all. And when I had to up anchor and come alongside the dock yesterday, the windlass worked like fury, with no tripping out, even against a 25-knot breeze. Big thanks! And big thanks to all family and friends who offered concern, loving support, strong vibes and stronger mast-supporting angels to help me through.

There was only one other yacht in the anchorage when I arrived, a yacht even smaller than *Shanti*, which always makes me feel better about my diminutive size. *Beguine* is only 27' and is circumnavigating with father and son, Ron and Mark, from Florida. It was a long-held dream of the father's, and his son had put his own life on hold for a year to support him in fulfilling it. This was the longest they had stayed in one place since leaving.

Fortunately for me, both are engineers with decades of experience of dealing with every conceivable problem that might beset anything. They are the kind of guys who once faced with a problem will gnaw away at it until the best solution is found. And so they did for three days after looking up at the rat's nest of my unravelling rigging, each morning presenting me with different options to consider. They were totally respectful and left it to me to accept or reject their ideas. When such experienced engineers offer advice, naturally I take it. Likewise, when someone other than me is willing to climb the mast, which is out of bounds to me with my fear of heights. I always say that if anything goes wrong up there, it will have to stay wrong, because there's no way I'm going up to fix it.

Father and son arrived with all the tools for the job, including bosun's chair, miles of rope and blocks and tackle, everything needed to pull oneself up the mast unaided. God only knows where they stowed all that gear on their tiny boat. I would have struggled to fit it on *Shanti*.

After some contemplation, they decided to hacksaw the T toggles off the upper ends of the stays, re-lay the unravelled wires, wrap something strong around the mast above the spreaders and join them together with D-clamps, or "bulldog" clamps. A lot of this kind of temporary fix depends on what's available. Luckily there's a Chinese "hole in the wall" store in town, well hidden behind a red steel door, that seems to sell a mixed bag of everything, from eggs to hardware.

About an hour after finishing the job, the huge red Canadian yacht *Dream Catcher* arrived. Norm was glad to find nothing remaining to be done apart from giving it the thumbs up. I was still very appreciative of his support all the way here, knowing they were only a few days behind me and ready to rescue me if needed, although Norm did confess to not feeling particularly comfortable with that plan.

We leave today, me at 0900 for Mauritius, *Dream Catcher* at midday for La Reunion. Ron and Mark, who have already been here for 7 weeks, leave Friday for Durban. With continuing good luck, I should find the recommended rigger in Mauritius, who will have all the necessary parts to replace our jury rig for something more permanent. A short hop of only 350 nautical miles, I should be there by Saturday morning. However ...

That was definitely the most harrowing passage so far, with me so much on edge as to almost fall over the unseen precipice into the realm of chaotic confusion. Waiting for something unknowably imminent to happen is perhaps one of life's greatest stressors. All that you know is it's as inexorable as the next sunset, but you don't know when or how or to what extent its impact will be.

It was raining, at times heavily in gun-fire squalls as I lifted the anchor. Wearing shorts and a thin rain jacket I was quickly soaked to the skin. I'll change as soon as I get out of the channel, I thought. Once out of the protected harbour, the ocean swell was topped with short, steep waves, tumbling every which way, tossing

Shanti about like a cork. I was feeding the fish for hours.

Darkness intensified my misery. I cannot predict any wave direction, nor *Shanti's* reaction and the inside of my head is a whirligig, that has completely lost centre.

I could hear the turnbuckles clanking against the chainplates and the mast vibrating. I knew the rig was too loose but there was nothing I could do about it in my just-let-me-die-now state. At dawn the next morning I forced myself to go up on deck with screwdriver and shifter in hand to tighten them.

A lot of this journey is to do with overcoming inner resistance, digging deeper than ever asked to before, seeking that extra ounce of fortitude that might still be in reserve. There didn't feel like much left to prop me up, that's for sure. But that mast needed propping up.

In the milky morning light, I could see the stays and mast swaying like strands of limp spaghetti. How could those engineers possibly think it would hold up like this? Was it their intention that there be this amount of play, followed by a violent snatch and grab, which at the last moment would jerk it back upright? Surely not. I often trust others' opinions more than my own, especially the so-called experts of the world. Experts, someone since told me, are the very ones to be wary of, since they are expert in doing things in a certain way that they know, and may not be able to see beyond that. But at that moment, I wasn't luxuriating in such ruminations. I tightened the stays up just enough to take out the slack, hoping that I wasn't doing the wrong thing. I still trusted others more than myself.

Two days later, with a sharp gunshot crack, the windward lower shroud let go. It was a sound I had been dreading to hear. Fear of the mast falling at any second overwhelmed me. Would it hole the boat and would she quickly sink? Would I be able to cut it away in time to prevent that? I had heard of muscle-bound crew struggling with bolt cutters, hacksaws or grinders. All these thoughts flashed through my mind in that initial moment. What to do, what to do? First I panicked, then I cried. Both highly practical. Not! I just kept staring at it in some strange disbelief, as if that would change it. I needed someone to slap my cheek or throw a bucket of cold water over me. But it's just me. Just me to snap me out of it, like a hypnotist, to bring me back to now.

An angry voice shouted inside me: *Stop panicking and mop up your tears! Take the one remaining halyard from the end of the boom and attach it to the port toe-rail. Lead it round the coach-house winch, the only one not in use and tighten it as much as possible. NOW!!!*

The mast was creaking and groaning like a haunted house. I felt sure it would fall at any second. My stomach was filled with ravens, not butterflies, as I gauged the effectiveness of the support. There was so much more load on it than it should ever have; the rope was strong; perhaps the hole in the aluminium toe-rail would rip out. There was nothing more I could do, other than to stand and watch and wait. Seconds passed in slow motion, and gradually eased into a minute, then two. Ever so slowly, the moment of crisis shifted from its chilling immediacy to a latent threat, a possibility which may or may not happen. *Stop imagining the worst and deal with what is!*

I furled in most of the headsail and started the engine to motor the remaining 100 nautical miles to Mauritius. I wasn't sure if it was ok to do this, given the possibility of the rig getting tangled in the propeller if it fell. My silent mantra became, *if it falls—quickly, instantly, immediately, urgently, throttle back to neutral.* I couldn't impress upon myself strongly enough the urgency of this, yet still, it was amazing how often that thought vanished and needed to be reinstated. Such is the weakness of the mind. Or mine at least, in that time of mixed emotions, with moments of pending disaster interspersed with improbable moments of tranquil acceptance.

It was a seemingly interminable 26 hours of roller-coasting along, using every resource I had to visualise a safe arrival. The wind had dropped to around 18 knots and the sea state was the best it had been on this passage, with waves of only around 2 metres. The forecast was for it to abate, but that was wrong. It came in more strongly overnight, up to 25 knots. Each wave that slammed against the port quarter caused the mast to lurch to starboard, lifting a good half-inch off the deck. Again, this was echoed in every fibre of my being and I wondered how we could stand it. If only I had stayed with what I had, which was a million times better than this. But what was done was done, and I could only hope and pray and watch intently, as if my eyes had the power to create my desired outcome. It took a lot to keep on seeing it upright, instead of over the side. We *will* make it! Never doubt it for even one second. Don't go to sleep until we are there.

Miraculously, the mast was still standing as we motored into Port Louis in Mauritius. Tied up safely at the Customs wharf, I took a moment to give thanks, to feel immensely grateful that the mast had been saved, along with the rigging and sails, not to mention *Shanti*.

Surveying the damage, I found the base of the mast had several small splits and one larger crack on the left. The whole mast had moved about an inch to the right. Looking up at it through the middle hatch, I saw it had a distinct S bend in it. I felt devastated as if I had worked so hard to save it, but it was wrecked anyway. Later, it occurred to me that this was still a preferable outcome, since it could have caused a lot more damage to the boat or me in falling, and I still had the boom, the sails, the internal wiring, lights and wind instruments intact.

In Rodrigues, I had been given the contact of a good rigger, a famous Vendee Globe sailor, Herve Laurent, and this recommendation was confirmed by other cruisers in the usual marine equivalent of the good old Aussie bush telegraph. They were not wrong. Herve and his English-speaking wife, Sophie, were standing dockside at the Caudan Marina on Sunday afternoon. They asked me my time frame and I half-jokingly said two days. It seems he took me literally, arriving first thing on Monday morning, cannibalising old bits to make new. The necessary parts were not available on the island, so he welded new to old in another temporary fix, which would hopefully get me to South Africa. At the point where he loosened off all rigging to move the mast back into position, I couldn't bring myself to watch so went shopping. Such a girl!

Incredibly, two days later, I am patched up yet again and ready to continue. They say that cruising is mainly about doing boat jobs in exotic locations—which sadly we often don't get to see much of. This is true, not just of smaller, older boats but also the magnificent floating apartments, such as the 43' Island Packet, *Infanta*, berthed behind me. The owner is clearly no gentleman, ("gentlemen don't sail to windward") sailing the wrong way around back home to Perth. He's had engine overheating problems, water-maker failure, etc, etc. Same same—only I don't have most of his extras—or resources. But we're all out here, facing similar challenges. Lisa Blair, the solo sailor attempting to circumnavigate Antarctica, lost her mast off South Africa. So I count my blessings.

The next stop for me is also South Africa, either Richards Bay or Durban, depending on the wind. Either way, it will be a grand moment to get there and be done with this wild Indian ocean. I have heard tell that the Atlantic is much gentler. We'll see.

I departed Mauritius on November 11, anticipating two weeks of uneventful (even boring) sailing to South Africa. Alas, it was not to be. There were half a dozen other yachts on the same passage and I joined them on the HF radio on the "Indian Ocean Crossing Magellan Net". If nothing else, it lets me know that I am not an orphan when it comes to boat problems. Various common breakdowns assailed many of the others, from autopilot to rig failure, to complete engine seizure. Eve, on *Auntie*, whom I had met in Bundaberg, had to turn back from almost halfway and bash against the wind back to La Reunion with steering problems. That had to hurt.

The Indian Ocean is crowded with commercial shipping—Japanese, Maltese, Greek, Italian, Liberian—trading whatever from here to there and back again, because obviously whatever another country has must be better than what we have, but luckily they want that, so send their ships to get it. It's a curious and growing phenomenon. What it means for small yachts is that there's more likely to be a watch on the bridge who is awake and watching out. A great many left a track detouring around *Shanti*.

The AIS has done for radar what the GPS did for the sextant—practically rendered it obsolete. If not for me having a two-way AIS transceiver onboard *Shanti*, which lets ships see me, I would have been squished like a bug on a windscreen so many times—well, I guess really only once. Setting my watch alarm to wake me every hour seems pointless. Often when I get up and go out on deck, there is at least one ship nearby, if not four flanking me. Or there is one ten miles past, which means they were next to me half an hour ago, while I was asleep. I might just as well sleep all night. If one did slip past my AIS and I woke to find it bearing down on me, I would be a goner anyway. So what am I looking for? What do I expect to see? Oh look, there's a ship crossing my stern, or bow, or more often parallel to my course. Then it's gone, and I set my alarm again. Not really sensible. But I will continue to do so if only to check the sails, the wind, and so on. At 1630, a Norwegian ship changed course to go behind me; CPA of 1.4 miles in 16 minutes. Thank God I bought a two-way AIS.

The seabirds here are so tame they will sit on my finger and land on my head. They come and go. How does a pea-brained bird know how to find *Shanti* again in a vast open ocean, to recognise her and return to their bidden nestling spot? One tried to commandeer the cockpit and pecked at my legs if I approached but I quickly put paid to that cheekiness and it settled later in the sheltered crook of the dinghy tube on the bow.

There is a well-respected South African weather adviser, Des, who guides his "chicks", as he calls them, safely in. He sends out individual 3-day forecasts, based on each vessel's position. It was Norm on *Dream Catcher* who gave me this contact and I was very grateful for it. Des is a fascinatingly rare character, highly intelligent and well-read. When he discovered my status, he spiced his brief messages with humorous feminist quips, such as *"Women who aspire to equal men, lack ambition"*. Deeper philosophical musings were limited by my Inmarsat Sat-phone which only accepts texts up to 160 characters. Still, it was enough to inspire and encourage until we were able to meet in person. It was comforting to know someone was keeping an eye on things, even if in the end I had to face it alone.

Thursday, November 16. The day everyone has been edgy about, with a low-pressure system forming between South Africa and Madagascar. It seems to be moving south quite quickly. For *Shanti* there is a 20-knot sou' westerly forecast, bringing perhaps 24 hours of wind on the nose, commencing whenever it does. No-one seems to know exactly when. Another Damocles' sword swinging above me. Options suggested by the "net" included taking refuge in Fort Dauphin Bay on the east coast of Madagascar. This is about 150 miles from here. Were I closer, with a chance of getting in before the change, I would do it, but I think not.

Another option is to go closer to the South African coast, where there will be less current against wind and possibly less wind, but that is also quite far off and I don't like the idea of being too near to the land in a storm. There has been a lot of scary talk about the Agulhas current, which flows down the east coast of Africa between 27 and 40 degrees south. Strong southerly winds, spawned off Antarctica, oppose this current, producing immense rogue waves up to several metres high, reputably breaking the backs of supertankers. This sounds like something to avoid at all costs. The initial advice Des gave me was to slow down, which I did. Later on, he sent another text saying it wouldn't help—there was no avoiding it. I was going to get smacked. At least I was forewarned.

Friday, 1000 hours. A bird landed in the cockpit, appearing to have broken her wing. I'm not sure what to do with her; she will probably die there. Each time I approached, she tried to peck me with her needle-sharp beak, as if it were her cockpit. I decided to try and put her in a bucket, to contain her territory, and her pooping. I threw a small towel over her and scooped her up. She wasn't having it; flapping and squawking, she eyed me threateningly. Perhaps she had not been able to get airborne because she needed air beneath her wings, or perhaps she just wanted a rest.

I lifted the bucket, intending to set her aloft, but accidentally lost the lot overboard. It flashed briefly through my mind to turn back for my bucket, but within seconds it was far behind (as would be the case with a W.O.B.—Woman Over Board). The malingerer soared off, only to return ten minutes later. She made another crash landing on the cabin top and sat there with wings folded looking smugly at me. "OK, you can have that", I said, "but the cockpit's mine". Every big wave that slews *Shanti* sideways upsets her, but she clings on tenaciously.

An eerie calm is draped over the sea like a suffocating blanket. It feels very creepy, like the ominous approach of something big. I'm only expecting around 20 knots from the SW, but still not sure if I should drop the mainsail and put out the headsail, which is easier to furl away. We're still doing better than 6 knots SOG with the current, even though it feels like we're hardly moving. Distance to go is 840 nautical miles, around 8 days if we can average 100 miles a day. I transferred 20 litres of diesel from a jerry can into the tank and began motoring in the lull before the front.

A gentle rain is falling in practically no wind. Feeling *so* tired, I slept for an hour. Wow! What a gift. I don't know how long it will last, but for now, it's a huge gift. I cooked some baked beans on toast for dinner, washed up and cleaned my teeth—all without bracing myself. Another *wow*. And more thanks—a solitary dolphin just popped up to say hello.

I'm tempted to leave everything as it is for the night, with only one reef in the main. It's such a chore putting the second reef in. But no, I know something is coming, so I had better do it, while it's still relatively calm and there's a smidgeon of daylight left. I just finished when the wind piped up to 27 knots and I was glad I did it.

We went south-ish overnight with the current, until at 0400, when we were pushed more East, away from our destination. I hove to for a couple of hours and slept. I woke to see the lights of a ship close by. It's so busy here.

Later, on the HF radio "sked", (schedule), there was talk of another front coming next week. The sked gives me the position of other boats in our small fleet, and the conditions they currently have, so that too is a bit of a head's up as to what to expect. Some of them are limping along with rig problems in strong winds, one heading for shelter in Madagascar. They have far more wind up there than I have here. Just the luck of the draw.

The bird goes and comes, happy to perch up on the bow until it gets too bouncy. Then she tries the boom bag, which offers a broader platform. She has far fewer cares than I do, and I contemplate life as a bird. Meanwhile, as an earth-bound human, I'm worried about passing too close to the land—25 miles off the southern tip of Madagascar—with shoals and whales, so I tacked away. But that was no good as I couldn't manage a better course than due South, so tacked back again. While handling the ropes, I observed the tiller waggling to and fro, unaided. I adjusted the sails and she's doing fine. I won't tempt fate and mention this to *Tilly*, but I remember having made this discovery back in the Whitsunday Islands, a lifetime ago. I wish I had been doing this all day, saving power, although the sun is blazing. Following the wind, the course has come up 20 degrees and if it continues, we may just be able to hold this round the Cape. Surprisingly, there is a Panamanian cargo ship *Peace Garden* in this close to land, in only 50 metres of water.

Sunday 0340. I put the clock back an hour. A Hong Kong-registered ship *Great Link*, passed within half a mile to starboard. Too close! I could practically see what they were having for breakfast. I called them on the radio to check if they could see me. They said they would alter course, but didn't, causing lots of unnecessary wake.

0700. Rounding the bottom of Madagascar, I saw a whale. Two delights! This morning's sked induced some further anxiety regarding the weather. The forecast was for a southerly of 25 – 30 knots over the next few days. The reassurance was that this was just a trough, not a low. I already had 25 knots with mounting seas.

Wednesday, November 22. Today is the kind of day when I feel that I never want to return to the land. The sea is that glorious deep Indian ink blue, with just a touch of white frosting. There is a gentle 15-knot breeze and not too much rolling about. I have just made a rolling lunch/dinner. It began with flour and yeast. I have been thinking of baking a loaf of bread for a while now and today it was calm enough to try. The first course was an orange. Next, while waiting for the bread, was a cup of soup, Pumpkin, and a rice cake. Next was a sushi roll, another first. Leftover rice, tuna, cucumber and soy sauce, rolled in a sheet of Nori seaweed. The bread is nearly ready, but I will have to resist temptation and let it cool first. It's a shame I have no butter.

There are lots of questions around the weather at the moment. Is this another case of me deferring to the experts? Partly, but they do have a forecast in front of them, whereas I only have the clouds and sea and wind and barometer. As far as strategies go, it's over to me. This is not something I have a lot of past experience in. Late in the afternoon, motoring in next to no wind, I decided to pack away my mainsail and did up the zip. I left a tiny amount of headsail out to let me know when the wind returned. This turned out to be a mistake.

It was just after dark when the sheet lightning began, lighting the entire seascape for miles in a fleeting incandescence. With blinding flashes, it lit the horizon and spread to encompass everything. I had thoughts of a strike to *Shanti* or me, either going up in flames or melted down to the bones. This continued for a couple of hours, a ghostly harbinger of the approaching front. Next came the rain, hammering like hundreds of rocks on the cabin top. I cowered below in the companionway, watching the deluge through the Perspex storm boards. Then came the wind. It shot up from zero to the mid 20's, within minutes passed 30 and quickly reached over 40 knots. *Shanti* was shoved rudely on her side, the whole boat juddering as if about to fall apart. It happened so suddenly I scarcely had time to register what was going on. I had never seen anything like it before. The noise was deafening; the torrential rain, the shrieking wind, the quaking rig, all blurred in a cacophony of indecipherable chaos.

I knew I had to go out into the cockpit to deal with it, but that was the last place I wanted to be. Far preferable to hide down below and hope for the best. Or to send another crewman up. But, it's just me. And *Shanti* needs me. Donning the heaviest wet weather jacket, I shrank up inside. The moment I stepped out, the wind snatched off the hood and sharp needles of rain tattooed my scalp. Within seconds, I was soaked through to the skin, shivering as if every filling might shake out of my teeth. I felt completely disorientated in the enveloping blackness.

Tilly, the autopilot, squawked her refusal to deal with such demands, and *Shanti* veered off course. Grabbing a short length of rope, I lashed the tiller to one side, then went below to start the engine. It was hard to know which way to go, confused as I was. Somehow, more by instinct than design, I got it right. *Shanti* turned closer to the wind and hove-to. One right move. That at least bought me a few minutes to try and make sense of things.

We were far from secure. The sheets of the partially unfurled headsail had come loose and were flailing about like demented snakes, whip-cracking the plastic clears on the front of the dodger. It was far too dangerous to go anywhere near them. The headsail unfurled itself a few feet more, adding to the mayhem. It would be nothing short of a miracle if it didn't shred to pieces. The whole boat was shaking violently as if a toy in the hands of an angry giant. If the mast hadn't toppled before, this would certainly test it. The wind was now up around 50 knots, the seas mounting rapidly.

The starboard jib sheet had become tightly tangled up with the flag halyard and other ropes, knotting itself into a rock-hard monkey fist, which at least subdued its crazed conniption. The outer casing was completely shredded and small scraps were festooned in the rigging like patches of sticky cotton wool. Try as I might, the sheet simply could not be retrieved. The ironclad interlacings were cinched far beyond anything my frozen fingers could even begin to prise loose.

I managed to use the furling line winch to get the headsail in, despite the enormous load on it. My wilted hands had hardly any strength and could only push the handle a fraction of a turn at a time, all the while, praying that the line wouldn't break. In the midst of all of this, the AIS alarm was going off, warning me of at least half a dozen ships nearby. I certainly couldn't go down below to check the computer or to disable the stressful alarms. There was no time to worry about that. It was enough to comprehend the more urgent need of the moment and figure out how to deal with it.

The mounting seas were telling me that the wind and current were opposed, so I needed to make a decision as to which way to go. Unlashing the helm, I found *Shanti* could make some slight headway under motor. Each time I opened the companionway, gallons of water would gush in. I would have to mop up later. Standing there, dripping wet, it was not high on the list of immediate concerns. More important was checking our position and course and trying to slow my panting breath so I didn't have a heart attack.

The waves mounted even higher, with the south-westerly wind fighting against the current. Knowing now where I was, the best tactic was to try and push through and get closer to the coast. Progress was almost non-existent, but at least we were relatively stable. Going below to rest was out of the question. It was just a matter of hanging on and praying things didn't get any worse.

After another five or six hellish hours, the storm abated slightly. It's amazing the difference that the reduction of a few knots makes to one's sense of relief. It has to be psychological because gale force winds are fierce enough when they first hit. Perhaps it's because when they are encountered on the way down, rather than up, there is comfort in knowing conditions are improving. They might still be horrendous, but they are passing.

When the rain stopped, I managed to change into some dry clothes and eventually stopped shivering. In the pitch-black night, I crawled forward on the deck to run the port sheet over to the starboard side to replace the tangled line so we could stop burning diesel and sail. Unfurling even the tiniest triangle of headsail relieved *Yani* of her struggle and we began to make some headway.

It was a long slow bash to windward for the last 50 miles with the wind holding a fairly constant 30 knots. Des sent a few anxious texts, querying my safety. There was no possibility of reply; like me, he would just have to trust. He told me later, that also like me, he had no sleep until I was safely in.

Never was I more relieved than to thread my way through the hordes of anchored or slowly moving ships and enter the channel into Richards Bay. The harbour was full of boats, with several rafted two or three deep. Being the smallest, it was no problem for *Shanti* to add on. A silver Vervet monkey wandered by, with tail raised high. *Welcome to Africa.*

Shanti will rest in the Tuzi Gazi Marina for the next two months while I fly back to Melbourne for Christmas and then over to New Zealand for my father's 100th birthday celebrations at the end of January. Family are coming from everywhere for this exceptional occasion. The highly esteemed Mr Jack Hope is an inspiration to us all, still taking walks and a daily swim in the sea.

Chapter 12

Cape of Storms

After about 40 hours of flying backwards in time from New Zealand, I reboarded the patiently-waiting good ship *Shanti* on February 3. This trip back home was a kind of demarcation, a time to reflect on what's been and what's ahead, making me question my ability to endure another trouncing out on the ocean. I even entertained thoughts of selling *Shanti* here in her birthplace of South Africa.

Friday was a typical South African summer's day, high humidity and temperatures topping 40. The Boardwalk mall seemed a good place to take shelter from the heat. Seen from the street, the mall is a vast, grey, slab-sided monolith that appears to be set in several acres of wasteland and car parks. Not a window adorns its featureless concrete exterior. Inside, it is the same brightly lit, air-conditioned spaciousness as found in any modern shopping centre. All the mega department stores, supermarkets, restaurants, book stores, toy shops, boutique fashion parlours, electronics stores, arcade gaming dens are there, all blaringly loud and glaringly seductive.

I needed a post office to return the door keys which I had inadvertently brought back with me from Melbourne. Surely any self-respecting modern shopping mall has a post office? I was directed to take one of the corridor exits, stepping into what seemed like Dante's Inferno. Crossing a narrow street, it was as if I went back in time, entering what must have been the old shopping centre before it was plasticised. Suddenly I was shoulder to shoulder with hordes of dark-skinned people swarming in all directions. Those that were stationary were standing in long queues at the ubiquitous ATMs. Friday must be payday.

When I finally found the well-hidden post office, I could scarcely believe my eyes: a queue as long as for an international flight, with the same crowd-controlling belt barriers, winding back and forth, several layers deep. Surely this couldn't simply be a post office? A man was directing traffic, sending those next in line to form shorter lines in front of each counter. There were about ten narrow counters, each behind an old fashioned, timber-framed sash window. I half expected those serving to be wearing a green plastic visor and stretchy armbands on long-sleeved shirts.

And it was HOT. No air conditioning in this antiquated building. Sweat dripped from every brow. I had no idea what they were all there for. There was no sign of any mail being handled. In fact, there was no sign of any prepaid postbags and I was starting to get worried that such things didn't exist here. But fortunately, half an hour's melting later, my turn came and the large woman serving me disappeared out the back for no more than another ten minutes to locate such an uncommon request.

On my way back to coolness I passed yet another thick queue, the longest and saddest yet, lining up before what was little more than a hole in the wall, with a handwritten sign for some government-subsidised medications for long-term communicable diseases. This was the side of Africa I hadn't yet encountered.

———

The following week, I motored around to Zululand Yacht Club where *Shanti* was hauled out at on the club "dolly" (trolly) to replace a broken seacock and through-hull skin fitting. At $AU120 in and out, it's got to be the cheapest place to lift out of the water in the world—although it does feel a little precarious, kind of like careening on wheels.

Once *Shanti* was high and dry, the fitting was quickly replaced, along with a couple of other small jobs. The new stays which were sent up from Cape Town yesterday should be here tomorrow if the local version of "Island time" doesn't prevail. So now I'm almost ready to continue my coastal hopping south. Clearing out takes a full day, so with any luck, I may be doing an overnighter of the 90 miles to Durban by this Friday.

The new stays arrived on time, and the rigger came to fit them. Unfortunately, he had either measured wrongly or miscommunicated his start and endpoints, so the stays are too short. A few shackles can fix this problem to get me around the coast, but they will need replacing again when I get to Cape Town. This is becoming a bit of a habit.

Sailing around the southern coast of South Africa is mostly done in small bites, involving at least half a dozen stopovers along the way. From Richards Bay to Cape Town is over 1000 nautical miles and the timing for each bite is entirely determined by the weather. At least once or twice a week the strong sou' westerlies blow, which is not a good time to be out there. The wonderfully helpful Agulhas current runs south-westerly at up to 6 knots making it easier to gobble up the miles.

Weather watching takes on a whole new meaning. As the two tail runners, *Shanti* and *Argonauta* have the advantage of Des' undivided attention, as well as less crowded marinas. His response to my enquiry was, "it would be unconscionable to abandon the last of my "chicks" as the rest (64 boats this year), with two exceptions, are all safe in Cape Town, and some already over the pond in South America."

It's good to be sailing in company with one other boat, even though at 44', *Argonauta* is much faster than *Shanti*. It's also good to share the bureaucratic nonsense that must be gone through at each port with reams of documentation describing some oft-repeated "flight plan". At least it's all free, apart from shoe leather and time, which is not in short supply.

Several of the earlier fleet had to bypass Durban after it was closed due to storm damage. That made their first bite a big one, 360nm from Richards Bay to East London. So I was happy to make my first overnighter only 90 miles. It was a boisterous sail with winds up to 30 knots and lumpy seas, and I was pleased to keep my insides in.

There was still evidence of the damage to the floating pontoons in Durban Marina, as well as no power or water. Not a bother at all; I was just glad to find shelter and rest. It's little wonder these marinas fall apart so easily. They might just as well be held together with string and chewing gum, the way they are anchored with rusty chains to the seabed. When the wind blows, it's a symphony in motion, with moored boats and pontoons swaying together.

Some boats had to wait several weeks for the next suitable weather window, so we were fortunate to be able to move on in only 3 days. It gave us just enough time to do all we had to do. I had 2 new batteries home delivered to the boat and spent several hours fitting them. The near-new old ones I gave away.

After running around to all the usual rubber-stampers, Marina office, Ports, Immigration, Customs, then back to Ports and to the Marina office (anyone would think we were leaving the country), we were ready to cast off by 1100. The next hop, to East London, is 260 nm, which takes about 46 hours, with speeds of up to 9 knots in the current. There was very little wind so lots of diesel-burning for the first 24 hours, but with a nasty washing machine sea and waves coming at us from all directions. There were a few dramas en-route. *Argonauta's* engine overheated a couple of times, she blew a cooling hose and had some weird explosion in the engine room that blackened the ceiling. Luckily for them, the wind arrived in time for them to sail. (She is, after all, a yacht.)

We both arrived at 0600, only to be told we had to stand off and wait 3 hours for shipping movement in and out of the port. The wind was forecast to come in strongly at 0900 and already the sea and current were messing us about. *Argonauta* was told to drop their anchor (in 46 metres—not long before that was dragging) and *Shanti* was running out of fuel. What a fiasco. Eventually, they took pity on us. A disabled tanker was asked to anchor off, two tug boats towed *Argonauta* in, and *Shanti* just made it in under her own steam.

We are now anchored in the Coca Cola coloured Buffalo River, wondering if we should bother putting our dinghies in. The nearby yacht club is closed and the town is an hour's walk away. I might just stay on board and do boat jobs. It's the first time I've sat at anchor since Rodrigues, although the wind is now 30 plus knots and there are lots of whitecaps foaming the anchorage. This should abate around midnight. A sou' westerly change is forecast in the morning.

Dockside provides entertainment, watching hundreds of brand-new cars being loaded onto ships, those massive, Lego-block-style car carriers that bear no resemblance at all to anything marine. Dozens of drivers would arrive by bus, each hop into a car and drive it onto the ship, later to exit the loading-ramp via another bus for another rotation. It was quite a sleek operation that continued day and night. The cars being delivered to the dock are mostly white, clearly the preferred colour. Some drivers spark up their day, giving a slight burst of testosterone peddle-planting, just a tad less conservative in their approach, almost doing a spin-out wheelie at the stand-still point. I try to count the rows of cars. More than 500. Drivers? Around 50. Interestingly the ship doesn't appear any lower in the water as they load tons and tons of cars into its gaping maw. It just swallows them whole and says bring me more.

Sunday, February 18. 0430. Approaching Port Elizabeth in the pre-dawn light I saw a bright green, translucent light spread in a wide band across the sea, directly in front of me. I figured it was either a surfacing submarine or the powerful spotlight of a hovering alien spacecraft, about to beam me up. FEAR is an acronym for False Evidence Appearing Real. I am tired, too tired for such nonsense. A weary mind diverts easily, gathering up long lost memories that bear no relevance to now, other than perhaps through some slender association with fear. At least the eerie glow slowly dissipated without harm, as did my unhelpful ruminations.

The Algoa Bay Yacht Club marina in Port Elizabeth has got to win first prize for being the marina most likely to be condemned. Apparently, a gale almost destroyed it in 2009 and they have been (slowly) rebuilding it ever since. Such projects have low priority in South Africa. The mega-money spinner here is the adjacent manganese ore terminal, which doesn't help matters in the marina, where nothing is spared its sticky grey dust. So the handful of sadly neglected boats left to rot here wear this added coat of dismal despair. Even the fierce south-easterlies can't blow them clean; only threaten to blow them and their fragile pontoons away. Despite this, the locals made Port Elizabeth one of the friendliest stopovers I have encountered.

From there, fellow cruisers, Sheri and Giorgio, on *Argonauta* encouraged me to alter my plans and take the 4-day weather window directly to Cape Town. It meant more sleeplessness for me but still turned out to be a wise call. Rounding the Cape of Good Hope, the infamous Cape of Storms, was awe-inspiring for its reputation more than its hostility. I caused some slight concern to the others, losing radio and mobile phone contact for a few days. They called the Coast Guard, who eventually got through to me. Apparently, a fishing boat had circled me while I was sleeping, then later spotted me on deck wrangling with sails, while *Shanti* bucked wildly in the face of high seas. I can understand how it could have looked as if I was in trouble, even though it was situation normal for me. I thanked them for their concern and rang the others as soon as I was back in range. We were staying in different marinas, it being necessary for me to be at the Royal Cape for my mast to be removed, and rigging once again replaced.

Cape Town takes the appellation of 'windy city' to new heights, with fierce katabatics funnelling wind-shear to a toppling assault. It's never easy to arrange things around it. You know that wind is coming when thick banks of cloud cover the magnificent Table Mountain like sheets of snowdrift.

The crane was booked for 0900, but the wind was still blowing the crabs off the rocks, so it was cancelled. A couple of hours later, in a slight lull, they were able to lift me and the works began. Aside from the mast and rigging repair, I took the opportunity to replace reef lines, sheets and halyards. A new dripless shaft seal was fitted, new solar panels, and best of all, *four* new 100Ah deep cycle batteries. I bit the bullet on this one, even though I had only bought two new batteries a few weeks ago in Durban. Having four of the same type has been something I've wanted for years.

Probably the worst news is nothing to do with *Shanti* or my small problems, but all to do with the recalcitrant rain gods, who haven't opened the skies here for more than 3 years. Cape Town is on Level 6 water restrictions, with rations of 50 litres per person per day. (I could give lessons in *Shanti*-board consumption of 2-3 litres per day). The marina taps are turned on for one hour, 3 times a week, and of course, no washing boats down. Who does that, when a salt-water dousing is only a day away?

Toilets are all fitted with dispensers of hand sanitizers instead of soap (the suppliers of this must be making a killing) and things like swimming pools, laundromats, car wash places, etc. are out of business. It is the most talked-about topic here, with forecasts of reservoirs running dry in a few months. The hierarchy of disaster is first the land, then the plants, the animals, then the poor people. There's a lot of tension in the air and people speak of corrupt governments and mismanagement, but those things are not new here. Only the drought adds its punch.

I took a 45-minute walk this morning to the local produce market near the upbeat V & A Waterfront Marina where Sheri and Giorgio are staying. It was one of the best markets I've seen, with vast displays of gourmet edibles, making me wish I'd gone on an empty belly. I filled my shopping jeep with last-minute fresh goods, like unripe tomatoes and bananas, home-made cheeses (hope the fridge plays along), non-sulphur dried fruits and nuts. It's hard to resist munching immediately.

From there it was to the Ports, Immigration and Customs and I am now officially checked out of the country. It's funny how you can wander about freely with your passport stamped out. Compare this to the fuss at an airport, if you ask to turn around after passing through Customs and Immigration to go back for something you'd forgotten.

From Cape Town to St Helena is about 1800 nautical miles. The weather looks about as good as it gets on this coast, with light winds to begin with, which should send me off on a good start. Indeed, with 7 knots of wind on the beam and SOG of 5.5 knots (thanks to the Benguela Current), sunshine, hardly any swell or waves, it's the most beautiful sailing I have ever had on the open sea. If only it could always be like this. But of course, nothing stays the same.

Some people said if I went directly from Cape Town to St Helena, I would get hammered. Others said it was best to sail north as far as Namibia, or to 20 degrees before turning left, to avoid the high pressure, no wind zone. Some advised getting as far offshore as quickly as possible, just in case a nasty nor' westerly blew up. I hedged my bets, sailed north about 100 miles off the coast, before turning away. I still got becalmed and hammered. Sometimes there's just no winning.

The magnificent sailing was a short-lived pleasure, with what little wind there was dwindling to nothing in the evening. Once again, this turned out to be the calm before the storm. Running the engine in the night, I felt a dull thump, as if the propeller hit something. Today I see what it is—great clumps of sea-weed; not just floating like a thick log on the surface, but dangling down a couple of metres below, with a large, fibrous bulb on the end. It doesn't seem to have done any damage, but I'm not going over to look.

Whoever said the Atlantic Ocean is a "gentleman's ocean", with steady 15 knot SE Trade Winds obviously went on a different day to me. Three days after leaving Cape Town I was in huge seas, up around 6 metres, with 35 plus knots of wind. Oh great! Here we go again! It was a wild slalom ride, slewing off to left and right, gybing at the bottom of each wave as poor *Tilly* struggled to hold course, no matter how many degrees off I gave her.

Every few waves, one would slam violently against the hull like hitting a brick wall. A sideswipe from one of those Mack trucks bursts open storage lockers and all contents go flying. Butternut pumpkin missiles are lethal. Torrents of water douse the entire boat, cascading through the middle hatch over me if I happen to be in my bunk. The forward hatch might just as well not be there. Everything is soaking wet. A bathtub-full of seawater floods into the boat at every slam dunk or broach. The bilge pump can't deal with it as water sloshes from side to side up the walls. The floorboards are awash and of course, everything is on the floor. Back to bailing out; the good news being I found my missing reading glasses in the bilge.

I'm losing my sense of humour. A backrest cushion flops down on me and I push it away with petulant irritation: *Get off me!*

An edible-sized squid has given up its last gasp, spraying indelible ink all over the cockpit, the white dodger, ropes, bimini (how did it get up there?), but I don't feel like calamari for breakfast. I use every known cleaning product to try and remove it. I make a mental note, *Squid ink is forever*. It could be a song or the title of this book, but it's said in jest, as a challenge to the immutable fact of impermanence. Because as we all know, nothing is forever. Perhaps the oceans come as close to it as is possible here on earth. What of love? Ah, if that was so, I wouldn't be out here, alone, in the mid-Atlantic, scrubbing ink off the decks of this little yacht. In a world of constant change, non-attachment is the only way to avoid suffering. Easier said than done, but worth remembering.

I just hove-to to change sails and discovered the screws that anchor both ends of *Tilly* have come loose. Nothing stays the same.

Saying "nothing lasts forever" alludes to the nature of transience. It's most often used in reference to things that are, rather than things that are not. Thus, a thing, like an ocean, or a mountain lasts not forever. But looking at the absent, then it's possible to see that the loss of a child is forever, the loss of a left breast is forever. Attachment to what is no longer present may be the cause of pain. But the loss is forever.

More useful is the saying, "This too will change" which has more bearing on our *perception* of what is, or what is not. Such truisms only have value if they are useful in our everyday experience. My favourite: "This too will pass", is helpful in the thick of an Atlantic storm. It also helps me to remember that this experience is rare, unique and very short-lived in relation to the whole of my life. A 6-week passage may seem like an eternity, but put into context of decades of life, it is a drop in the ocean.

There are moments within that droplet, that have such intensity as to seem like a lifetime. It is *Action*—acting now, in direct response to the immediate challenge. Action, that life or death hangs so tenuously upon, demanding the corralling of every animal survival instinct. Following those adrenaline-packed moments of action are blissful highs, not found in too many other places. Where else, other than alone at sea can one look for answers? Of course, one needs to know the questions first.

Three times the wild ocean has rudely tried to claim the blue canvas cloths from the sides of the cockpit, as well as the newly side-mounted solar panel. Whilst trying to secure it, balancing half in and half out of the boat, I heard a thunderous wave approaching. There was nothing I could do but hang on tight and get soaked to the skin; luckily not swept overboard as *Shanti* again gets knocked down.

I feel at a very low ebb, having had little sleep or food for three long days and nights. During one short doze, I imagined someone else was with me and I was begging him to do things for me, like bail out please. Of course, he didn't because that's my job. A large part of my job here is damage control. Firstly, prepare *Shanti* as best as possible, then pick up the pieces along the way. At least I'm not having to worry about the mast falling down. I don't recall it being quite so harsh in the Indian Ocean, but then, bad memories fade as the sun comes out.

I cracked my scone a beauty coming up the companionway steps; how could I forget the hatch was closed? Ouch! A big duck egg is forming. *Please take more care!*

I'm thinking about a circumnavigation, and what is it for? A tick-box? To experience solitude on the ocean? To see new places and meet new people? To recover from all the things that have ever hurt me? To learn about sailing, about weather, hardship, about joy, about myself? About overcoming boredom, tiredness, hunger, loneliness, fear, adversity....

Most cruisers seem to want to make the ocean passages as quick as possible. You can overhear conversations like "how long did it take you to get from Galapagos to the Marquesas?" "Oh, we did it in 19 days", one might boast, while those on smaller boats might admit, "It took us 6 weeks." Oh dear.

Of course, there's the awareness of finite resources on board, food, water, fuel, tolerance. And the fact is, it *is* a bit of an endurance test. But what if the attitude was changed to embrace slow travel, to stopping along the way, not just to fly home for a break or to visit family or to take care of business? Then it wouldn't matter if I put another 10 degrees to port to help stop the dead downwind sail collapse, flog, gybe, stress. It might add another 300 miles, but what's that in the overall scheme of things—another 2 or 3 days? *Patience!*

A lot of cruisers distract themselves from the immediacy of the experience by reading, talking, watching movies, Sundowners, etc. They simply enjoy the lifestyle, the camaraderie of the cruising fraternity, where everyone is always quick to lend a hand or share expertise, knowing it may be them in need next time.

But what of the BIG questions that I hoped to gain insight into out here alone? The "Who am I?", "Why am I here?", "What's my purpose?" questions that motivate our search for meaning in a seemingly meaningless world. Looking for answers, usually in all the wrong places.

My father is inspirational. Why? Because he is 100 years old and still swims in the sea every day. He pushes himself to do it; never allowing himself to slack off or be soft on himself. He knows it gives him back more than it takes. So too, this sailing alone, with purpose.

———

It has been a busy day, with good enough conditions to do some boat jobs, sorting out reef lines, the uphaul and downhaul for the spinnaker pole. I tried poling out the headsail after getting it all sorted, but the plastic fitting that connects the downhaul to the pole broke, so that's the end of that. I'm not too unhappy, as it's precarious up on the foredeck, wrangling the pole, jib sheets and other ropes by myself. I always seem to get to a point where some other hand is needed to free something or pull on something. But it's just me. The sun is shining, the sea not too boisterous; it's warm enough to peel off a layer, and I'm feeling happy enough to sing.

I made a cheese and tomato omelette with lettuce and honeydew melon salad. Delicious! It's impressive how well the fresh food from the Cape Town farmers' market is keeping, with no fridge for the past 11 days. I have green beans, zucchini, eggplant, lettuce and tomatoes, stowed in breathable baskets on various shelves, and have only lost 2 small cucumbers. There are about 8 tomatoes left and they all look good. I guess it's still quite cool weather here.

In the brief snatches of sleep I get, my dreams are vivid technicolour, big-budget productions, peopled with scores of larger-than-life characters, often dressed in period costume, making brilliant, original utterances, far beyond my ken. My son, Baillie, has been experimenting a lot with lucid dreaming, which can supposedly teleport one into other dimensions or parallel universes. I have had this experience before. It takes a bit of intention to be able to remember and helps to write it down as soon as possible. This is not always possible for me. One second I'm snug and warm and dry in my bunk, the next I'm out on deck in a cold, wet, blustery, bucking world, reducing sails, altering course, tending to business. At least there is very little traffic to watch out for here. I haven't seen one ship since I left.

Saturday, March 24. 1500. Crossed the Prime Meridian of 000 and we are now at longitude West, instead of East—all rather arbitrary, but I guess the globe had to be dissected in some logical way. I had a relatively good night, only gybing once at 2300. I don't know why they call it the South East Trades; one minute it's

7 knots from the SW, the next it's 27 knots from the SSE. One minute there's total cloud cover; the next sunshine; the next rain. It could be Melbourne!

Sometimes it feels as if we are smoothly gliding along as if on greased rails. Then a knock, a twist, a lurch, and we are back to the dreadful coly-wobbles, the mast a pendulum, arcing across the sky. I cry out to *Shanti*, "Settle!" With my body tossed to and fro, every bit of me is aching. We're so close, yet so far. With another 130 miles to go, I should have just enough fuel to motor if need be. I was prepared to sit and wait for wind, but by 0230, a glassy opal sea was listlessly bulging under the half-moon. Billions of stars pierce the profundity above, reminding me of my complete insignificance.

At midday, the dead calm sea is completely and utterly windless. Peacock plumage, discs of iridescent aquamarine, silver, turquoise and opal, burnish its lazy loll in the hot midday sun. It is unbelievably beautiful. And there's that deep blue bottomless well alongside, with shafts of light penetrating its unknowable depths. This fascinating phenomenon can only be seen in deep calm, rays of sunlight converging, as if being poured into a mysterious funnel, as seductive as a siren's call. It's mesmerising to watch, strangely enticing, inviting one to plunge into its promise of cool tranquillity.

I just had a very disorientating thought that tomorrow I will be in a different country. That little rock on the chart has U.K. written next to it. I had better hoist the British courtesy flag above the yellow Q flag. It feels most peculiar. I wonder what affiliation with the home country means to this tiny island today? Or has it served its purpose as an unassailable bastion in bygone days, an inescapable place of exile for Napoleon Bonaparte?

Wednesday, March 28. 0400. At first, I thought it was a ship in the distance, but later the flickering pricks of red lights merged into rows of lights across the horizon. Land ho! There is nothing quite so surreal as the sight of a lump of rock rising out of an empty ocean in the pre-dawn light. The tall granite weather face is flat-topped, like Table Mountain, with rocky clefts and knobbly protuberances. The even higher mountains beyond are green, with a sprinkling of white dwellings. People live here! Up close, the granite cliffs look like the saggy skin of an ancient woolly mammoth.

It was fortunate that the total becalming happened at the end of the passage, and not the middle, so I could burn the rest of my small reserve of diesel to motor in. Another positive side of this lull is that the mooring field at St Helena is relatively peaceful. I heard that a few weeks ago it had a 3-metre swell upsetting everyone. Then they closed the harbour. Going ashore is challenge enough in good weather, and impossible in rough. There is no beach or protected harbour to disembark; just a rugged, inhospitable concrete landing which the surge sometimes drowns. There are ropes dangling from above to assist with the leap ashore, which one needs to time with the upswell. A robust little wooden ferry offers a commuter service for 2 GBP (Great Britain Pounds), which is the more worldly currency; the other being St Helena pounds, which are only of any use on this rock, so it pays to watch your change. I gave all mine to the ferryman before leaving, to sweeten his sometimes-surly mood.

The town itself has a quaint, olde-world charm, with beautifully-preserved historical buildings clinging to its steep slopes. A British colony, with around 4,500 residents, everyone is super friendly and helpful. It is Easter now, and the whole island has gone camping. Some fellow cruisers and I are hiring a car to explore further afield. The interior is a constantly changing landscape, from barren, windswept rock, to verdant fields and cool canopies of dense forest. We visited the blighted, narrow strip of the airfield, ending abruptly at the edge of a sheer precipice, built on the most turbulent side of the island and subject to much criticism, but providing a necessary link with the outside world. Also, the house where Napoleon was exiled and the tomb where his body once lay before being taken back to France.

The *Ocean Adventurer* arrived in the anchorage. It looks a bit like a miniature cruise liner, but is, in fact, an ice-breaker, taking 50 paying guests on an 8-week cruise from Ushuaia in Argentina to the Falklands and Cape Verde in the Caribbean. They pause briefly here at St Helena, then go on to Ascension and other remote islands on the way. It sounds more interesting than your usual floating hotel cruises, but give me my own tiny bubble any day.

The evening before departing St Helena, a fellow cruiser incited me to lunacy, climbing the 690 near-vertical steps of Jacob's Ladder. Given that it was to be the last serious exercise I'd get for the next 3 weeks, it wasn't a bad thing. The view down to the tiny boats dotted around the mooring field was vertiginous.

Hurgen is slim and sprightly, with bright eyes and a laughing intelligence. Despite his German heritage, he speaks with that adorable, lilting South African accent that for some strange reason resonates with me. His yacht, *Morwenna* is a sky blue steelie, rather squarish and clunky-looking, with the usual rust streaks crying ochre tears down the sides. She doesn't sail well to windward and when I ask his destination, he replies, "wherever the wind takes me." Nice to be so free.

Chapter 13

Vertical Time

Most other yachts have already left St Helena, so once again, I am a tail runner, on my own, the wide, empty ocean ahead of me. I really felt this solitude, perhaps exacerbated by the lengthy calms and slow progress. Perhaps it is also because of having spent some time in the company of others. I'm happy to be leaving port, but these light airs are testing. This must be the gentleman's Atlantic I had heard about.

The first week out, the wind teased me with fluctuations between 2 knots and 20 knots. On day 3, after the frustrations of chasing its every nuance, I overcame my apathy and dug out the spinnaker from under the V berth up in the bow. I wasn't exactly sure what I was going to do with it, as I had never even seen it, never mind flown it before. It took a good 2 hours to unearth it, work it out and set it up, but oh boy, was it worth it! With 6 – 8 knots of wind from behind, boat speed got up between 3 – 4 knots. I realised it was going to be a long, slow passage. The 100-mile days I was used to seeing were to be a thing of the past. I was lucky to see 70 or 80 at best.

The spinnaker, or "kite" is not asymmetrical, meaning it can only be used with *Shanti* running square or with the wind dead astern. The smaller "whisker pole" doesn't push the kite out far enough not to chafe on the furled headsail. The big pole is much heavier and more awkward to manhandle but I'm getting used to it. I always douse the kite at dusk, in case the wind increases overnight, which seems to happen a lot.

I am beginning to learn the subtle shifts in wind and wave directions with wind tending more E in the day and more SE at night. The waves are often larger than the wind would suggest, indicating stronger blows further away, or coming. There is always a garland of puffy white clouds around the rim of my world and often thick black storm cells which suck the wind out before belching it back violently. This is almost like the doldrums, not usually found so far south of the equator.

I made the mistake of plotting waypoints on my course—lots of them! It was almost depressing to see the number of potential days inching or millimetering across the map. With no idea what winds I might get, this really was the unanswerable question of how long is a piece of string? It could be 3 weeks; it could be a month (I didn't like to even entertain the thought of more than that). It "should" be 18 days. Hah!

With scarcely enough wind to fly the kite, it often collapses and wraps itself in a "wine glass" around the forestay, which is a nightmare to free. Sometimes starting the engine and driving the boat round in counter-wise circles can unwind it. Another trick I conceived was to fly only half a kite, leaving it still partially contained in the "sock" that snuffs it. I am physically sapped from constantly changing sails, trying to eek that minuscule forward motion from whatever fleeting zephyr flutters by.

At 0350, I was woken by an English-accented male voice calling "Hey Twinkle, Twinkle! Suse!" I leapt up expecting to see someone nearby who had obviously mistaken *Shanti* for another boat, but of course, no-one was there. The wind had increased to 18 knots, so I happily put up more sail and began moving in earnest. There are thick black clouds around the horizon, so this breeze may be due to them cheekily tantalizing.

I started watching my mind more closely and found my thoughts are runaway trains, creating a weirdly entertaining, yet unreal world. It's a bit like that line in the song: "everywhere you go, you always take the weather with you." I am beginning to see that this tendency to dwell in the past or look toward the future, is not only stealing the richness of what is here and now but is also imprisoning me. Here, alone on the ocean, I have a wonderful opportunity to work with this, stepping out of the time dimension as much as possible, looking whatever I'm presented with squarely in the face. The rest is just a fantasy, only existing in the mind, but with hugely destructive power.

Attitude is everything. If I lament my slow progress, I can make it much harder on myself. My strategy is to give myself a tiny pinch on the forearm and say "Stop it!" Then I turn my attention to the here and now—the sounds of water gurgling past the hull, the wind—the strength of which I can tell pretty accurately now by the pitch of its hum through the rigging. I know I WILL get there. When? is becoming less important.

Eckhart Tolle refers to "vertical time", rather than horizontal time. Stripped of its normal linearity, vertical time spreads upwards and down, like a shaft of light, illuminating the present moment, providing greater depth of awareness into the blissful "isness" of now. This awareness is more available to us in nature, away from the distractions of everyday life. I couldn't be any further removed if I tried. My 10-day Vipassana silent retreat has got nothing on this. The outer silence is the easy part; it's the inner silence that is so elusive.

The beginning of week 3 saw some steadier 10-12 knot winds. It was almost as if I had passed through the doldrums, the storm cells, the black clouds, the shafts of rain like pearly curtains daubed on the horizon. It is a very humbling experience, being out here alone on the sea. Some friends have expected me to feel proud of what I have achieved so far, but I don't. Sure I have the sailing skills, or at least enough so far to keep me out of too much trouble. Sure I have the tenacity and perseverance to push on through the testing times. I am pig-headed and determined enough to refuse (so far) to quit. But the enormity of the ocean, which has the power to squish me like an ant, prevents anything but gratitude to it for not having (yet) done so. The magnitude of the heavens, the unimaginable vastness of space, the stars, planets and galaxies that enthral me at night, shrink me to less than a molecule of dust. I feel it is a great privilege to be able to be out here. The shell of my egoic view of self is slowly breaking down.

The sea is a magnificent deep blue with licks of white frosting. There is a garland of puffy white clouds around the rim of the horizon, and all feels perfect. On two occasions, when there has been a gap in the ring of cloud, I have seen the elusive "green flash" that so many sailors watch for at sunset. At the precise moment when the blood orange orb dips below the horizon, like a fireball being extinguished by the sea, a pale greenish flare momentarily smudges the sky. Chances are it's an optical illusion or complementary colour after-image, but its rarity gives an uplifting thrill. Similarly (but differently) exciting are the flying fish. What on earth inspired these bizarrely prehistoric creatures to take to the air—to leave their first medium, water, for another? Perhaps some predator was sizing them up for breakfast, chasing them faster than they could run, and suddenly, they take to the sky, skimming above the waves, their gossamer wings beating madly, only barely keeping them aloft, their tail trailing like a rudder, then sploosh! a head-on crash into a wave, but farther from danger. Crazy critters—they always make me laugh out loud! It's such a shame a few gasp their last on *Shanti's* deck. I wouldn't have thought they could fly that high, but some have even made it into the boom bag or whacked me in the face at night. Now there's a good wake-up call.

As the coast of Brazil and the end of this passage drew nearer, I was in no hurry to get there. I had broken through that sense of urgency and was happily enjoying "Groundhog Day". The flat disc of sea stretching all round, the curved dome of sky above, with only tiny *Shanti*, day after day in the same apparent spot, as if pinned to the exact centre, a visual solipsism. The relative position never changes, never gets further from one horizon or closer to the other—always the same, dead centre. With not another living soul in sight for weeks on end, just me—encapsulated in this tiny space, like an interstellar life-support pod (only at times, buffeted more boisterously)—I greatly appreciate this rare opportunity, away from distractions of people and things. It disentangles brain cells, reassembles in a new and wondrous way the kaleidoscope of a lifetime of esoteric rabbit holes I have been down.

My hair is growing longer and, perhaps due to this, or to a lack of protein, is falling out. The longer than usual silvery hairs lurking around the cabin annoy me. Goenka, the founder of Vipassana, tells a story of an Indian prince who adores his wife's luxurious thick black hair—but only so long as it is on her head and not in his soup. This morning, in recognition of what is, I elected to clean it all up. Action, instead of complaint. You can't argue with reality.

Life is inherently imperfect in all its forms. Firstly, try to accept the form that this moment takes, rather than wanting a better or different one. Eckhart Tolle says that this then becomes a portal into the formless. At times I know exactly what he means by this. There is this longing for freedom in everyone. But it is not found by running away from the world of form. Every form has its limitations. Pass through limitation, face it, accept it, surrender—and everything changes. Krishnamurti's profound secret to happiness is: "I don't mind what happens." I wonder if I can ever achieve such equilibrium? Perhaps from time to time out here, on my own, but is it possible to sustain once immersed back in the frenetic noise of life ashore? Even here, it often seems to be two steps forward and one step backwards. Or sometimes three steps backwards. But it is the journey, not the destination.

Two days out from Cabedelo, I looked up and noticed the masthead light fitting was dangling like a marionette on a frayed wire. Either a big-footed booby bird had tried to dance on it, or the rigger back in Cape Town didn't secure it well (I notice my first reaction is to blame). The eventual fall from grace came the night before my approach to land (no navigation lights), but the good fortune within the misfortune was that it didn't plop straight overboard (which by all accounts it should have) but hit the deck and was still there on arrival, albeit in many pieces.

Jacare Marina is about 8 miles up a river. Its bushy banks and murky waters give the feel of going up the Amazon (not that I ever have) and it's a surprise when at the turn of a bend there is a modern-ish marina, and not too far away, the bustle of a busy metropolis, Joao Pessoa.

The weather was kind to me for my arrival, calm and sunny. The day after, the skies opened up to dump a deluge of tropical rain with strong winds. I was lucky also that some fellow cruisers invited me to raft up against their boat until the Marina office was able to allocate me a berth. The boats are tightly packed in side by side, with no walkways in between, using laid lines from behind to hold them back from the dock. In other ways, it's similar to Bundaberg, being in a fast-flowing tidal river. It feels very odd to be still, almost as if on concrete, after the constant motion of the past weeks.

The Marina is run by a couple of French men, who have created a wonderful dockside environment in which to relax. The open space has comfortable couches and lounge chairs. There is a small bar and a restaurant run by an attractive Portuguese woman, whose jet-black hair cascades in soft ripples down her brown back. I was surprised to learn she was older than me, her firm flesh exposed as much as decently possible.

Yesterday, the entire day was devoted to long walks and bus rides to do the usual visits to Immigration, Customs and Port Captain. It would have helped had I spent some time learning a few words of Spanish or Portuguese. The couple who had been anxiously watching for my arrival were checking out of the country. They invited me to tag along with them to find the well-concealed offices scattered at great distances apart. I would have struggled to find these by myself.

As always, it was an interesting experience. After having our photos taken, we sat for a long time in the few plastic chairs in the foyer of the Immigration office. I wasn't sure what we were waiting for, as no-one else seemed to be ahead of us. After a couple of hours, we were called to a small office, fortunately together, so my helpers could translate for me. I made some slight efforts to at least gather the Portuguese words for hello, goodbye and thank-you. The young man sitting opposite us seemed to have dyslexia or some other disability that made him form his letters painstakingly slowly, gripping the pen in his fist as if to strangle it.

From there we caught a bus to Customs, a tiny, unidentified room hidden behind a featureless concrete warehouse. I sat back while the others were subjected to an aggressive tirade of complaint from a phlegmy, tight-collared officer, who at least had some English that I could understand. It's hard to imagine checking in and out of foreign countries without a common language or a guide. I managed to get through the pre-departure formalities by myself a few weeks later.

―――――

For the first few days after leaving Cabedelo, I was unwell. Not just the usual mal-de-mer, but something more, a localised pain around the navel. I dug out my ancient copy of the "Ship Captain's Medical Guide", which offered several possible diagnoses, from hernia to appendicitis, with the recommendation to radio for medical advice (?) and head to the nearest hospital (??). Luckily it passed of its own accord, but it brought home to me the additional risks of this lifestyle that I generally ignore.

Despite her ailing skipper, *Shanti* sped off jauntily, taking full advantage of the Equatorial Current, which flows NW at up to 4 knots, setting unheard-of records for me of 165 miles a day—a positive start to covering the 2,000 miles directly to the Caribbean.

Then, on day 4, came the doldrums, this time for real. Getting through the doldrums with less than 150 litres of diesel is a challenge, constantly working at changing sails to keep the boat moving, taking advantage of every subtle offering. At 1312 I received a call on the VHF radio from the ship *Golden Arion*. The Indian

2nd officer, recognising the name *Shanti*, wanted to explain its meaning to me. "Do you know it means peace?" he asked in his lilting, head-wobbling way. He then wanted to chat about how is it to be sailing a small yacht? "How might he get one?" "And what is your good name?" It kept a smile on my face for several more miles.

Day 5, May 7. I crossed the equator—00° 00' It was hotter than expected, so I didn't bake a roast dinner but did have a private party, with cold libations, offerings to Neptune, the gods of the four compass quarters, music and song. I cut the engine to actually sail, rather than motor across that invisible line. I drew a couple of 0's on two eggs and took some selfies but decided against the bare-breasted version for public view.

On day 9, I tried flying the spinnaker again, but with no success. There was just not quite enough wind. Whilst wrangling it, the pole swung wildly and banged me hard on the head. It took my breath away for a moment (to give thanks that I was not knocked out, or overboard). The very next minute, it tried again. I quickly sprouted two large duck eggs, about an inch apart. All this before breakfast!

There are vast patches of yellowish Sargassum weed everywhere, which have an ethereal beauty. I wonder where they all come from, perhaps the Amazon. Some are the size of a football field and stretch for miles, in disparate clumps, joined by a narrow chain, like a giant string of pearls. They almost have the appearance of dry land, or an erupting, newly born, sandy quay. The colour is totally uniform, as is the structure, like upturned gorse bushes. When the rising sun catches these, they glint like spun gold. At first, they were a worry, lest they foul the propeller or get sucked into the water intake when motoring through them, parting a semi-solid path. Neither of these happened, so I just enjoyed the extraordinary sight.

On day 11 one of the especially fierce rain squalls hit and had *Shanti* screaming along at a great rate of knots as the rain pelted the sea into a rolling roundness. The second after the rain stopped, she gybed. I went up to sort it out but was unable to. No matter what I did, gybing kept on happening. It was as if either *Tilly* had gone nuts or we were in the eye of the squall, with circular winds veering and backing constantly. After about 10 minutes of the main crashing left and right (*Make up your mind!* I railed), we were away again. Thankfully we had no more of that nonsense overnight. It was another opportunity for practising acceptance of what is.

Day 13: At 1530, I rounded the imaginary "turning mark" and began heading inshore, toward the Suriname River. It was not my original intention to go there, but others had sung its praises and it seemed an attractive prospect to break the 2000 miles to Trinidad and Tobago. I had been buddy boating with another single-hander, Paul, on a Jeanneau 44, *Hierbabuena*, since leaving Jacare. We had been keeping a good distance between us, with the two boats generally out of sight of each other, but at 0330 my AIS alarm (which was set for a range of half a mile) went off. I called Paul on the VHF radio and found out the furling line for his genoa had broken, letting the sail run fully out. He was now unable to reduce speed and was way over-canvassed for the conditions.

We discussed his options and concluded that he would need to drop the sail completely. This was not going to be easy, balancing on the foredeck, trying to contain yards of wildly flapping canvas on a pitch-black, moonless night. The shoal water waves were steep, sharp and confused. To top it off, it started to bucket down with rain. Then on top of that, his engine failed.

An hour later he called back on the radio to say he was utterly exhausted. I told him to sleep for 2 hours while I kept a lookout for fishing boats. I sailed in a broad holding pattern, going round in circles, trying to stay close. When he awoke, we discussed the engine failure. There was no way he could go up the Suriname River without it, and *Shanti* was too small to tow him. He had to get it going. The symptoms he described (going slow, then fast), sounded like what is known as "hunting" for fuel, requiring changing the fuel filters and bleeding the lines—something I have had lots of experience with. Despite being relatively new to boating, he was able to do it, which was just as well. Even though sailing in company gives the illusion of safety, really, there is little practical hands-on help possible, with wind and waves preventing close contact.

Meanwhile, *Shanti* had made up her mind that Suriname was not for her. My AIS track looked as if I had fallen into some Bermudan Triangle, going round in circles, all the while drifting north. Try as I might to head back, the strong equatorial current dictated that North West was the only way for a little boat with little power to go. So at 0930, we bade *Hierbabuena* farewell and headed back out to sea, alone again. This was a perfect case of "the best-laid plans of mice and men …." We had studied the charts intently, laid down waypoints, checked the tides at the river, calculated time and distance, plotted alternative routes for contingencies, only for me to have to abort, 100 miles off the destination. It's another lesson for me in staying in the present moment. Make plans, but don't be surprised if they change. Let go of attachment to outcomes.

My spirits are high, delighting in sailing *Shanti* on this glorious day. Just as when the German buddy-boats left me, I feel relieved that it's just me again, that there's no need to adjust pace and course to suit others. The choppy waves have given way to a longer swell, clear blue sky and brilliant sunshine. A pure white bird with bright red lipstick and a stingray tail is madly flapping its wings, circling *Shanti* as if to find a resting platform. One dolphin has joined us, much smaller than usual, with unusual colouring of pale greyish-brown patches.

We were almost run over by a ship last night. I'm so very glad that I thought to change the AIS range from half a mile to 4 miles. When the alarm went off, the ship, *Marguerita*, was directly in front with 10 minutes to CPA (collision). I called on the VHF radio to ask his intentions (a polite way of asking, do you intend running me over?) For about 10 seconds my heart stood still, as I listened to silence. What could I do? Alter course? Pointless. Then, in a matter-of-fact tone came the reply, "My intentions are to pass port to port; turning to starboard now." I realised as he passed within metres of me that he hadn't seen me. I lay in my bunk and re-enacted that near disaster several times, imagining the worst, before finally getting myself back to the present and calming down.

It is only another 510 miles to Tobago, Checking-in after hours or on weekends incurs heavy overtime penalties. With the favourable South Equatorial current adding up to 4 knots of speed over ground I could possibly arrive on Friday afternoon. However, the current could disappear, the wind change, or anything, so I won't count on it. I'm learning that things never go quite the way I think, so best not to think.

With only 8 miles between me and a good night's sleep, an ear-piercing alarm brought me instantly back to the present. I had no idea what it was, other than a painfully deafening noise that could have been coming from anywhere. My mind raced for a few moments, touching briefly on all kinds of madness, from warships to air-raid. Inside the cabin, the sound was amplified to a supersonic pitch, as if magnified by bouncing off the confining walls. It was a demonic shriek, an undeniable call to panic. In panic mode, I turned things off, first the VHF radio (no difference), then *Tilly* (likewise).

In hindsight, it's amazing how slow my mind was to recognise the source of this noise as coming from the engine. I have only ever heard it once before in that embarrassing moment at Sandringham Yacht Club when the high-temperature alarm shrieked its objections to my leaving home. There are processes to go through before shutting down the engine and I could scarcely remember them, but within another minute, the ignition key was turned off and the dreadful noise ceased. The pounding of my heart took a bit longer. Then came the need to calm down and consider the situation. No engine. A coal-black night, a lee shore close by, the wind holding strong (which was reassuring), a very strung out and overtired skipper. *What to do?*

One possibility was to keep on sailing north to Grenada. A second option was to head south-west to Trinidad. Either way, it was going to be another sleepless night. I opted for Trinidad, where I already had a booking to haul out at the end of June for the hurricane season. It would mean arriving a few weeks earlier than planned but at least I would be there.

The wind held steady through the night but at dawn, it dropped to less than 5 knots. It was raining and there was very little wind, with the usual roll—just enough to slide tools, engine covers, me, from side to side across the wet floor. The last time the impeller was changed was on the day of my grand departure from Melbourne. Thankfully, despite the current conditions and my ignorance, there was no alarm when I restarted the engine.

Six hours later, I was doing 1.5 knots through the narrow channel with the tide against me and the odd 25-knot katabatic gust blasting right on the nose. There was no way I could have sailed through there.

Even though I am here a few weeks earlier than intended, I don't think I will suffer by it. There are plenty of things to be done on *Shanti*, such as replacing the masthead lights that fell down, removing and repairing *Min*, the Fleming wind vane, etc. Other friends I have met along the way (the two Germans, Wolfgang and Klaus) will arrive here in a few days, also to leave their boats on the hardstand.

Early one morning I decided to take *Guppy*, my inflatable dinghy for a row, with the vague notion of checking out the Coral Cove lifting bay. It's always helpful to have some idea of where to go when the time comes. To my surprise, I discovered a familiar blue ketch nestled in there, with Cape Town painted on its broad stern. Knocking on the rough metal hull, I called, "Hey Hurgen, are you awake?" Within seconds a bare torso appeared.

"Oh hi there," he greeted with a warm smile.

"So the wind blew you this way I see."

He laughed. "Climb aboard if you can."

I glanced around for a way, finally spotting a rusty vertical ladder that led through a wooden platform overhanging the back of the boat.

"You're very agile," he observed as if expecting me to struggle.

"Boat life," I laughed, feeling nonetheless pleased.

The cockpit was small for such a large boat and vertical-edged. The coamings overhung the backrests so it wasn't as comfortable as I'm used to on *Shanti*. Hurgen passed up some cushions while he brewed a pot of herbal tea. We already knew from our brief time together in St Helena that we had similarities, not the least being our love of music. Hurgen has had a long history of involvement in music production and teaching dance. He makes exquisite pan flutes from bamboo. Pursing his lips across the raft of pipes, he produces hauntingly beautiful melodies. I was absolutely in awe of his talent and the vast range of sounds that could be formed from such a tiny instrument.

Even more interesting was his spontaneous Kundalini awakening, something that simply happened to him a few years ago, and which took several more years for him to come to understand. It is not something that many people get to experience, so there are not too many signposts or rational explanations available. In the Hindu tradition, it is described as an extremely powerful energy, the central creative force of the universe. It is depicted as a serpent coiled in the sacrum, which once awakened, rises up the spine and exits through the crown of the head, removing lifetimes of negative patterns. It forcibly brings multiple layers of past blockages to the surface for healing, producing a rapid evolution of consciousness. It is generally triggered by our own higher self, and only at such a time as when we are ready for it. We don't actually cause it, in the sense of wanting to make it happen.

Hurgen shared some of his thoughts about his experience with me, trying as far as possible to demystify it. He spoke softly, without self-aggrandisement.

"The Kundalini awakening is given at random. It is a doorway for spiritual awakening, or in other words, a means by which we become more conscious. Awakening of consciousness is an ongoing process, and it includes the awakening of the body, which is the Kundalini. The physical awakening can be argued to be simply an opening or free-flowing of energy centres, or chakras. When energy flows more freely through the body it has various effects. First, it is incredibly pleasurable, like a continuous whole-body orgasm, pulling the body into spasms of delight that tears at the muscles and tendons until we can get it under control. The second effect is healing. In my case, I grew a few inches taller, my eyes improved, the deterioration of glaucoma halted and bones repaired. It does not prevent illness but does offer an improved healing condition, unless I block the energy flow, thinking I want to be "normal", forgetting that open chakras should be the norm. Spiritual awakening is easier to attain, or at least there is a known method to get going on a path of enlightenment or gradual awakening of our consciousness. Physical awakening seems more random. I have experimented with others to get them to experience it and I found one technique that works, at least temporarily."

We sipped our tea in silence for a while, allowing the mountain of information to sit quietly in its profundity. What he had shared seemed so full of meaning, like a mountain or an ocean, or a bird. It would take a while to digest and I gave thanks for the impulse that had led me to get up early, hop in *Guppy* and row in this particular direction this morning. Like me, Hurgen is hauling *Morwenna* out and leaving her for a few months, so our time together will be brief.

"Man plans and God laughs." Things change and plans seem especially prone to those Divine chuckles. Fortunately, to date, most minor modifications have been peripheral to the grand design. Had I been paying closer attention to my inner knowing, I might have been more aware of the overambitious timing of this exeat. It started out according to plan, with me toting 7 months' worth of personal belongings into the sky, the final stopover being New Zealand, as per usual, for my father's 101st birthday. This would delay my return to *Shanti* until early February.

The realisation that this was totally impractical slowly seeped into my waterlogged brain and eventually shaped my decision. The Panama Canal transit is best done around March. Returning to *Shanti* in February would scarcely leave time to sail directly there (over 2,000 nautical miles away), not to mention the work that needs to be done before setting sail.

It will be the first birthday of my father's that I have missed for a long time and I feel pretty bad about that, but sometimes practicalities prevail. If not, I could end up spending the rest of my days, like Wolfgang and Klaus, going up and down the Caribbean island chain for years (not such a bad fate, but not my intention). They, and most other cruisers, are returning to their boats around mid-September to resume sailing the following month.

If I returned in February next year, I would not just be the tail runner, but completely left behind. Reports of increased piracy off the coast of Venezuela make it safer to sail in company with others if possible. So I opted for a more condensed excursion to Europe instead, visiting friends and relatives, and attending French school in Montpellier.

Chapter 14

Close Encounters

Returning to Trinidad in early September, I found *Shanti* pretty much as I left her, despite there having been major flooding and a 7.3 earthquake in the interim. It's nothing short of a miracle that all this reclaimed land held together and boats stayed standing on their metal props while the earth shook violently.

The jobs' list spread itself into the available time, as per usual, with "Island-time" and the rainy season contributing to delays. A typical tropical pattern saw generally sunny mornings, dense clouds building ominously behind the eastern hills toward midday, a torrential downpour followed by soaring humidity—with a possible repeat performance later in the day. Temperatures in the mid to high 30's with relative humidity around 90%, are more conducive to snoozing than working. Most of the liveaboards have hired an air-conditioning unit to make life "on the hard" more bearable. No such luxury onboard *Shanti*, but my excellent Caframo fans run 24/7.

Labour is relatively inexpensive here so it's a good opportunity to give *Shanti* a new coat of paint. Others are also sprucing up their boats. Wolfgang has contracted the same local painter he uses every year while Klaus does it all himself. Steelies like *Dream Catcher* and *Morwenna* are being sandblasted before emerging from their crustaceous shells, ready to take flight like butterflies in glistening blood red and sky blue. It's such a satisfying transformation to behold, even on boats other than one's own.

I can't say that Chaguaramus has been without diversions to make me appreciate spending more time here. A well-organised group of cruisers from all over the world conspire to ensure there's always plenty to do, from "pot luck" dinners, Mexican train dominoes to "noodling" in the pool. My favourite, of course, is the Friday night jam session, where I get a microphone stuck in front of me and get to sing loudly to my heart's content, while rows of Congas and Jimbos and Bongos and other island drums keep the beat.

Hurgen's pan flute often joined in, enthralling us all with its raspy richness. By now most people assumed he and I to be husband and wife, so often were we seen together. It was just a comfortable friendship, with each of us holding some loyalty elsewhere, me to Luke and he to one of several would-be girlfriends spread throughout the world. He explained how this new-found popularity had come about since the Kundalini awakening, which left him free of the need of women. It's interesting how that works; the greater the need, the less the attraction.

Every Friday evening, two excellent guitarists set up sound systems in the open pavilion at the back of Power Boats' yard, with professional amplifiers, large speaker bins and microphones. I would like to say that it was at one of those riotous events that I damaged my ankle, but no, there wasn't even any dancing or alcohol involved. I simply slipped off the edge of a wobbly wooden step, rolled the ankle to the accompaniment of a loud cracking sound, and fell, rather dramatically. It was the kindness of others that got me up the ladder onto *Shanti*, where I felt somewhat trapped for the next week.

There were other jobs I was waiting on anyway, which also had their own share of frustrations. In Chaguaramas, local workers invariably bite off far more than they can chew, promise deadlines they can't keep, seldom turn up when they say they will, and are quite arbitrary in their pricing. I didn't think it was such a big ask—just a 5' long stainless-steel pipe with a small plate welded onto the base—yet it took weeks longer than planned. I am now happy to introduce the latest addition to the all-girl crew: *Blewy*—a second-hand Silentwind wind generator, (painted blue). Coupled with a new charge controller, (which I bought from Portugal and had it shipped to me in France), she now augments my power bank. I'm halfway around the world and only just starting to feel as if I have sorted out the balance of power supply and consumption.

Close to schedule, *Shanti* 'splashed' on Wednesday, October 3. *Blewy* sang her heart out as we motored down to the nearby anchorage of Scotland Bay. It seemed prudent to spend a few quiet days alone in this bay, resting (*sure*), getting shipshape, checking systems and rediscovering my sea legs. The continuing tasks of cleaning mould from decks and dinghy etc. were made easier with a peaceful seascape and cooling breeze. I love being back out on the water again, enjoying that gentle motion of fluidity beneath. As friends have told me, "the land is dangerous".

On Monday, October 8, I will visit Customs and Immigration to clear-out of the country, then do an overnight sail to Grenada. Large numbers of cruisers are already beginning their northern jaunt up the Windward Isles, pending the end of hurricane season next month. This is a seasonally dictated digression for me, a chance to explore some of the Caribbean islands before turning south and heading toward the Panama Canal next year.

The colour of one's urine is always a good indication of one's state of hydration and on the morning of my arrival in Grenada, mine was dark orange. I hastily downed 3 cups of water and 10 minutes later promptly regurgitated them, for no apparent reason, other than perhaps shock to the system, or a delayed reaction to the calamitous overnight sail here. Being the first sail after months off the water, things were bound to go wrong. I could list them:

Casting off the mooring, one of my thongs went overboard. (I was wearing them to keep the bandage on my sprained ankle dry). Retrieving the deeply buried boathook from the cockpit locker (in semi-panic as *Shanti* drifts back toward the boat behind), the hook catches on the fridge wiring and pulls it out.

Tilly, the tiller pilot, notices the shiny new red ropes on *Min*, the wind pilot, and decides to retire. This is a critical piece of equipment, which is why I carry a spare. Ripping into the sub-bunk black hole, (in the next stage beyond semi-panic as we become a "vessel not under command"), hauling out everything that's so neatly stowed there, I unearth the large bubble-wrapped, unopened box, housing who? —*Tilly 2*. This is a darker-skinned version of her forebear, and untested. Now, I ask you, who in their right mind, doesn't pre-test? Recalcitrant, petulant, obstinate, or perhaps just comically whimsical, *Tilly 2* wants to steer *Shanti* round in circles. That's OK, I have known such things to happen with new autopilots; it's called "swinging the compass", so the inbuilt fluxgate compass can get its bearings. But right at this moment, it's incredibly annoying, with all the large steel vessels moored nearby.

After 3 more circles, I say, *enough already! Let's just get going*, but she won't oblige. (It's not her fault; I haven't given the instructions more than a glazed glance, and later discover she needs an extension push rod). So I toss her back down below, grab a can of WD40, spray *Tilly 1's* connection points and give her another chance. This yields a last gasp of about half an hour before all function lights finally fade into autopilot oblivion.

The sea-state outside of the Bocas is lumpy in the breathless afternoon, so *Yani* must pitch and roll us through this slop. "At least she's working," I think— followed quickly by, *"Don't tempt fate!"*

The current is pushing strongly West, so we must push against it to avoid ending up in Venezuela. I try not to clench my jaw, my neck, or anything else, contemplating this precarious situation of a strong current, no wind and a long-idle engine, whose every variance in pitch causes me alarm.

One of the worst things about single-handing is enforced steering, with no autopilot. Being stuck at the helm is said by some to be the maritime version of wearing a ball and chain. There's probably more of a psychological aspect to this than the physical restraint warrants, but I certainly felt uncomfortably fettered, being harnessed to the jerking tiller as each wave tried to yank it from my hand. Of course, it's possible to lash it momentarily or simply abandon it to dash below to check the course.

And so we motored on, until eventually, just after a scarlet sunset, a mirage-like rainbow and a brief deluge, a thick curtain of darkness wrapped the world up and packed it away out of sight. The wind came and *Yani* was hushed—always a peaceful moment—except at this time, for *Blewy*, who was whirling like a turbo-charged demented dervish, making, or so I believed, mega-amps of wonderful power. However, on checking the readout on the charge controller, I discovered, zilch, zip, zero input. Why?? Screaming like a banshee, or jet engine, or wind-generator, there went *Blewy*, making all that unconscionable commotion for no power production. The battery monitor showed 12.2 volts and draining. What on earth?? And then, as if becoming suddenly aware of her disgraceful performance, *Blewy* did an Isadora Duncan, wrapping the hobbling-string round her neck and thwacking to a strangled halt. Ah, peace at last.

Now it was *Min's* turn to shine. It would have been preferable to be testing the rebuilt Fleming self-steering wind vane in daylight, and there was not even a sliver or a shimmering shaving of the outermost rim of a new moon to prick the clouds. Nonetheless, with the breeze building and veering north-east, for the first time, something untested seemed to be playing the game.

Tired as I was, the most I could trust leaving everything to its own devices at this stage was only 10 minutes. There were interesting distractions. A pod of dolphins sheered up some sparkling bioluminescence in their wake and before long, the brilliant Stella-nova-lights of the oil drilling platforms lit the horizon. I aimed to sail between them, but an American service ship was directly in my path, moving at 2 knots to the east, and it seemed prudent to pass behind it. This was a big mistake, which I didn't realise until later. At around 0500, my course over ground showed the full extent of the current, which had practically swept me beyond making any possible landfall on Grenada. At the same time, the ebb tide added a further 2 knots to the West, and the wind went to the Northeast. All of which meant that even with *Yani* fully roused and roaring, the headway was scarcely 2-3 knots.

This circus ride went on for about another 9 hours until finally, the reef-bound pass through into the anchorage at Hog Island was breasted. It's been a long while since I felt such a tremendous sense of relief at reaching a safe harbour, reminding me of the struggle up the east coast of Australia and other coastal passages, where time and tide wait for no-one.

Wolfgang and Klaus were already anchored alongside one another, having completed their world circumnavigations here. At 82 years of age, Klaus must be one of the oldest of mariners to sail around the world, but his momentous achievement went unremarked. I suspect I will likewise skulk quietly back into Australia one day in the future, setting no records, satisfying no expectations other than my own. Not such a bad way to be. Much of the hoo-ha is of very short-lived recognition anyway, soon becoming yesterday's news.

Wolfgang was quick to zoom me off in his big dinghy to fulfil all the clearing-in formalities in a typically relaxed Caribbean mode. Never mind that we were miles from the designated arrival port, that they couldn't view my boat to check my fruit and vegetables or any of those other bureaucratic revenue generators. The Immigration officer wasn't even there and we were told to come back and complete the process tomorrow.

Hog Island and the encircling reefs make this a very secure hurricane hole. There are literally dozens of boats packed cheek to jowl, rather like the crowded anchorage colloquially known as "Bum's Bay" in Queensland, only multiplied tenfold. A few of us arranged a private bus tour of the island, with a very informative local guide by the name of Cutty. This filled in some of the gaping gaps in my knowledge of Grenada, as well as taking in the spectacular scenery of the interior that we yachties seldom see. At the Rivers rum distillery, I bought a couple of bottles of the 73% proof firewater to give as gifts to Wolfgang and Klaus. Perhaps the greatest thrill after getting settled here was finding a resident yachtie who was able to re-gas my fridge in less than 5 minutes. Once again, I can enjoy chilled white wine. These small luxuries that shore-people take so much for granted are like rare jewels to me.

In their usual helpful way, Wolfgang and Klaus were able to resurrect *Blewy*, the wind-generator, discovering that the power cables had not been well secured in the connecting box. She's humming away to my favourite amp-loading tune, keeping the fridge going day and night. Fridge and power! What more could I ask for? Happy-hour for all on board *Shanti* with iced wine and freshly baked cheese and coconut scones. Ah, the immense, small pleasures! How good is life once you stop banging your head against walls!

St Vincent and the Grenadines. November 3, 2018

One great advantage of the Caribbean chain of Windward Islands is their proximity to each other, often less than 10 miles apart. Leaving Hog Island, it was a very pleasant 3-hour sail, just around the corner to the capital of Grenada, St George's Bay. As per usual, Wolfgang picked me up in his big dinghy, the 15 hp outboard easily getting us up on the plane. There's benefit to both of us, my weight helping to keep the boat balanced, though I know Wolfgang likes to see my delight. It's an exciting ride, the thrilling speed, the wind in my hair, the almost out-of-control bouncing up and down on the firm rubber tubes. I can't take the grin off my face and always feel like singing. It's better than a roller-coaster ride. It would take me five times as long in *Guppy* with her 3.5 hp outboard to get from the anchorage to the town. It's not as slow as Hurgen's tender, which is an old inflatable kayak. When he's feeling extra hospitable, Wolfgang picks Hurgen up too.

The next day called for an earlier start for the slightly longer haul of 35 miles to the island of Carriacou. With 4 boats heading in the same direction, it's always a bit of an unspoken race, and the conditions were ideal for *Shanti* to shine. I haven't done much windward sailing on this circumnavigation, so it was a novelty to be punching into a stiff breeze at a perfect angle off the bow. Our fearless leader, Wolfgang, had already given us the benefit of his previous experience in this area and directed us to the less densely-populated spots. As we watched the crimson sunset from the warm sand, I lay back and gave thanks for a perfect day in a perfect place in a perfect life. How lucky am I?

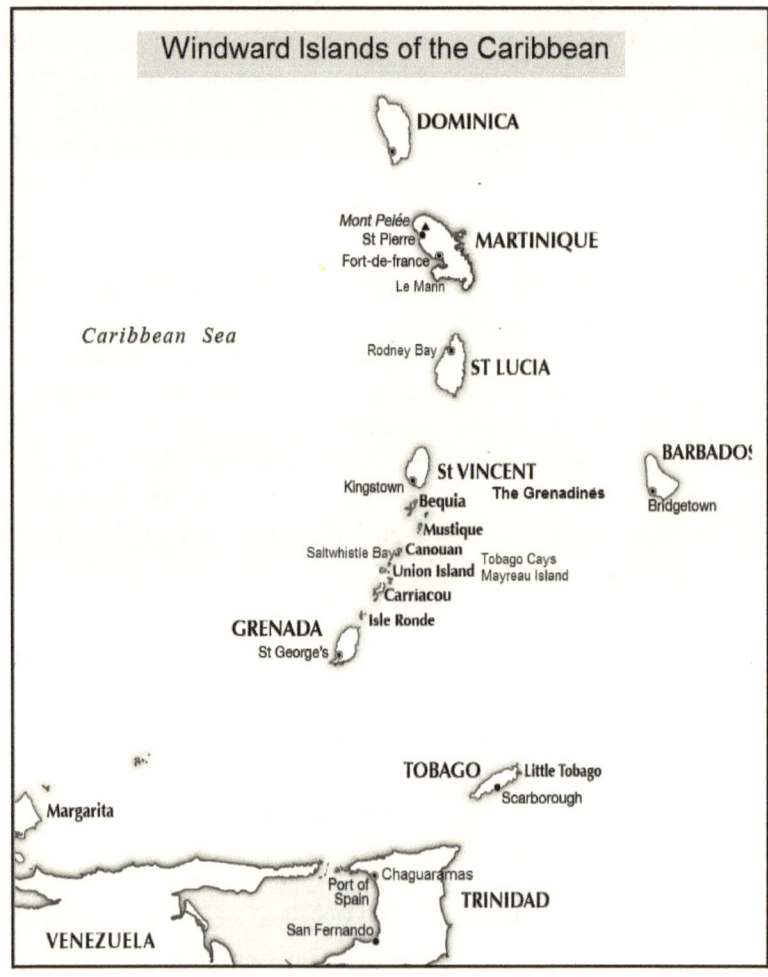

Strange as it may seem, many of the Windward Islands are independent countries, and it is necessary to go through all the formalities of checking out, clearing customs and immigration, getting passports stamped, etc, only to sail 6 miles or so to the next check-in. Carriacou is part of Grenada; Union Island is the start of St Vincent and the Grenadines. The islands of this country continue up as far as St Lucia (British), before Martinique (French).

From Union Island, we anchored out near the fringing reef of Tobago Cays, which is kind of like being in the open sea, especially at high tide, when it can get a bit rolly poly. There are reefs everywhere in this area, which I discovered later to my peril.

But let me tell you first about last night. We had sailed around to the leeward side of Mayreau Island, (also part of Tobago Cays) where at first it seemed a bit more sheltered, especially in close to the cliffs. But later the rebounding swell made it unpleasant, so I moved in closer to the beach, perhaps a bit too close to the ferry wharf, which Wolfgang assured me only saw a daily bread delivery by a smallish vessel. *Ba-boom!!* Wrong!

Just after 9 pm, a loud horn blast announced the arrival of the not insignificant inter-island vehicular ferry. The wind had swung *Shanti* even closer to where she should not be. With lights splitting the darkness, the ferry was doing one of those ten-point turns, with engines in reverse, lining up the vehicle-loading ramp with the wharf—but as we know, "operating astern propulsion" does not necessarily mean going backwards. For heart-stopping moments it loomed nearer and nearer until I almost wondered if I should do something to fend off. It was a terrifying thing to be in the billion candle-power spotlight, as the sheer metal cliff-face of this monster's bow came within metres of running into me. I could practically see the whites of the captain's eyes, who was no doubt wondering what on earth this little insect was that was sitting directly in his path. But these ferry-drivers are highly skilled operators and so no paint was lost. The moment after he had docked, I leapt into action, fired up my engine, lifted anchor and reversed blindly through the darkness, amongst mooring buoys and other boats to get as far away as possible, without courting further coronary. That was last night. This morning—close encounters with the hard stuff...

We are now in Salt Whistle Bay, which will forever be known for the loss of *Shanti's* virginity to going on a reef. Ouch! That is such a painful experience.

Yani, the trusty Yanmar engine has developed this nasty little idiosyncrasy of stalling during, or just after lifting the anchor. It could be due to old age, low compression, being a bit "cokey", or any number of other possibilities. I have learnt certain tricks to get around this, such as putting her into slow reverse gear first, which mostly works, but sometimes not.

This morning was a NOT. And with the reef only metres away, the timing could not have been worse. I had gotten myself into a tight corner and dropped the pick in weed, too close to the reef behind, so had to re-anchor. But halfway through the first hoist, I heard the high-pitched squeal of the engine alarm, telling me she had stalled. I ran back to the cockpit and started her up again but once the anchor was free, again, no power, and we were drifting reefward. I watched in horror as the depth sounder showed 0.5, 0.3, 0.1, 0.0. Bump, bump!! Aaargghh!

Luckily the wind was not strong, and with the aid of a local fishing boat and Wolfgang's dinghy, we managed to get back into floating depth. I dove immediately after and couldn't see any damage—just a few inches with slightly less slime on the keel. It could have been worse, but it's still a very distressing thing to have happen. Such is the price of trying to edge into a calmer corner of the bay.

The 60-mile passage from Bequia to St Lucia via the windward side of St Vincent took us back into the Atlantic Ocean, as big and bold and boisterous as ever. The seas were a lumpy 2-3 metres with an agitated cross pattern on top; all of which conspired to stop *Shanti* dead in her tracks, wallowing up and down, going more sideways than forwards. Arriving just on sunset, worn and weary, I made an uncommon mistake—I forgot to turn off the engine saltwater intake valve. It was a very rolly poly night with katabatic gusts reaching 40 knots; ideal conditions for siphoning water up into the engine. (I do believe the anti-siphon valve is supposed to prevent this, but after fitting two new ones to no avail, I suspect the height above water level is an issue). Anyway, sure enough, the next morning when I opened the engine cover to turn the water on and discovered it *still* on, I knew that spelt trouble. *Trouble with a capital T.*

This is how it goes—put the gear lever in neutral, full-throttle; turn key to the reassuring shriek of the oil pressure alarm, push start button; and *clunk*. Nothing. Or at least nothing that's supposed to happen. Not the sweet grumble-rumble of cold metal turning over; just the jarring thud of metal cogs refusing to mesh.

Now, here again, is the good fortune in the bad, where something is learned (and remembered) from past experience. It is also extremely fortunate that *Yani* the 3-cylinder Yanmar diesel has 3 decompression levers on top, which when flicked up, allow a water-logged engine to turn over without firing, and gradually expel all the water from the cylinders. Success! On the move again.

The next exciting challenge had far more good fortune within the bad, which could have ended disastrously.

It is not possible to anchor in the marine reserve of the Pitons, where the water close to the shore is around 40 metres deep, so it's necessary to pick up a mooring. The locals say the Pitons are the breasts of St Lucia that the town is nestled between. The wind funnels fiercely down these buxom breasts and there's a strong current swirling through the bay, so boats are often facing in all different directions. After one uncomfortable night, I decided to move in closer to shore. I started up the engine, released the mooring, and backed away from it slowly. About halfway in toward the new mooring the engine suddenly stopped dead. I tried restarting it but got nothing. The gear lever was jammed tight and wouldn't budge.

My mind was racing as we drifted powerlessly at the mercy of wind and tide. Wolfgang was nearby in his dinghy and called out to me to turn toward another free mooring that was downwind. He lined himself up there ready to catch us. *Shanti* was still moving at about 2 knots and I wondered if he'd be able to stop her. He did. And the second bit of good luck was I had had two lines set up at the bow, so he could grab one and quickly attach it to the heavy mooring rope before I sailed on by toward the rocks.

My other line had blown off the deck as I reversed away from the first mooring, gone overboard and gotten wrapped around the propeller. I try not to beat myself up too much over this stupid mistake that could have cost me the boat. So many things hang off one thin thread. Another "cat's life" burned, another barrelful of gratitude and outpouring of heartfelt thanks to the mortal and immortal guardian angels that are watching over *Shanti*.

Later that day, the third musketeer of our impromptu band, Hurgen, appeared around the headland in *Morwenna*, with his engine failed. It was impossible to sail into the bay with the wind coming from all directions, so he needed to be towed in. Wolfgang helped, but the 16-ton steel ketch put a hefty strain on his outboard, which has never been the same since. But that's what we do, help each other when we can, and Hurgen was safely in on a nearby mooring.

The next day, Wolfgang took the three of us around a rocky headland to the town to pay our dues. It was a slower, wetter ride than I've been used to with three of us in the dinghy and the ailing outboard, so we had lots to thank Wolfgang for. We decided to chip in for a hire car to explore more of the interior. The "Breasts of St Lucia" are sumptuously clad in vibrant floral hues splashed over sensuously verdant rises. Wolfgang knows an exclusive resort overlooking all of this, so lunch was in one of the most amazing restaurants I have ever seen. The tables and chairs were practically hung in mid-air, with just a timber balcony railing between us and a drop of thousands of metres to the sea. The majestic uprisings of the mighty Pitons flanked either side of us, their cleavage funnelling our attention to the seemingly miniature toy yachts, our own yachts, on the moorings so far down below. What a view!

All of the towns on each of the Caribbean islands are completely different from each other, with the one common feature being the kaleidoscope of diverse colours. No boring covenants of conformity in place here; more of a complementary palette of artistic licence, splashing sea-greens with coral sand and sky-blue in a reverent echo of the enveloping climate.

The next stop was Anse la Raye, a quaint village with many small houses that are just like a child would draw, with pitched roof and two windows each side of a door. Hurgen jagged off in search of a new fuel pump for his ailing engine, while Wolfgang and I hunted down a quiet waterfront café. Several young locals plied their wares or offered their services, transport, tour-guiding, or anything else designed to get cash from our pockets to theirs. The majority nestled in the warmth of inactivity and acceptance of just-enough.

From there, it was another windward bash to Rodney Bay, which again, is a totally different scene, more like a mega tourist destination with money written all over it. There is a vast marina development not unlike Queensland's Gold Coast with pricey waterfront properties and private jetties lining man-made canals.

Much as I'm enjoying this Caribbean caper, it does feel as if I'm biding my time—which in many ways I am—until I can get sailing again in earnest. Occasionally I feel very nervous about what lies ahead, the uncertainty of another big ocean crossing. Despite its name, the Pacific holds no guarantee of being the peaceful ocean and several other cruisers who have crossed it recently have reported adverse conditions.

Yet I fully understand the lure to be back on the open sea. This coastal hopping up the aptly named Windward Isles is mainly motor-sailing directly into wind and wave, and then anchoring in blustery bays with poor holding. Plus, it is a great way to blow off heaps of cash.

The shopping malls are glossy and full of everything except customers (waiting for the tourist season to begin in earnest). Rodney Bay has a well-stocked Island Water World chandlery, which is good news for me. Over the past few anchorages, my anchor winch has been struggling to lift anything heavier than a walnut and I decided a new motor might not be a bad idea before it ground to a halt completely. Luckily the very helpful store manager tracked one down for me in the USA, which should get Fed Ex'd here in a couple of days.

If you take your ship's papers and customs documents with you the prices are ex tax, so I did that this morning, once again with the help of Wolfgang's bigger dinghy and now temperamental outboard. The not-so-good-luck was we both took a tumble into the briny as he was stepping back aboard, using my shoulder to balance himself. It was impossible to avoid falling in and I even took the two bags of shopping with me as I went. Sinking deeper, I struggled to remove my backpack and toss it back into the dinghy. All my documents, passports, money and mobile phone were inside. Wolfgang didn't see the funny side of it, but I couldn't stop laughing. Back onboard *Shanti*, everything is spread to dry and the waterproof case on my iPhone seems to have done its job. Just lucky!

Most passages up the Windward Isles seldom enjoy the benefit of a rare southerly component to the prevailing north-easterlies, so when one is forecast, everyone grabs it. It was too good an opportunity to miss by hanging around waiting for my anchor winch motor to arrive, so we cleared out of St Lucia and had a glorious 25-mile sail up to Martinique. This has got to be one of the quickest and easiest places in the world to clear into, where filling in a form on a self-help, dedicated computer takes a few minutes. This made it easier for me to clear back out again a couple of days later to go back to St Lucia for my anchor winch motor when it arrived.

For the first time in a while, I sailed by myself while the others enjoyed the quiet anchorage of Le Marin. It should have been a fantastic downwind run with the north-easterly behind me, but the rolly seas kept throwing *Tilly 2* off course, laying *Shanti* on her ear, and sending everything down below flying. I resolved to wait for a good weather window to return. If the others wanted to go on without me, they could. Wolfgang's friend, Klaus, had already continued on further north to meet up with his "girlfriend", a thought which rather tickled my fancy, for some strange reason. Why shouldn't an 82-year-old have a love life? Just because I don't.

Tomorrow would have been perfect wind to sail back up, but further delays to my delivery thwarted that. In the end, it came through, in the rather remarkable Island-time of less than 3 weeks.

Beating my way north again, the sailing was surprisingly enjoyable, the main reason being me. The sea conditions were just as rugged, the wind up to 25 knots, 3-metre waves tossing *Shanti* about just as carelessly, but I had taken the opportunity while waiting on anchor to do a few long meditations. Facing the full brunt of wind and waves, I feel as if everything is just as it's meant to be, right here, right now. Yes, life will always present challenges, but accepting this removes the hardship. I open my arms and heart, and cry: *Welcome!*

The scudding cloud-shapes enthral me. They are a perfect reminder of transience as they gather, drift and fray. An eternity resides in each tuft. How can so much profundity exist in so little solidity? And somehow, I am inextricably entwined in this pulsating rhythm. The clouds, the sky, the sea, the earth, Mother Nature—are interdependent existences, each held by the other. The song in my heart spills forth joyously against the blustery wind and I am happier than I can remember being for a long time. I AM happiness. How I love this life!

Le Marin on Martinique is the most crowded anchorage I have ever seen, with literally a forest of masts spread for miles and many expats living out their days on all manner of immovable craft. Hurgen unkindly compares them to rotting cabbages. Several sunken wrecks border the mangroves as testimony to old age, atrophy, natural attrition and hurricane devastation.

The anchorage is one of the safest, the soft mud providing good holding for most anchors. Most, that is, apart from Hurgen's Bruce anchor, which is no match for his 16-ton steel ketch in a good blow. We came back after doing a hire car tour of the island to find *Morwenna* had dragged over 200 metres, practically onto the wreck-strewn reef behind, a strong reminder of how easily one can lose everything.

Shanti too seems slightly closer to the boat behind than she was. Once again, I am a nervous Nelly, checking constantly for any closing of that small gap that would cause me to spring into action, start the engine, lift the anchor, and move— though move where, in this dark night and crowded anchorage? I just pray that she stays put and wait for the strong winds to abate. In many ways, the open sea is less stressful. I'll be there soon enough, and probably wishing I was here.

From Le Marin, it was a short sail around the coast to Grande Anse. One of those ominously uncertain dark clouds dumped its worst, with strong winds, torrential rain and zero visibility. I had to stand outside to keep a lookout for any oncoming boat that might suddenly appear in front of me, as well as for the ubiquitous fish traps. These clear plastic bottles strung off metres of floating twine are near-impossible to spot and several boats have gotten caught up in them, even with more than one pair of eyes looking out.

Arriving in the crowded anchorage, drenched to the skin and teeth-chatteringly cold, I didn't do my usual dive on the anchor to check if it had dug in well. As it turned out, it had landed in a patch of weed instead of sand and had no hope of holding. But I wasn't the only one; *Morwenna*, naturally, went slowly backwards throughout the night, missing all others, while Wolfgang's anchor caught on another's chain. Sometimes you can be lucky. I saw Hurgen up-anchor at 0500 and move closer in. What a night! Boats are so precarious and uncertain. If you live in a house, storms rarely threaten to drag your house down the street. Land dwellers seldom have to worry about crashing into another house in the middle of the night.

The anchorage at the capital of Martinique, Fort de France, was much better, and I did dive this time to check if the anchor was well-bedded. Here, we met other interesting sailors, a young French woman, Margot, on a small 28' yacht, and my first other Australian, Trevor, on a 35' steelie, *Ironbark II*. He was about as different from your average cruiser as one can get, having spent a couple of years in Antarctica, then sailing directly from there to Ireland. He prefers the cooler latitudes and has no sunshade over his cockpit at all.

The town itself is that fascinating blend of first and third world, with iconic buildings, like the pale green cylindrical high-rise on the waterfront, the vaulted Cathedral and the Schoelcher Bibliotèque presiding proudly amidst spacious grounds. It's interesting how the least typical are the most eye-catching and form an image in the mind of the place, even though they are completely unrepresentative. Creeping up the hills behind are the shanty shacks with the million-dollar views.

Many happy Sundowners were had on each other's boats, watching intently for the elusive green flash as the sun kissed a cloud-free horizon.

Each of us occupied our days with the usual boat chores, sometimes lending each other a hand, sometimes wandering around the streets hunting for treasures. I bought a sturdy plastic bucket with a steel handle that seems impervious to rust. It's something I have long wanted, to secure a rope to, throw overboard, collect saltwater to wash the desks and myself. The man in the shop demonstrated its intended use by holding it behind, squatting slightly and making grunting noises. I would make good use of that later.

Hurgen, me and Wolfgang.

Chapter 15

Homeward Bound

Farewells are part of a cruiser's life and so our little gypsy troupe disbanded, some to stay in the Caribbean for another season, others to head further north before leaving. For me, it was time to begin my move West to the island of Bonaire in the ABC's in the Dutch Lesser Antilles. The parting was sad, as I had developed a fondness for these friends whom I may never see again. We all say we'll keep in touch, but eventually, the tyranny of distance will water that down and all that remains are the fond memories.

It was calm initially as I sailed off by myself, but then one of those wicked storm cells hit, bringing 30+ knots with 3-metre waves. I was not prepared for it but was very happy to find I seem to be (relatively) free of my old "mal de mer". The 470-mile passage to Bonaire, which I expected to take 4 days took only 3, with strong winds and current assisting.

Rounding the lighthouse at the southernmost reef of the island, the turbulent seas subsided, so I enjoyed some fantastic beam-reach sailing in flat water. Colourful kite surfers skimmed like insects across the broad bays off to my right. I took a moment to look about me, give thanks and appreciate arriving in a new country, before the anxiety of where to go took over. That part is always a bit nerve-wracking.

Bonaire is the "B" of the ABC's, the others being Aruba and Curacao. The capital, Kralendijk, is sheltered by the large island of Klein Bonaire directly opposite. Anchoring is prohibited, so one must either go into the small Harbour Village Marina or pick up a mooring. Other cruisers had warned me that there may be none available, but luckily I found several free. The crystal-clear waters shallow quickly, making it possible to see the huge concrete blocks that the mooring lines are tied to. Just as I was about to pick one up, a man on the boat next door warned me off it, saying that the next one, further along, was better. I thanked him and grabbed hold of that one instead. It's great the way this sailing community watches out for one another. Later we shared sundowners together and I learnt that he and his wife were keen divers, who had been living on their boat in this area for the past ten years.

It's easy to see why Bonaire is a world-famous dive-site, the waters being so translucent as to almost not be there. Dozens of colourful angel fish mill around *Shanti's* keel in the day. After dark, the eerie luminescent green lights of night divers diffuse through the water like a Martian probe.

Sheri and Giorgio on *Argonauta* are due to arrive in the next day or so. We haven't crossed paths since South Africa, so it's an unexpectedly fortuitous coincidence. Coming back against the wind from Curacao they had a rough trip and tore their headsail. The boat is a shambles, even worse than the usual post-passage chaos. Their daughter is flying in to stay awhile, so everything needs to be put back where it belongs, or at least in concealment.

Once settled, we strolled along the foreshore, looking for a restaurant that's not fully booked for Christmas dinner. Finally, we discovered a secluded, vine-shrouded enclave in the back streets, serving vegan Indian cuisine; not exactly to Giorgio's taste but perfect for we women. The special Christmas Day menu included many different delicacies to share, each dish bathing the taste buds in delightfully subtle flavours. An open seating arrangement encouraged diners to mingle if they so desired, and the atmosphere was festive, yet casual. It turned out to be one of the best Christmas dinners I've had.

Sheri shared her latest insights into the awakening consciousness on planet Earth and I gave the example of my friend Hurgen, with his Kundalini experience. I don't profess to understand it but try to keep an open mind. It was a subject Sheri knew well, without me having to go into any great detail. Hurgen once asked me if I had ever met a man who could have a full-body orgasm that lasted half an hour, which apparently can happen following a Kundalini awakening. I omitted these tender morsels from the conversation; there's always plenty else to cover and more to learn.

The next ports for me are Curacao and Aruba, then Santa Marta in Colombia, and the San Blas Islands en-route to Panama. So I'm homeward bound, and once again, must bid my adieus.

———

Cruising "plans" are perhaps the most flexible of all plans, and where and when we go is pretty much dictated by the weather. Spotting a break in the perpetually strong winds we'd been having, I made the short dash across from Bonaire to Curacao on Boxing Day. This is a Dutch offshoot of Holland in the Lesser Antilles, a vibrant island with that typically Caribbean use of colour that singles each building out from its neighbour. A row of multi-storied terraces presents a façade of what could be a theatrical artifice, a manufactured film set, with pale jade, muted ruby and soft amber adding frivolity.

I anchored in a wonderfully protected anchorage, Spanish Waters, about ten miles from the capital. A great many yachts shelter here in this hurricane-free area. A young Chinese woman spotted me doing my usual anchoring antics and called to her Portuguese husband, "She alone! Invite her over."

Their three-year-old daughter is a fearless nymph, leaping over the side and swimming unaided around the boat. Each morning she would ask her parents, "Where the lady? Tell her to come here." Youngsters living aboard cruising yachts are generally precocious for their years, able to hold their own in any gathering of adults without needing to dominate. They also provide me with the cuddles I'm missing from my own grandchildren.

So I have good company for New Year's Eve, a small group of us taking the bus into town just after dusk. Unsure what to expect, I'm glad to be in the company of people I trust. There is an atmosphere of excitement, uncertainty and risk.

The crowds are already thronging, beginning the celebrations, lighting firecracker wicks, tossing them down and leaping aside. An unearthly white blaze shards the streets as thousands of throwable crackers go off in staccato gunfire. They remind me of the firecrackers of my childhood: "Tom Thumbs" and "Jumping Jacks"—snapping and flaring, leaving a smoky red carpet from their spent cartridge cases. This highly dangerous entertainment is completely unregulated here, just as I remember it being in New Zealand before small children started losing fingers or eyes. Kicking our way through the dross, every so often an unexploded cracker would ignite, scaring the wits out of me.

Later, a few of us reconvened aboard the young family's yacht. Others brought food, drink and various instruments, guitars, flutes, violin and even a piano accordion. We played and sang into the wee hours, always my happiest way to spend time. I took photos of several pages from a Dutch woman's songbook and made it my resolution to learn a new song each week. In the past, I have always relied on looking at the chords and lyrics, which is a sure way not to learn them. This prevents me from having anything to offer at twilight beach parties where it's too dark to read. I am always in awe of others who can play and sing dozens of popular tunes off the top of their head. At least I can sing along.

The surrounding wealthy Venezuelan homes put on an ongoing spectacle of fireworks' displays every night, as if in competition with each other. Fireworks like I've never seen them. Uncontrolled, wild, excessive, never-ending, without climax. Days and days of them, all around the bay. Rotating our heads, pointing delightedly, we gave our ratings. *This one is the best; no, look there! Don't you just love the way those white spirals change their mind halfway up! Hilarious.*

I received a "Happy New Year" email from my French friend, Catherine, which closed on a positive note, wishing me *"an incredible 2019 with safe adventure, great sea and wind—and, knowing your ability to make friends, great friendships."* It got me thinking about the transient nature of a cruiser's friendships. They come; they go. Most are more like acquaintances than friends. Sheri and Giorgio, in the twelve years of their circumnavigation, collected but a handful of special friends, among which I am honoured to be included. But who knows when we will see each other again?

Occasionally, some of us, like Wolfgang, Klaus and Hurgen stay a little longer in one spot or sail in company for a while, in which case the friendship grows. Then the parting is harder. Then it helps to remember Catherine's observations on my ability to make friends easily. As with infants, who so blithely embody the spirit of "out of sight, out of mind", non-attachment eases the way. Certainly, while trying to stay more in the present moment—leaving the past and future to their place as mental constructs—what is here now is all that there is. Ever so gradually, the Monastery of the sea is training me to understand this, but still there is a residual feeling of loss when I continue on alone.

My original intention was to visit all 3 of the ABC's, the next island being Aruba. From there, my course was set for Santa Marta in Colombia, then the San Blas Islands before arriving in Panama. But, as mentioned, the weather is the boss. Advice from others who had been before me warned of the brutal winds and waves that are common in the Colombian basin, with many saying they faced the scariest conditions of their entire sailing lives. I wasn't keen on putting *Shanti* (or me) there, so I watched the forecasts closely for a good weather window.

To go directly to Panama was about 750 nautical miles, about a week to ten days of sailing for *Shanti*. It seemed a shame to miss out on seeing those other places, but there was also the fact that a couple of large rallies were hot on my heels, which would clog up the Panama Canal transits.

I think I prayed too hard for calms because that's what I got. Motoring across the top of Colombia, the wind down to 6 knots, I saw a couple of whales ahead. Such rare encounters with these gigantic creatures always lift my spirits. I had been thinking about how long-distance voyaging wears boats out—engine, sails, rudder bearings, which have started making a worrying clunking sound. It's no use saying they were new only two years ago. Similarly with my body—not so new—but feeling the wear and tear, my left shoulder and right knee making their presence felt.

Some very big rollers have started mounting from behind. The wind is still only 7 knots, but the forecast is for 15 knots at 1600. This didn't arrive until 1800 the next day. There seems to be a counter-current against me; the boat speed is 4.5 knots, the SOG only 3.5. (Sad face in the logbook). The sun is sinking, there's not a cloud in the sky; just a slight fuzz around the rim.

The following day the wind was up to 18 knots from behind. We should have been doing 5.5 knots, but still only seeing 3.5. I don't know what's going on. Perhaps it's something to do with passing the mouth of Barranquilla and Ciénaga Grande de Santa Marta. I have been warned to watch out for large logs being washed out to sea. It's a bit hard at night.

I just figured out why I'm not seeing the green flash each evening—the sun is setting behind land! The Colombian basin is virtually land-locked, funnelling the Caribbean Sea down toward Panama. When the Trade Winds blow strongly, this can become an extremely wild patch of water, influenced by counter currents and deep ocean trenches with depths up to 7,000 metres—which is almost equal to the height of Mt Everest. A fellow cruiser told me she saw gusts of over 60 knots here, so I'm doing well now with only 30.

The main problem is the waves, now up over 4 metres high. I'm very tired but find it hard to sleep. I'm growing a cluster of cold sores on my lower lip and have prickling pains in my stomach.

The following day, at 0330, I was thrown out of my bunk and landed hard against the fold-down table with both knees. Ouch! I had just fallen into a deep sleep and it was as if *Shanti* had said, *Oh no, she's asleep and dreaming she's not here alone—quick, wake her up!* I haven't put up a lee cloth on the port bunk before because when we are on starboard tack *Shanti* is heeled over to port and my nose is jammed up against the locker. But with strong wind and very big rollers from directly behind, it's more of a side to side motion. It's not easy to sleep at all, being tossed about like this. It takes its toll on me. The face in the mirror looks every bit as old as my father's 100 years—only more lined and with cold sores! Ah, joy! I think the pain in my stomach last night was due to lack of sleep and nervous tension, not knowing quite what's coming in this capricious sea.

I read in the cruising guide:

> *"The prevailing current for offshore is the Caribbean counter-current, flowing Eastward. Closer to shore, the currents are stronger and unsteady. At Los Farallones and Isla Tambor, current varies from none to a strong eastward flowing current that can reach over 2 knots. This counter-current is greatly influenced by wind conditions in the Caribbean; generally the stronger the Trades, the more current."*

At least that explained something of what's going on in this washing machine.

Monday, January 14. 0630. The AIS alarm sounded loudly for the first time in ages. Checking the computer, I saw an unnamed ship crossing my bow at only 200 metres distance, doing only 4 knots. This is an unusually slow speed for a cargo ship, but it gave me time to alter my course slightly. He could easily have gone behind me so I don't know if it was some kind of deliberate scare tactic. Most ships are more courteous. I called on the VHF radio but got no reply. As he passed within spitting distance, I could clearly read the name on the bow: *Spirit of Tokyo*. I expected to get up close and personal in Panama but this was ridiculous.

———

January 15. Shelter Bay Marina is the first marina I've been in since Cape Town, so I was pleasantly surprised that I was able to back *Shanti* into the tight berth without mishap. I received hearty applause from the couples on the catamarans on either side of me. Just lucky!

I had been told that there could be a 4-6 week wait to transit the canal at this time of year. Indeed, with each passing day, the delays increase, so it was just as well that I arrived when I did. They are working hard to push boats through quickly before the World ARC rally boats arrive at the end of this month, which will certainly slow things down.

On the recommendation of the couple on the catamaran next door, I hired a local agent. I hadn't planned to do this, but it took a lot of pressure off, having everything organised for me. It can be extremely dangerous taking large sums of cash into the banks in Colon; much better to simply hand a couple of thousand dollars to the agent on the dock. His fee didn't add all that much to the overall cost and obviated the need to pay a bond of another thousand dollars, which may or may not be returned sometime in the future. There were plenty of other things for me to do, preparing for the transit.

It is mandatory to have four line handlers on board each boat, two for the bow and two for the stern. Given the fact that most yachts normally transit in a raft of two or three tied together, it's likely that only the two outer lines will get used, if that. The biggest boat is generally put in the middle of the raft and all four lines can be run from them. I am hiring two professionals from the agent at $US100 each, and getting two other cruisers to come along, who volunteer for the experience.

Rachel and her husband Josh have their own boat on the Pacific side of the canal, in the newly opened Vista Mar Marina. At first, they were both coming, but Josh was busy preparing their boat for the South Pacific, so we became an all-girl crew with the substitution of their good friend, Becca, a highly qualified young lady with her 100-ton Captain's licence. Both proved to be exceptional young women and great company. Another huge benefit was their willingness to help in the galley. Providing meals for everyone for two days presented quite a challenge, thinking what and how to cook, accustomed as I am to feeding only one. All five crew also have to sleep overnight, which is a bit of a squeeze on *Shanti*, but luckily the guys prefer sleeping out in the cockpit.

Meanwhile, I wander around the marina, chatting to others, gathering menu ideas, as well as information on who is doing what and going where after. I'm looking for my buddy boats, asking who else is transiting tomorrow but can't find any. There is a buzz of anticipation like Christmas eve. A few horror stories add to the atmosphere, tales of pilot boats rolling over on top of small yachts in the locks.

There are 3 "up-locks" from the Atlantic (Caribbean side), leading into Lake Gatun, where we will spend tomorrow night. The following day we traverse the 40 odd miles across the Lake, then, sometime late in the afternoon, descend the 3 "down-locks" to the Pacific. All very exciting!!!

Rachel provided a brief history for our edification:

"The Panama Canal is one of the great wonders of the world. You cannot fully grasp its magnitude until you see it in person. It operates continuously, 24 hours a day, 365 days of the year; this past year they had a total of 13,785 transits, everything from massive freighters to small sailing vessels like our own. This forty-mile artificial waterway saves ships sailing between the east and west coasts, a trip around Cape Horn, a journey of about 8,000 nautical miles.

Traffic through the Panama Canal tends to be a barometer of world trade, rising in times of economic prosperity and declining in times of recession; from a low of 807 transits in 1916, traffic rose to a high point of 15,523 transits in 1970. While the Canal was under U.S. control, tolls for its use were set at rates calculated to cover the cost of maintenance and operation and not for profit, making the Canal self-financing. The rates established back in 1914 remained virtually unchanged for 60 years, until 2016 when the Panamanian government made it a for-profit operation. Large container ships using the new, larger set of locks today can pay upwards of a million dollars to transit".

Yet again, plans are as fluid as water. A few moments before my volunteer line-handlers arrived, the agent appeared on the dock to tell me my transit had been rescheduled for the following day. At first, this seemed a low blow, but good came of it, giving the girls a day off to relax by the pool and for us get to know one another. We had drinks and pizzas at the marina restaurant that evening and they got to sleep for two nights onboard *Shanti* instead of one. It felt rather strange, hearing the sounds of others sharing the tiny space that has been my solitary home for so long.

On Thursday at midday, the two hired hands, Leroy and Jackson arrived, and I fed everyone some lunch before heading out to the "flats" to await our Advisor. The 60' yacht, *Sauvage* that we were to transit alongside was already anchored there. The next few hours were the beginning of the waiting game. I was impressed with Leroy and Jackson's ability to intersperse periods of dozing with sudden springing to action.

At 1630, a large black Pilot vessel approached, looking for all the world like it was going to plough us down, but stopped within inches to allow our Advisor, Edward, to step nimbly aboard.

Action stations! Start the engine, lift the anchor and begin heading towards the entrance to the locks, about 7 miles away. It's to be a night-time manoeuvre. We are scheduled to begin our transit of the first three Gatun locks at 1800, following a very rusty looking ship that was anchored on the other side of the channel. Edward kept us informed of its movements (or lack thereof).

This is where confusion comes in. After gunning the engine full tilt to cover the distance, we find ourselves stuck in a "holding pattern" near the lock entrance for a couple of hours, driving slowly round in circles, while two other tankers proceed before us. Nobody knows why.

Finally, we spot "our ship" coming and it's time to raft up to our buddy boat. Her skipper approaches *Shanti* painfully slowly and I wish we were doing it the other way round, with *Shanti* using them as the moving dock. There are plenty of hands and fenders, and even though one of their crew accidentally lets our stern line slip, with much yelling, and the next monster ship is blasting us to get out of its way, we finally proceed as one, into the lock.

The "up locks" are vast chambers, waiting to be filled with 26 million gallons of water to lift us 10 metres to the next lock. The turbulence of this rapid inflow is huge, swirling around us like rapids. It's a very unnerving feeling looking back at the lights of Colon from our new height.

At 60' long, *Sauvage* is big enough to take all four lines from both sides of her bows and stern, so nothing is required of us; we will just be dragged through like a limpet alongside.

This is where further confusion arises. Our rusty ship has a large tugboat behind it, tied up against the starboard wall, which for some unknown reason, we were expected to tie to. Hence no lines are being thrown to our port side; in other words, nothing to stop *Shanti* from getting ever nearer the 30' high concrete wall to our right. Again, much yelling, before in the nick of time we are secured.

The system is very human dependent. Four men, looking like little Lego men, way up high above us on the top edge of the lock throw the "monkey fists" at us. These are heavy balls of woven twine with metal centres that carry the thin trace lines, hopefully avoiding windows, hatches, solar panels, wind generators, and people. I was glad they were primarily being aimed at *Sauvage*, although we did have to transfer a couple that didn't quite make the distance.

The line-handlers onboard their boat then have to speedily tie these to the heavy 140-foot long dock lines they have prepared earlier, laying them out carefully without twists or tangles. These are thrown overboard and the Lego men above pull them up and secure them to a bollard at the top of the lock. The people on the boat take up the slack, constantly monitoring the change in tension as the water rises. It's a demanding job. I watched a very muscle-bound woman next door frantically working to free some tangles as if trying to detach a determined boa constrictor.

Fortunately, the monkey fists are only thrown once for the first of the three

Gatun locks. Having risen to the top, the massive gates in front are opened, the heavy ropes are dropped back to us and we motor through, with the Lego men walking quickly along the wall with the trace lines in tow. All rather remarkable, and generally proceeding smoothly, contrary to all the horror stories we heard beforehand.

After passing through the third lock, we entered Lake Gatun, where we were to spend the night. Unusually, we remained nested against *Sauvage*, who dragged us speedily through the darkness. Using powerful torches they managed to spot one of the giant round mooring buoys to tie up to. The two yachts stayed snugged up together, which made for some uncomfortable rolling and jerking as ships continued to transit the lake all night long. Leroy and Jackson slept out in the cockpit and luckily it didn't rain.

Normally, there are different Advisors each day, but to our pleasure, we had Edward again, who returned at 0830 on Friday, ready to go. He brought a big black plastic bag full of ice to cool the dozens of bottles of water and soft drinks that I was required to provide. Scrambled eggs and croissants were eaten underway, thanks to my wonderful female crew, who handled that side of things fantastically.

One of my greatest stresses now faced me; could *Shanti* with her small engine and extra load of 6 bodies keep up in motoring across the lake? I had deliberately avoided filling the extra jerry cans of diesel and water tanks to keep the weight off.

Our appointed ship was due to follow us into the Pedro Miguel "down-lock" at 1330, which was 30 miles away. Leaving at 0830 gave us 5 hours to get there, which meant averaging 6 knots of boat speed across the lake; a very big ask. I was pleased to find that *Yani*, the trusty little Yanmar was capable of around 5.7 knots, but it was not enough. The two Advisors had already agreed that the bigger yacht would peg back its speed and wait for us.

That didn't happen. Quite early in the route, they passed us and slowly pulled away—very disheartening. Edward's two main comments were, "Can you go any faster?" and "Move further over to the edge of the channel." Neither was particularly helpful. I wasn't prepared to risk total engine failure for the sake of a bit more speed nor running aground on the rocks that were within spitting distance in places.

I thought we made pretty good time, but as our ship passed us, I asked Edward if they knew they were supposed to be locking with us. His reply was, "they don't care." He said we would just have to wait for another ship to go through with. Luckily a massive car carrier was fast approaching, so without missing a beat, we drove straight into the Pedro Miguel lock in front of it.

We spotted our now non-buddy boat, *Sauvage* in the adjacent lock, tied alongside a small passenger ship. The girls made a few saucy remarks but were glad to be on red alert, ready to test their knot-tying skills. The monkey fists were thrown, the first one missed completely and landed in the water, the next one wrapped itself several times around one of the stays, the next one hit the aluminium bottom of the upturned dinghy on the foredeck with a percussive diiinngg. One of them Rachel caught perfectly, to much cheering.

This process had to be done twice for this set of locks as there is a greater distance between the first and second, so more missiles came hurtling at us, but all were fielded beautifully. *Go, girls!*

If anything is going to go wrong, they say it will be in the Miraflores, where the current swirls and gushes incredibly strongly, as if in a rush to reach the Pacific. It pinned the rudder hard across, almost forcing the tiller from my hands.

As we descended, I looked up at the sheer black walls of the 100-year old concrete sides of the lock, marvelling at the engineering of those times and considering the enormous cost in human lives to build this mighty canal. About 40 ships would pass through today. I felt unspeakably grateful for this almost surreal experience, grateful to my wonderful crew and to the valiant little *Shanti* for getting us through.

Taking a moment to reflect on all this, I noticed that the trace line from my port stern was caught on one of the bollards recessed into the sides of the lock wall. The linesman above could not see this. I pointed it out to Edward, who told me not to worry, they would free it.

So, the bells ring, the massive lock gates in front of us open, the current swirls and pushes us forward, the line handlers above release the lines—and, sure enough, one is caught. The ship behind us begins to move and Edward tells me to go. But how? We are still tied to the wall.

Well, I need not embellish the panic and confusion that ensued, with Rachel telling us to take deep "Yoga breaths" and stay calm. Easily said when about to be squished like a bug by a Goliath.

It was her line that was caught, and as much as the guy on top of the wall flicked and whipped, it stayed caught. As we moved forward, she played out more and more of the heavy line that we still had on board, fully prepared to lose the whole lot if necessary, rather than see *Shanti* pulled back against the wall, or worse still, run over by the ship. Of course, the ship wouldn't be happy to tangle our rope around his propeller, so it was good that she didn't have to.

Eventually, after what seemed like several lifetimes, the little Lego man above had the good sense to let go of his end. It could still have been wrapped too tightly to release, or gotten stuck with the monkey fist, but praise be to all the powers that be, it slipped free, trailing in the water behind us. Hallelujah! Following this adrenaline spike, we were fast approaching the gates of the final lock, with only one stern line. These are the most important lines to hold us back, so it was a mad scramble to retrieve and secure the lost line. Rachel did a sterling job of this, while I had the engine hard in reverse.

As they say, it will all be alright in the end, and if it's not alright, it's not the end. We managed to avoid all the hard concrete and steel bits; nothing got broken, no one was hurt, and in the end, it was all alright, with a story to tell our children.

We crossed under the iconic 'Bridge of Americas', and were in the Pacific, with its 5 – 6-metre tides! So much stress left behind and SO thrilled to have made it.

With seamless precision, our trusty Advisor was picked up shortly after, followed by a taxi boat to take the ropes, fenders, and ultimately proven-worthy line-handlers, Leroy and Jackson. The girls and I continued on alone to anchor off La Playita for an "arrival survival" drink, to unwind, laugh, chat and debrief. Then they left via the dinghy of friends anchored nearby and caught a taxi back to their own boats and husbands. And then it was just me again, back to being alone, after the only time others had set foot aboard *Shanti* since leaving Bundaberg.

I slept the sleep of the dead, woke early and set sail to Vista Mar Marina, to refuel, put on more water and provisions in readiness for the next big hop. My trusty line-handlers were there to help further with driving us around to various shops. The great thing was I arrived in time to phone my father in New Zealand and send my absentee best wishes for his 101st birthday. It was such a shame that for the first time in years I could not be there to help celebrate it, but such is the price of being where I am now.

Tomorrow morning, I head out into the Pacific, with a brief stop at Las Perlas Islands before the 4,000-mile crossing to Gambier Islands. This will be the longest leg I have ever done, alone or in company, and I'm hoping I have enough food and water for what could be 2 – 3 months, depending on how long it takes to get through the doldrums.

Chapter 16

No-Go Zone

Crossing half of the Pacific Ocean in one go was never my intention, but as always, Mother Nature dictates, and I merely follow. Earlier, I had considered the possibility of being 2 - 3 months at sea, but I think I was secretly hoping that was an exaggeration. As it transpired, it took exactly 7 weeks, or 49 days and 49 nights (just to make the point that I didn't sleep through half of it) to do the 5,000 nautical mile passage from Panama to Tahiti—which is not too shabby really, making my customary average of 100 miles a day.

February 2. I left Las Perlas bound for Gambier Islands in French Polynesia, 4,000 miles away. Wolfgang and Klaus had stopped there and recommended it highly as a pristine and easy stopover. If you draw a straight line between Panama and Australia, the first half of the ocean is noticeably devoid of stepping stones where a tired sailor might take refuge. The route that most cruisers take to break the journey across the Pacific is to the Galapagos Islands, a short hop of only 800 miles. Then it's another 3,000 miles to the Marquesas. There's no avoiding that one, so what's another 1000 miles on top? Gambier is further south of that imaginary Rhumb line, but it's somewhere new to go, which is always a drawcard.

Stopping at Galapagos held no appeal for me this time. I had already seen the Darwinian mega species about 10 years ago when the costs and bureaucracies were not prohibitive. Lately it has gotten ridiculous, with stories of boats being sent back out to sea to have their bottoms scrubbed by divers that could charge up to $1,000 for the pleasure. Engaging a local agent to fill in the arrival forms is now mandatory, also at great expense. Movements to the neighbouring islands are restricted, and food, water and diesel are scarce. I know of others who felt it was worthwhile stopping there anyway and there's no denying, it is a unique and fascinating place. But I decided against it and set my course for Gambier, not without some trepidation, facing my longest period of isolation at sea.

It began as it was to end—motoring. Of course it's not possible to "drive" that distance, with a supply of only 150 litres of diesel. So a lot of demands were made on me to use what little wind there was and keep the boat moving. This was to become my mantra—*just keep the boat moving*—no matter how slowly. And only turn the key when actually stopped—assuming of course that there's still some fuel left. That would change later.

It was a beautiful day, with the Las Perlas pelican convoys paragliding by en masse. A perfectly proportioned, solitary dolphin arced across the bow, always a good omen. That night I set my timer for 30-minute intervals but didn't get any sleep, there being plenty of fishing boats and ships around. Despite the slow start, I covered 115 nautical miles in 24 hours. It helped enormously to have up to 2 knots of current with me.

By day 4, the wind had dropped to 8 knots and I had the kite (spinnaker) flying. Thanks for the courage to try, the energy to dig it out from under the V berth, and the memory of how. It was to become my best ally over the next few weeks.

Initially I used the smaller "whisker pole", but eventually had to muscle up to manhandle the big pole—not so easy on one's own (nothing is). After a few tangles and lines running the wrong way, it was up and ballooning magnificently. I dropped the main completely to give it full air. What a glorious sight! The blue and white panels stretched broadly before us, replete as a laughing Buddha. *Shanti* was racing along doing 7's and 8's of speed over ground. The wind was around 12 to 15 knots. When it peaked at 18, it was time to douse the kite. Easier said than done!

I got it under control eventually but it all could have gone horribly wrong. I dread to think of all the possibilities, from "wine glass" wraps around the forestay to it going into the sea, to tangling lines around the rudder and prop. Oh dear! I must work out a better way to snuff it. There is a fibreglass yoke, or "sock", which slides down from the top, but sometimes there is so much pressure from the billowing sail that the control line lifts me off the deck. I need to eat more.

Over the next few days a new danger appeared—massive cut logs, presumably fallen off a ship, still with big metal staples in them. The fifth one passed within a metre of *Shanti* —about 2-metre diameter and 10 metres long, with a forked branch of similar size, which could easily have been a game-ender. Again, luck is with me.

I'm contemplating those who read the future—soothsayers, oracles, clairvoyants, shamans, gypsies, witches burnt at the stake for their premonitions—demonized by Christians. Yet what of the prophets of old? And today's weather forecasters—those who tell me what wind I can expect in three days from now? A black magic science. (Not diminishing my scientist daughter, Pandora, with a doctorate in paleoclimate). But here and now, these two-metre rollers from the north are much too big for the present 10 knots of wind and foretell of something stronger to come.

The price of sleep is high. I lay down for a half-hour nap on day 6, only to wake to blissful silence—which of course is only blissful for a second, because it usually presages something wrong. Sure enough, the kite (which I never leave unattended) had an almighty "wine glass" wrapped around the furled headsail. I started the engine and drove slowly round in circles to unwrap it. Luckily there was no damage. Just a quiet reminder to never take my eyes off it. Communications with the outside world are limited as the Sat phone is struggling to find satellites.

Day 7. I woke at 0100 to *Tilly 2* squealing. No forward motion equals no steering. We're totally becalmed for the first time on this passage. I turned the key and felt uneasy motoring through the coal blackness, knowing that logs are around. I lay back down but couldn't sleep. Two hours later I turned the engine off and just drifted until sunup. It gave a good indication of the current. In 3 hours, *Shanti* drifted 6.6 nautical miles due West.

Friends on *Halcyon* had set up an HF radio sked to try to maintain some contact amongst a small fleet of yachts heading more or less in the same direction. I spoke to Becca (one of my Panama Canal line-handlers) and she gave me a couple of waypoints to head for, where there might be some wind. The first is 80 miles due south, the second 190 miles SW. Apparently they think I'm a speed boat. There's supposed to be 10 knots where I am now. *Try two!*

I could just turn the key and motor directly to their waypoint, but there are no guarantees of wind there, and I prefer to conserve my fuel. I'm currently 18 miles from the equator.

1100 hours: This doldrum sailing is not too bad, all things considered. Today, here, right now, I have 4 – 5 knots of southerly wind, doing 2.5 knots of boat speed and 4.5 speed over ground. It's a magnificent sunny day. I did the laundry, had a saltwater shower, rinsed with a cup of freshwater and I'm feeling good. *Shanti* is slipping along smoothly—loving it!

1430. A very special occasion—once again, crossing the Equator, homeward bound. Back into the Southern hemisphere. Yay! Party time! A few South Pacific dolphins joined in. I put on my best dress, made a Pina Colada, listened to music, sang and danced, then topped it all off with fresh home-made bread and cheese. Perfect. The distance to Gambier is 3190 miles. Who cares?

Three white birds, amazingly iridescent, lit up as if in a night club, stayed with me all night. They match the glistening phosphorescence in the water. This is as close to heaven as it gets. My world is the right way up again, back in the Southern hemisphere and I recognise more celestial bodies. The "pointers" give a friendly nod toward the Southern Cross while the "Big Pot", or "Orion" has become my lead, high in the West. The Milky Way is a mix of sharp pointillism against a remote blur, like the spatter on an artist's canvas. Each tiny speck of light is a cluster of hundreds of galaxies, each containing billions of stars and possibly millions of planets capable of sustaining life. How could anyone take themselves seriously beneath all this?

Day 9. I'm approaching Jimmy Cornell's "danger zone", a rectangular patch of open sea in which other cruisers have reported adverse conditions. Do I avoid it or take my chances and blunder on through? *Halcyon* advise that the weather forecast shows nothing untoward in that area.

It's incredibly hot. The temperature inside the cabin is 37 degrees, humidity 60%. Outside it is 42 degrees, so going out on deck in the midday sun is madness. The sweat drips off me and runs into my eyes, almost blinding me. I have to ask myself if it's worth it for 3 hours of kite speed. I'm getting quicker—it now only takes me 45 minutes to get it up, and with no tangles. It went up in 6 knots of breeze with the resolve to snuff it at 12 knots, which I just did—of course, just as I lay down to rest. *Shanti* seems to know this. I rely on her more and more these days and nights, rather than the digital kitchen timer. I know I can trust her to call when she needs me.

I can almost catch the satellites but not quite. It's possible that everyone with whom I have been in contact will be worried by this sudden silence. John and Becca have a more reliable Iridium Sat phone onboard *Halcyon* so I asked them to send out a couple of emails for me, advising that I'm without shore communication. I found out later that Luke had been able to get my position from "Marine Traffic" and was posting this on Facebook, which relieved a lot of anxiety. It also created some confusion, with Facebook saying he is "with me"—sure, he just dropped in via parachute! Such is the power of social media and the printed word to convince believers of the unbelievable.

I'm feeling at a low ebb, probably due to the heat and lack of sleep. It also disturbs me when I know I'm causing others to worry about me. But there's nothing I can do about it right now. I have started using some "Imiquimod" cream to treat a tiny spot on my nose which had been diagnosed as a BCC, or Basal Cell Carcinoma. The cream is supposed to only identify pre-cancerous cells but my entire nose is raw and burning. I figured it was a good opportunity to do it on this long passage, out of sight of the world for a few weeks. But the cracked skin is becoming more painful each day, suppurating and bleeding, preventing me from sleeping well. It may not have been such a good idea, but I thought it was worth a try, hoping to avoid surgery.

A couple of large Galapagian Booby birds have made their roost on my pulpit. It seems they know to avoid the rear solar panels, (usually a favourite) as *Blewy* made mincemeat of some poor hitchhiker a few days ago—just left a few feathers and visceral smear as a deterrent. When I wake early, I see those two Boobies are still there, asleep with their heads tucked in, like fuzzy footballs. It's amazing how they can hang on in their sleep, with all this rolling. I guess I do the same, though not quite so precariously.

They woke some time after me, lazy sods, at around 0700, which is fair enough because I am still on a different time zone to them and the sun is only rising now.

0900: They are still here, my twin mascots on the bow. The wind is 16 – 18 knots NE. Very nice! Now, what to do with this day? I lay back down and slept for an hour, then got out my guitar and learnt a new song—Sam Cooke, "Bring it on home to me". I played and sang for a couple of hours. I'm happy with the progress of my New Year's resolution so far. It's very satisfying to know a few songs off by heart.

1200: The birds are still here. They seem to spend their time preening their feathers or sleeping. Are they living stress-free lives? Do they need to drink fresh water? Where from? They are hundreds of miles from the nearest land. I wonder how far away from home they will travel on *Shanti*. On closer inspection, I notice one is definitely younger, with a smoother, softer downy skullcap, while the larger bird is grizzlier.

At 1600 hours I give them my two bits' worth: "Come on now; you can't hitch a ride all the way to Australia! You must be getting hungry and thirsty by now. Your home is over there—that way to Galapagos. Fly!"

And as if listening, off she went, leaving Junior opening and closing his mouth in a mute plea, *"Mama, mama!"*

"Don't worry," I soothed. "She'll be back soon with some dinner for you."

I watched her swoop and reel, marvelling at the ease, the grace of flight before she made a wide curve and flapped back for a perfect landing on the pulpit perch. No sign of supper. *"Go get your own!"*

"Mama!" Junior is mawing or silently crying.

Sadly I had to evict the squatters on Day 11. They squawked in loud protest as the spinnaker billowed toward them. They may return later or find another free ride to wherever. My good NE breeze dropped out around 0300 and by 0630 was gone. Even the kite is struggling in 5 knots and is swaying side to side like a Toreador's cape. Still, it is giving us 3 knots of speed over ground, which is better than nothing. If it drops any more we'll have to burn a little diesel.

The sked with *Halcyon* suggests some SE Trade Wind is coming in about 8 hours. I'm not exactly sure if it's coming or if I have to get to it, but I'll keep on doing all I can do. I have just crossed the northern edge of Jimmy Cornell's "no-go" area, so hopefully that won't delay things further. There are a few dark smudges on the horizon.

I don't know if I was feeling bad about evicting the birds, but for some reason, I was having more trouble than usual getting the kite to set. At midday, just as I was beginning to think about lunch, I noticed one of the birds circling *Shanti* and lining up for a landing. Coming in on a perfect windward approach, she made it, only to have a sudden flap of the kite scare her off. This was repeated three times and it seemed as if she had no intention of giving up.

Just then, on her third landing, the snap-shackle at the top of the spinnaker halyard let go and the whole kit and caboodle fell into the water. I could hardly believe my eyes! One moment, the vertical blue and white stripes were flying proudly, the next moment, gone! Luckily, I had been watching as it happened or within seconds it would have disappeared under the boat. I raced forward and began grabbing great handfuls of the waterlogged cloth, pulling it back on board. Its weight was enormous, dragging us to a standstill like an effective sea anchor. The fibreglass yoke of the scrunched-up "sock" was already several metres deep, with the sea trying its best to claim it.

Another pair of hands at this point would have been very welcome. I daren't let go of the gains I'd made to get a rope to a winch or even to lash down the sections I had gathered, so it was just a matter of keeping on hauling with all my might. My arms were starting to feel rubbery. I was vaguely aware of the dangerous position I was in, with myself not tethered onto the boat and fighting a great whale that could pull me over at any lurch.

All the while, Madam Booby sat watching from her undisturbed perch, as if saying, "well, glad that's out of the way." When it was fully piled on the deck, I looked at her and cried, *"Did you have to do that?"* But of course, she just gave her hooded smile. Half an hour later, Queen Booby was dethroned as the kite was hoisted to dry on a spare halyard. I didn't leave it like that for long because I was sick of it, so once it was dry, it was doused and packed away, hopefully for the last time.

Today is Valentine's Day, a day when land-based lovers might give and/or receive special attention. Naturally, I ache for Luke. I know it's my choice to be out here alone, but sometimes I wonder if the price is a little too high. I miss human contact like an orphan. I miss my family and friends. I'm talking to Booby birds for heaven's sake! It's not forever. Singleness of purpose requires sacrifices and making oneself narrow.

Gradually the wind filled in and veered more to the south. By dusk, *Shanti* was scudding along in a 15 knots SE. *At last!* I thought, the *SE Trades!* Aware that we were now a good 300 miles into the "no-go" zone, trusting *Halcyon's* forecast of nothing untoward in the near future, I sailed blithely into a huge electrical storm.

At around midnight I woke to torrential rain hammering on the cabin top and *Tilly 2* squawking her resignation. Just as I stumbled into the cockpit to relieve her, lightning lit the entire world around me, and the deepest, most visceral boom of thunder shook me to the core. I slipped on the wet teak and half fell into the cockpit, still blurry with sleep. There was scarcely a moment to take stock of the situation. I flipped *Tilly 2* off the tiller and felt the weight that had overcome her. *What's going on out here?*

Suddenly, I'm right in it! With scarcely any warning, there's 30-plus knots of wind and a choppy sea mounting. *Shanti* is bucking like a wild brumby as if trying to escape this hellish patch we've been suddenly thrust into. Why does it always happen in the middle of the night? I'm soaked to the skin and shivering, frantically figuring what needs to be done. *Get rid of some sail!* But I'm attached to the tiller and we're surfing down the backs of rollers. It's all I can do to hold her from broaching.

Every flash of lightning gives a fleeting glimpse of the spray flying off the tops of the waves, the ankle-deep water rising in the sodden cockpit, the tiny boat that seems suddenly so much smaller. The thunder is like cannon fire, splitting my skull in two and drawing out my brains. It's almost in unison with the lightning, doubling the shock. First the explosive flash of light, so close; then a deafening sonic boom.

My whole body quivers uncontrollably as I grip the tiller. My thoughts are so skittish it would take a trawler's net to gather them back together. I can't see the compass and can only rely on my native sea-sense to direct me. The lightning gives a fleeting clue, but it's more of a rabbit-blinder, bursting through the darkness. The synchronised thunder punches my solar plexus with a deep bass note.

Gradually I realise that this is me panicking and I begin to search the distant horizon for a way out of this hole. Sheet lightning white-washes the entire circumference with a broad stroke and I can't see any break. Much as I strain and peer, all is pitch blackness, torn open briefly by a taunting flick of a switch in a staccato revelation. So much is happening within each second.

Everything is totally surreal as if seen for the first time in the split second of incandescence. I can see the whites of *Shanti's* topsides glistening, the blue canvas, all the colours I can't usually see at midnight. And they appear a thousand times brighter. It's like a blind man, shaken out of darkness into the light and suddenly able to see. The rain cascades like a silvery curtain, within which I can see each individual droplet. And then it's gone, swallowed again by the utterly absorbing blackness.

I have never seen anything like this before. It's all so close, around and above me, as if I'm actually inside it. Perhaps I've been consumed by a demon and these are his gastric juices dissolving me. I feel consumed, eaten up, exhausted. Jagged forks of lightning stab the sea as if in a mocking jibe: *"missed you this time; let's try again!"* How long before one realises that *Shanti's* aluminium mast is the tallest thing on this empty ocean? How long before *Shanti* or I crumble?

There's nothing I can do about it so it's best not to think about it. If lightning strikes, it strikes. If something gives, it gives. *Try to settle! Breathe! Focus on something familiar—hands, shrivelled and cold, a little numb, not really mine. Don't lose it.* A voice in my head speaks, *we're OK; we've got this.* But I'm not convinced.

I must focus on managing what's within my control, deciding the best course of action. Do I heave-to or run with it? For a while we continue to run, but I know we're borderline out of control, slewing dangerously broadside to the waves. I decide to heave-to, releasing the main halyard while shoving us round to face the onslaught, waves breaking over, the sail flaying wildly as it drops.

Lashing the tiller keeps the bow facing closer to the wind, hopefully avoiding being rolled. We jig up and down in our own vomit. I stand just slightly in the shelter of the dodger, shivering, trying to shrink from the rain, trying not to overthink it. Mountainous waves continue to press *Shanti* down, threatening at any moment to overcome her pitiful resistance. She lurches too far to one side, a heavy black monster cascading over. I am lost in a blind tunnel. *Is this it?*

Then, beyond the fear and panic, something strange happens. The terrifying instance is drawn out, disassembled and reconstructed, becoming part of some alternate reality. It is as if time is being stretched to beyond a standstill, to some undefined point in eternity. It exists, and yet it doesn't. I can feel the void like a black hole we have fallen into. Its emptiness is filled with utter silence, spreading a wash of calm which is completely at variance with the external violence. I can feel my tension begin to loosen. Tingling sensations vibrate through every cell as I am enveloped by the deepest sense of peace. And through this internal quietude comes a profound acceptance, a complete letting go of any need to change what is. Simply letting it be as it is.

Miraculously, what is, becomes less wild, not just subjectively, but outwardly too. From one moment to the next, wind and waves hush their furore. It is so far removed from what was going on before, I could be on another planet. I can almost feel Mother Nature breathe a sigh of relief with me. It is the most bizarre thing, yet at the same time, most perfectly natural. I recognise what is happening— it is the "saying yes" that Eckhart Tolle refers to, the acceptance of the present moment, no matter how unbearable. *"Extreme challenges have the ability, the potential, to push you, or force you into a state of Presence."* When every part of me is screaming NO, my resistance causes it to persist. By giving in to it in complete surrender, everything changes. It's only when pushed to the limit, scooped out and flattened, that this can happen.

This is something new I have learned. It is no longer just an abstract idea, but something I know now from direct experience. My logical mind will later rationalise it as the storm simply abating in the normal way, but the experience is one I will always remember. It is imprinted in my consciousness as a reminder of the more subtle realms. Steering *Shanti* through the darkness, there is much to give thanks for.

Dawn creeps in like a rarefied attenuation of the night, stretching what's left thinner.

We survived our first South Pacific storm unscathed, perhaps a little wiser and with perhaps a little more confidence in skipper and boat. The intense awareness that I had been thrust into at the peak of the storm has slipped back into the envelope of memory. That's the way it goes, when millennia of conditioned ways of seeing, lock tightly the familiar patterns. But I can still sense the memory, glowing quietly within me. The tiniest chink of light has cracked through.

As if to make up for the past couple of days and nights, there is a clear blue sky and sunshine presiding over an azure sea. The full mainsail is up again and headsail out. There is a gentle 10 knot SE wind, waves less than 2 metres, making for perfect sailing. I baked a very delicious coconut, ginger and honey cake to celebrate. I feel like a new woman, breathing more freely.

Chapter 17

Time and Motion

Two weeks out. I spent a relatively peaceful night, apart from the sails slatting when the wind drops below 7 knots. Luckily not too much of that. It looks like being another glorious day. Speed over ground is around 4 knots. I just had my last attempt at making yoghurt with the last little bit of culture. It hasn't been successful lately, perhaps the rocking upsets it. Anyway, it's resting out in the hot sun for the day, where the temperature is 41 degrees. I put the clocks back an hour and noted in the log "All is well on the good ship *Shanti*."

At around midnight I hoisted the main again in 9 knots of breeze, which continued to build through the night. I'm taking this more in my stride, accepting that it is my job to deal with constant change. Putting reefs in, shaking them out, just doing what needs to be done, no matter what time of day or night. There's no place for any victim mentality here. A smile, a laugh, a couple of lines of a song serve me better.

Just as I decided to name my hitchhiker "Bobby", it seems on closer inspection that it may not be the same bird that leaves and comes back each day. I have gone up close to him this morning and made a good study of his colours and plumage, so feel I know him intimately now. We shall see. I just had an interesting breakfast—a bowl of oats, soaked in semi-set, mainly whey yoghurt, with raisins, sunflower seeds, mung bean sprouts and coconut cake. I'm not too sure about it. As food stores dwindle, meals become more creative. I had the best day's run despite the calms, 133 nautical miles. My nose hurt too much to sleep.

I don't know how the information leaflet (in French) can say to use the cream for 6 weeks. After only 2 weeks, using it for 5 out of 7 days, it was as if my nose was on fire. I got up after the 10th application to wash it off as I couldn't stand it any longer. The cream somehow continues to work regardless over the "off" days and my entire nose is a giant raspberry. I can't see how a surgeon could possibly have cut out the small area that was of concern originally because the cream is showing up far more. They would have to cut off my entire nose to clear it all. It's gone scaly now, with bits cracking off—just like they used to when I was that young girl sailing in New Zealand. Ah, the sins of the past...

The sky is overcast (good for keeping my nose out of the sun)—not that I am going outside at all. The cockpit is wet, either from drizzle or incoming waves. The sea is a lumpy broadside swell, quite confused in direction. The wind is not strong, only around 18 – 20 knots, but I have triple-reefed the main and furled the headsail to storm jib size. This settled *Shanti* down enough for me to sleep for a good 5 hours last night. I'm still very tired, perhaps in part due to this savage chemotherapy attack on my poor schnoz. Hopefully, it will begin to heal now and not be too scary when I reach land, in another 3 weeks. Or is that an optimistic assumption?

It's hard to maintain crew morale when I'm so tired. I have had a pain in the abdomen for a day or two, which is also a bit of a worry. I'm sure it's just nervous tension, perhaps due to being right in the middle of nowhere, with 2,000 miles on either side. Where would help come from if I needed it? If anything should break down on *Shanti* or me?

I cut those dismal thoughts by giving myself a good talking to, which basically goes something like: *This is entirely your own choice*, etc. and then gets philosophical about death and loss. I remind myself, It's all part of the adventure, the danger, the risks. (I like that thought the best). Then I took some Rescue Remedy and some homeopathics for tummy pain, lay down and did some Reiki on myself, remembering that I am after all a Reiki Master, and fell asleep for an hour. When I awoke, the pain was gone and I felt much brighter.

For dinner I made lentil and vegetable stew in the pressure cooker, followed by coconut cake. Delicious! I'm finding that flavours are so much more flavoursome and satisfying. My body is like a gimbal and becoming quite adept at keeping plates of food and cups of drink on the level. The only trouble is I only have two hands, one of which is permanently engaged in hanging on, as the saying goes, "one hand for me; one for the boat." Thus I have to take it in turns, food or drink, with one or the other left waiting on the gimballed stovetop. Eating and drinking is not a relaxed, sit-down, fine-dining experience. But then those are best shared with good company.

Distance to Gambier is 1,948 miles. The wind dropped out overnight to only 7 knots, so we have slowed right down, with the sails slatting. The sea-state is less bouncy so I took the opportunity to make some treats—19 carob rum balls—one for each remaining day to reach Gambier. I'm changing my ETA to March 6. Just because it took Wolfgang and Klaus 39 days to do the 4,000 miles doesn't mean I will. I've been averaging 5 knots an hour, (120 miles a day) since the doldrums.

I'm just starting to get into the timelessness of it (this seems an ironic comment to make, following the previous entry). No, but really, I ask myself, how would it be if this *is* my life? (which of course it is); to freeze-frame a slice of it and consider it in that indefinite, semi-permanent way in which we regard our "normal" life, instead of seeing it as an abnormality, an interlude of finite time and distance, kind of like a holiday, interspersed between the start and end poles of reality? It is indeed so far removed from normal life as to almost be unreal. The infinite stretch of sea and sky, day after day, creates this rare sense of timelessness. At first, I resist it and count the days of its duration. Then, gradually, it takes on its own normality, its own pace and rhythm, and the question arises—*could this be my life?* I know an endless continuity of more of the same is an impossibility. And yet, within each expanded moment exists eternity, in such a way as is generally overlooked in the land of clocks and past and future.

The distance to Gambier 1828 miles, or 19 carob rum balls. The wind is 10 knots ESE so the second reef can go from the mainsail. I'm feeling a bit unwell. I was sitting in the cockpit thinking how easy it would be to succumb to anxiety at being alone out here, so far from the nearest help, when suddenly, dolphins! Now there's a sight to lift the spirits if ever there was one. They didn't stay long; just played with *Shanti* a while, then zoomed off as quickly as they came. It just shows, how even on the most magnificent of days, 'lonesome-me' moments can take hold. I breathe deeply, count my blessings and give thanks. There is so much to be thankful for.

The wind is a 6-knot easterly. We motored for 45 minutes this morning. I'm resisting turning the key more and more, not just to conserve fuel, but also because the noise shatters the silence so rudely. *Shanti* kept moving slowly through most of the night and the sails only started slatting at around 0300 when the wind dropped to 2 knots. I motored for 2 ½ hours until the wind crawled its way back up to 5 knots. Hoisting the sails again, we are mooching along doing the impressive speed of 2 knots over ground (basically the current). There's very little swell, so the sails are holding, which is great. When they start slatting it's as if my head is a walnut, only just resisting being cracked in a vice. The only recourse is to drop the sails completely. Then what? Motor or drift?

According to *Halcyon*, the forecast shows I'm stuck in a "hole", with nothing useful coming my way until next Tuesday. I try not to let this get me down. I did my laundry and washed myself too, which generally cheers me up. I lay down on the starboard deck to look over the side. There is a skirt of sucker barnacles all along the waterline, their fat pulpy fingers waving from bow to stern. I tied a plastic scraper to an extendable brush and tried to remove some. It's nigh impossible lying on my stomach and would be much easier from the water, but I don't want to risk that. I'm feeling very lethargic. For some reason, like the wind, I have run out of puff.

I'm back to contemplating distance and time equations. (It's actually quite an enjoyable preoccupation, regardless of its questionable value). The 4,000-mile passage should take 40 days if doing an average of 100 miles a day. I have been at sea for 21 days now, which leaves 19 more to go. Gambier is now 1620 miles away. If I divide that by 19, I only need to do 85 miles a day. That seems do-able.

The satellite hide-and-seek has allowed an intermittent breakthrough in the silence, and I finally managed to send and receive a few short messages. All of my weather-watchers have observed a "dead patch" with no wind to the south and advised staying more to the west. Luke has gone one step further, suggesting I change course to the Marquesas, rather than getting stuck in that hole, which looks like extending all the way to Gambier.

Now I really don't know what to do. My primary aim, and preference, was for Gambier. But I don't want to be flapping about on a windless sea for months on end, running out of water and food.

I changed course to the Marquesas and set both sails in 7 knots ENE. *Shanti* bounded off like a puppy let out and we both sang for joy. That lasted about half an hour. The wind is backing more to the east, so before long, I had to furl in the headsail and run square again, with the main flogging on every roll. I'm not prepared to head further north, which would be literally going backwards. So it's gybe and head back to the SW again. It's *so* frustrating!

Even if I wanted to, I can't fly the kite because the wind is so fickle. I don't have the energy to be changing sails every half hour, especially in this heat, when I melt and then drink tons of my precious water. I think I have answered my question—really, there is nothing I can do until I get some decent wind. And what if I get nearer to Marquesas and a big calm swallows me up? Do I then head back toward Gambier? Surely a calm can't last for months. How long can I stay out at sea? Good question.

Again I contemplate questions about the journey or destination and realise it must be both, for there is neither one without the other. I guess it depends on which one is your preferred focus. If you just want to be there, take a plane. Looking out at the horizon I see a wide band of thick haze to the SW, which looks like it could be the edge of the windless black hole. Or am I just being suggestible? I have lost radio contact with *Halcyon*. I sent them a Sat phone message but got no reply, so don't know if it went out or not.

A brief message bounced off an obliging satellite from my climatologist daughter, Dr Pandora Hope. Both she and her husband, Dr Andrew Watkins, confirmed the proscription in a succinct warning: "Do *not* go south of 10 degrees!" Sounded very ominous. Hmmm. Shame I am already at almost 12 degrees now. But when two highly qualified meteorologists concur (even if they do both specialise in climate, not weather, as they always tell me), I should take notice. Dammit!

It's not the time for petulance or pig-headedness or plaintive pleas about wanting to see Gambier. I must give up on that. Well, Luke will be happy anyway. He's been strongly encouraging me to head to the Marquesas, even if only for a few days' rest, which I most probably do need. I guess if I ask for advice I should be prepared to take it. Much as I tell myself *but I'm the one out here, in the reality rather than the supposed-to-be*. But my reality is a minuscule microcosm that doesn't take in the bigger picture, which I guess they can see. So, not without some spitting and stamping of feet, I changed course again toward the NW.

Despite my reluctance, I unearthed the kite. I have been wary of putting it up after the last fiasco but know it's my only chance of actually sailing in 6 knots of wind. I wasn't happy with the way it had been rubbing on the furled headsail, so am using the big spinnaker pole. It's long, heavy and unwieldy and takes a lot of tight-rope balancing. Two hours, and buckets of sweat later, it was finally set. I am so pleased with it. It's not swaying to and fro like before (which probably contributed to the snap-shackle letting go on that dreadful moment when it all fell into the water). I now feel almost confident enough not to have to watch it constantly and can almost relax. And best of all, I'm seeing speed over ground of 4 – 5 knots. Woo-hoo!

It's hard to imagine the stress of another cruiser that Luke told me about, who was caught in the lull en-route to Gambier before changing course to the Marquesas. He was 71 days at sea, with limited water supplies. I definitely don't want to go there! I just ate my last salad for lunch. The fresh produce has lasted very well, given that it was bought 4 weeks ago. I still have a few onions, some garlic, 2 carrots and a pumpkin left.

Day 24. There's just not quite enough wind to do anything with, and what little there is, is very fickle. I tried adding 10, 20, 30 degrees to windward to get some pressure in the mainsail, but a few minutes later, the wind indicator showed it dead astern, and then to the lee. So I gybe, and before long it's the same story the other way. I must have gybed a dozen times or more. An easterly swell kept us rolling. No, more like lurching, which means the boat, the boom, the sail, my body are all tossed from side to side—not at all conducive to sleep. At 0600 I gave up and turned the key.

Three hours later, there's 3-knots right on the nose. Speaking of which, my nose has a hard shell like a volcanic crust. Great chunks of crackly skin are peeling off and it's hard to resist the temptation to pick at it. Aside from the redness, it's not looking too bad, though I don't know if the cream has achieved the purpose. Time will tell—as with everything. *"All will become clear in the fullness of time"* is one of my pet sayings.

I have worked out a system of flying only half a kite as an asymmetrical. There's not enough wind to stop the full sail from collapsing, so I have improvised what I consider an ingenious solution. Pushing the "whisker pole" out at the bow and lashing it to the deck forms a make-shift bow-sprit, to which I attach one clew of the kite. The spinnaker "sock" is only half raised, the top half swaying like the engorged throat of a boa constrictor. Set free, the lower half of the spinnaker flies off to one side. It's a work of art, poetry in motion, beauty to behold—and gives us 1 – 2 knots. Whoopee!

It's settled into a magnificent looking day. I topped up the engine oil, cleaned under the sump and all around the engine bay and did a few other small jobs. A sublime sunset was my reward. It's becoming my favourite time of day, when I look forward to relaxing to music, having a drink and nibbling on whatever's left, perhaps a few dry crackers. I sit up on the windward cockpit coaming, soaking up the tranquillity, marvelling at the richness, the subtle nuances of colour—molten copper, bronze and gold—that adorn the horizon. There are not too many people on earth who, at this very moment, are filling their souls with such a magical sight.

How pleasant to wake to 9 knots of breeze instead of 2. Perhaps we're finally approaching the edge of the dead calm, and finally going to be getting some wind in the sails. At sunset yesterday I sat admiring the beautiful blue and white spinnaker doing its thing, and briefly considered leaving it up (or at least half up) overnight. But prudence won and I snuffed it down completely and set the headsail to port. I am learning a thing or two along the way, particularly about light wind sailing on a rolling ocean. The worst scenario is 4 knots of wind from behind, with a 4-metre sea.

I put the clocks back another hour; we are now at UTC -7 hours. I had fun working out where and when this changes, contemplating the sun glancing across each line of latitude as the earth spins around it. They were very smart, those early pioneers in astrophysics.

I was just about to drop the mainsail because when it flogs it jerks the mast and the rig and the whole boat (and me) so violently that something has to give. I tweaked it a bit more for the umpteenth time and thought I had it sussed, then slam, bam, whack, crack, that bone-crunching flogging again. There's just not enough wind to hold it. I feel as if I'm constantly fighting it, sometimes holding my breath in the few short silences between. I have tried absolutely everything to stop it, from bungee cords to preventers. There's that brief moment of suspense as *Shanti* lolls on one side, then the other, wondering if just maybe this time, she'll ease through it. It is testing me to the point of tears. I have gybed more than ten times this morning.

We are finally able to have the headsail out as well as the mainsail and stay on course. I hope it lasts. My thoughts are now wandering toward Tahiti as a potential place to fly home from for a few weeks in April, if I should make it there by then. There are things to attend to that were neglected by my choice not to go home last Christmas. If one stays away for too long, things start to fall apart at the seams. I want to get my nose (and teeth) checked, to see family and friends, to sort out my finances and several other land practicalities.

The distance to Tahiti is 1970 miles, which is 700 more than to the Marquesas. If I sail directly to there from here, it's a better wind angle. I have read that water in the Marquesas is not potable, that fresh vegetables and diesel are hard to come by, that the anchorages are not so good, that there are nasty, blood-sucking insects. Sounds appealing, *not*. I would only want to stop for water, fuel, fresh vegetables and a short physical and psychological rest. Then there's the dinghy that would need to be repaired before I can deploy it. *Blewy* needs attention but there's no guarantee I'll find anyone there to help me and if the anchorage is rolly it would be almost impossible to manhandle her down safely.

Crossing longitude 120° W, the clocks go back another hour. It's now UTC -8. I'm still undecided as to my destination. The distances are now quite similar—around 1000 miles—to Hiva Oa or to the Tuamotus. While the northerly component remains, the wind angle to Tahiti is better and faster. It's much of a muchness. Hiva Oa is only a strong temptation if I think I'm almost there—but I'm not. Adding another 7 days on top is not so daunting, as I'll be at the Tuamotus then, which are practically on the doorstep of Tahiti. It would be good to have someone to talk this over with. My 25-hour run was 128 miles.

The wind and waves increased around midday. I'm thinking of putting a reef in the mainsail. The anemometer is only showing 8 – 14 knots; I'm beginning to suspect it may have had too many Booby birds roosting on it. After lunch, the wind dropped right out and went more to the north so the rig started slatting again.

At 1430 things are settling down, with the wind back to the ENE around 8 knots. It's still very rolly in the residual slop of 3-metre waves. But we're back on course, doing 5 knots speed over ground.

There's only one small mirror on board *Shanti* that shows a disembodied reflection of my face and I don't like what I see in it. I notice how much more quickly I seem to be aging. My jowls are as saggy as a bulldog's and the laugh lines are not so laughable anymore. There are deep dark canyons under my eyes. Wind and sea and stress and lack of sleep are heartlessly piling on extra years.

But then I ask myself, did I think I was the only one getting older? Well, maybe more quickly. I certainly am not feeling at all attractive, even though my body is leaner and stronger than ever before. But I can't see that bit in the mirror. It's like at the hairdresser's when they wrap that black cape around you that pinches into the loose skin at your neck and only your face is exposed to carry the sum of who you are. Similarly, in learning French, I'm stripped to the bone, there being no witty conversation or vivacious personality to add to the whole.

All of which brings me back to *who am I?* Small wonder my sense of identity is fading out here, with no human interaction. Is that what it depends upon?

I recollect a poem by Robert Burns:

> *"Oh the gift that God could gie us,*
> *to see ourselves as others see us."*

In earlier times of my life, this seemed like a desirable virtue, perhaps because I was always feeling judged, but never knew exactly as what—clever or dull, attractive or plain, caring or indifferent? Now I ask the question, "seen by whom?"—a child, a close friend, a passer-by, a lover? Each will see me differently, to such an extent that the reality of who I am, becomes so blurred through such multi-perspectives as to be meaningless. One may flatter, another find fault.

The French philosopher, Jean-Paul Sartre, said that we can only know ourselves through the mediation of another. To base one's self-knowledge on such ephemera, on so many distortions and projections and subjective perceptions, one might just as well ask a spider for its opinion. For opinion is all you will get, an opinion that is coloured by so many extraneous influences as to have no inherent validity. Thus, give up this crazed mirror, and likewise, desist from inwardly judging others.

Trying to sum everything up in 160 characters, I managed to send a text to Luke. His reply was again pushing for Marquesas. I know he thinks I need a rest—and I do. So I replied, "OK, I will try it."

But after gybing onto that NW course, as suspected, it was impossible to hold the headsail. Speed dropped from 6 knots to 3. So it would take twice as long to sail the 1000 miles. I texted this, asking, "Is it worth it?" His reply, "Not sure honey."

Part of the trouble is that the conditions here are not the same as the forecasts he is looking at, which say I should have 15 knots easterly. I tell him I have 8 knots ENE. He's just going to have to trust me to run my own ship. It's funny how I almost feel as if I'm being unfaithful, going my own way. Compliance is a deeply ingrained habit. Tired as I am, I'm not the only person to sail 5,000 miles non-stop. And being told to rest somehow makes me feel more tired.

Day 31. 0630. The wind is up to 10 – 15 knots, which is such a thrill. We're running under full main only, speed averaging 5 knots. I will put a reef in the main later, before setting the headsail. *Je me demande*, I ask myself, I wonder—is there more stress out here or on land? I guess it depends on your position on land. I'm sure Pandora and Andrew would say on land, with their demanding jobs.

Out here, it is largely to do with the unknown and the unanswerable. How long will this passage take? Will the water, food, fuel last? What weather is looming on the horizon, to bash or becalm? How about the boat with all of its systems? And likewise me? I'd say the stresses are similar, the main difference being that life-threatening events are generally more easily dealt with on the land.

Yesterday afternoon *Tilly 2* was making strange noises as if she had a cold or a sore throat. Most likely just overheated. I have to rig up some shade to protect her, like me, from the scorching midday sun.

This evening, a sudden explosive crack made me jump. The headsail sheet cheek block exploded just as I was winching in the furling line, and bits of it went flying. I don't have a spare—it's not possible to carry spares of everything—so I must jury rig it somehow. It probably means no more poling out the headsail on the port side, which had been dragging us further south anyway, so we're probably better off without it.

After another sleepless night, being tossed from side to side, I wonder how long can a person survive without getting any deep sleep? I wonder what the symptoms of this are? How can I recognise what's going on with me, when it's just me looking from the inside?

0700. I reefed the main and gave away another 5 degrees. It's a bit better but very large, confused seas lift *Shanti's* stern and toss her about like a seesaw. She doesn't seem to mind, either way. I could take lessons.

Day 33. I managed to get some sleep last night, despite the heavy rolling, so hopefully that will stave off my inner collapse, or whatever is brewing deep down inside of me. We gybed several times across the course until 0200 when I'd had enough of it. I let her run NW until 0530, then got up to throw in another gybe. The wind veered and did a sudden crash gybe back. *Tilly 2* squawked. I felt like I should have stayed in bed until daylight and left well enough alone. I kept berating myself for it, *Stupid, stupid*, you should have waited, etc. and then finally said out loud, *"OK, I forgive you; let it go."*

What an amazing difference that made. There are a couple of good lessons for me in this. The first—leave well enough alone. The second—be less harsh on myself. The trouble is I forget these things as the sun comes out. Perhaps I should make a treasure-trove to put them in, a small but precious-looking box, with mother of pearl inlay? Or a notebook? But then I'd most probably forget to look in them. I guess life lessons have to become so deeply ingrained as to become part of ourselves, and thereby automatic first responses. No doubt there are many of these in there already, that I take for granted.

The satellites are being evasive so no messages for a while now. It makes me feel more vulnerable. No weather reports, no contact, no help if needed. I guess even the ship's Epirb, (which also relies on satellites to send out an emergency signal) wouldn't work here. So I'm completely on my own.

This morning, when I looked around at my watery world, the thought occurred to me that really there is little difference to being here than sitting on anchor, say at Great Keppel Island on the east coast of Australia, except for the fact of having a destination and some time around that. The weather is just the weather, the day is just the day. The days come and go, with little to distinguish them, aside from my moods. There are moments of blissful acceptance, endless frustration, potential panic and sheer terror. This is like a barometer of the external conditions, which is how most of us live our lives, laughing in the sunshine and crying in the rain. And then, this too passes.

Chapter 18

Still Waiting for my Epiphany

The lovely broad-reach that I was so enjoying drifted round to its favourite place, dead astern and both sails began flogging. I furled in the headsail. Back to situation normal, or as the acronym goes, SNAFU. (Situation Normal, All F---d Up). Checking the speed over ground it was between 1 – 3 knots. Hopeless! Instead of taking 3 days to get to the Marquesas, even to the closest island of Fatu Hiva, it would take a week. That, plus another week to Tahiti would completely eliminate any chances of getting to Melbourne for April. I might just as well gybe back and continue as before. Dismal.

I lay in my bunk making all kinds of trade-offs and pleas to the powers that be. I would even tolerate—no, *welcome* —the seesaw, rolly poly discomfort if only for a few days of 12 – 15 knots from a good enough angle to be able to hold my course. *Please*.

The main reason for stopping at Fatu Hiva was to clean the bottom. I'm sure the lengthy subterranean garden isn't helping matters, the fat tendrils swirling like a Polynesian dancer's grass skirt. I resolved to try again, lying on my stomach on the deck with a scraper cable-tied to the boat-hook. While I was lying there I noticed the rust at the base of the lower shroud was bulging and one strand of wire had already broken. *Oh no!!* Not again. So much for the top-quality stainless steel from South Africa.

I guess we have to expect things to break on such a long voyage, but I really didn't expect these new lowers to fail. Perhaps it was due to all the slatting and flogging. Luckily I still had a few of the bulldog clamps that I used last time and luckily the break was at the bottom and not the top of the wire, so it was easier to bolt the clamps on. I just hope and pray it all holds until I get to Tahiti. Now I have a good reason for heading there. I doubt I could find a rigger in the Marquesas and would have to stay there until new shrouds could be shipped in. So, yet again, Providence takes over and removes all my earlier doubts.

Spinnakers should come with instructions. (They probably do.) I managed to get 6 hours out of it, struggling the whole time to keep it from collapsing in only 3 - 4 knots of breeze. I finally gave up. It's SO HOT!! Sweat is pouring off me, running into my eyes. In the dead calm between flying the kite and the poled-out headsail, the water over the side looked so inviting I was tempted to jump in. It would be great to cool off and scrape the barnacles. There can't be that many sharks about here. I leaned as far as I could over the side and saw schools of weed-eating shark-bait swimming alongside. Hmmm, better not add to it.

Besides which I didn't have the energy to set up the swim ladder after so much sail-wangling. My heart was palpitating and I was shaking all over just from one hour's exertion in the full heat of the day. Heart-attack material. I won't do that again, I told myself, though knowing full well I most likely will.

In actual fact, we seem to be holding steadier and doing better now. The other good news is I found a bottle of Normandie Cidre Brut from Martinique, which is now chilling nicely in the fridge. That should keep me going for the next few days' Sundowners.

That's it! The hawk (masthead wind indicator) is doing 360's. We are officially becalmed. I wonder how long this is going to last. There were some "mare's tails" in the sky before, which often foretell wind. It must be the calm before—before the perfect 15-knot SE Trade Wind. Thanks. I can still cajole.

I just tipped a couple of buckets of saltwater over my head which feels much better. Then I used the coolness to bake a loaf of bread, which turned out to be not quite such a brick as the last one.

1800. I got all excited seeing 6 knots of wind, after absolutely nothing, so hoisted the mainsail again. I was surprised that it wasn't slatting but then realised that was because there was no big swell knocking us about. It's coming. Just saw 8 knots. *Woo-hoo!* Not sure whether to leave this sail as it is for the night or not. Long gone are the safe seamanship rules of reefing down at dusk.

Day 39—the magic number! This is how long it took Wolfgang and Klaus to get to Gambier, 3900 nautical miles from Panama, and how long it might have taken me to get to the Marquesas. But I am continuing on for another 800 miles, a total of 4,700, though in fact, probably closer to 5,000 with all the zig-zagging and course changes I'm doing. Theoretically, 5,000 should take 50 days—which is another 11 days. I am hoping for arrival on March 21, but that's very wind dependent, and the wind gods haven't been smiling on me lately.

There are some very dark clouds on the horizon behind. They brought nothing but a few fat splots of rain, a couple of unnecessary gybes, sucked the wind back to 4 knots, raised the humidity to a permanent sweat and left the main slatting violently. I'm very aware of not wanting to stress those damaged stays.

I'm thinking of how very different this voyage is to the one made 11 years ago with my former partner, when we had constant communication with other yachts via HF radio and daily emails home. But I learnt nothing.

"Know first thyself." It is impossible to get to the depths of one's being in the constant company of others. Hence the need for silent retreats.

1200. It's the law of nature—everything changes. Some things more slowly than others, but in due course, they will change. We now have the 15 knots I asked for and are on course. Yay! How long for? We'll see …. Don't get attached to either one or the other.

1300. The wind is building (YES!!—I can still get excited over getting what I want). The waves are mounting and *Tilly 2* is struggling. It's time to put the number 1 reef back in the main. The topping lift is caught on the top batten so the sail won't drop. Ah, more frustrations, hot labours, sweat and tears. Over such little things—ridiculous! Just as I got it all sorted and the reef in, the wind dropped back down to 6 knots. Never mind—back to my French lesson, and to evaporate some sweat before tidying up that tangle of ropes. And as for that reef, it can just stay in.

I've always been something of a perfectionist. I'm not sure if that's from being a Virgo or some genetic glitch, but it's hard for me to leave a snake-pit of ropes lying about, even if I have made a mental agreement to let it be as it is for a few minutes.

Being a perfectionist also entails trying to hide one's imperfections from others. Always hiding something is a bedfellow to guilt, that utterly useless emotion. And of course, there's also criticism, of self and of others. Perfectionists want to please others and to be seen in a good light. Being thought badly of is anathema. Trying to present an attractive image doesn't go well with this sudden aging thing that has been bugging me. Perfectionism must eventually soften its harsh expectations.

Now is a good time to practice acceptance of what is, and to swap some of the old tapes in my head for some new ones, ones that are more in line with reality, such as, *I'm not a used car salesman, trying to sell you a gleaming, shiny me or trying to convince you of all my wonderful merits. I make no apology for what is; if you don't like it, leave it.* Of course, all of this presupposes having overcome neediness and the vital necessity to be loved.

Now I know I can be alone. I don't have a perfect body or mind. But I do have a perfect soul, which is not solely mine, so I can make no claims on it. It is important to stay connected to that humility. I now have this mellow sense of goodwill to all. That's probably because there's no-one else here to test me.

Day 40, has a Biblical and Buddhist connotation of spiritual epiphany, following a period of 40 days of isolation, meditation and prayer. I'm waiting expectantly for the blinding flash of light.

There are so many variables affecting where and when I shall arrive that I have practically given up trying to work it out. It seems to be somewhere between 600 – 700 nautical miles to go, so maybe in another week. I have made the fundamental error that most cruisers eschew and written down an arrival date—March 21, but who knows. It's more of a request to the Universe, signalling my intention. April is a big month in Melbourne, with a few birthdays, Shoni's PhD completion, and Misha's headlining gigs, so I would love to make it.

Day 41. Still waiting for my epiphany, when all the deep and meaningful secrets of the Cosmos are revealed to me. Perhaps I have slept too much, or eaten too much?

The wind dropped out last night, so I was up many times changing things. Eventually, I gybed to a more SW course, dropped the slatting main and ran under half a poled-out headsail, doing 2 knots SOG. It was quite miraculous that I managed to cover 90 miles in 24 hours. There must be some current with me, or perhaps *Shanti* put on a bit of pace while I slept.

I have spent many hours drawing lines on the chart and contemplating possible routes through the barricade of the Tuamotu atolls. It's largely determined by wind angle; I don't want to be constantly gybing or going off course because some of the passes are quite narrow. I think I have picked a good one that is 600 miles to Tahiti from here, at 240°, with an adjustment of 10° more to the south if necessary.

An interesting thing has occurred. My world/seascape/perception has changed. I cannot describe how, but it is noticeably different. I first noticed it last night, around midnight, when I was up on deck dropping the main. Something felt different from before. At first, I thought it might have been due to lack of sleep. But today, it is as if I am in a different ocean. The wind is only 7 knots and there are large, long rollers, some of them breaking, coming from the SE. The wind is still ENE. But everything has a completely different quality to it. Perhaps it is my awakening slowly seeping in?

Day 42, 0830, I hear voices. Now I *know* I have cracked! Then I realise they are normal human voices, although unintelligible, coming over the VHF radio. It is a most unusual sound, the first I have heard in 6 weeks. There are no boats in sight. Perhaps it is coming from Napuka Island, which we just passed, only 20 miles off. There must be people there. That is a really weird thought.

The wind is light but enough to sail. I hope it doesn't abandon me. My turning waypoint is set for Katiu reef, 215 miles off, where I begin my pass between four island reefs, spread over a distance of 65 miles. Then it's another 243 miles to Tahiti. I have worked out distances and times and at this pace, we should go between the first two atolls (Raraka and Katiu) at around midnight tomorrow and the second two (Fakarava and Faaite) at around 1400 on Monday. I'm happy with this timing. The first pass is wider (20 miles) than the second (10 miles) and there is a waxing gibbous moon. I don't expect to get much sleep (do I ever?) as I will need to keep a very close eye on the course.

At 1000 hours, the AIS just picked up 3 Chinese ships 10 nautical miles to the north. This explains the unintelligible language on the radio.

I toasted the Universe and all the wonders within it with my last glass of wine at sunset. Then, buoyantly—let's see if we can gybe the headsail without furling it in first. Let's see how much of a mess we can get in; how many times the pole can bang me on the head, how much sweat the lowering sun can pour into my eyes? At least I'm still on board. Ah, the relaxing time of day. *"I forgive you."* Still no Sat phone.

Day 43. Another gorgeous sunny day, with the clearest deep blue water and schools of probably quite edible fish accompanying us. Sometimes I think some freshly-cooked fish could be nice, but right from the start I decided against fishing, mostly because I hate killing them, but also because of the bloody massacre in the cockpit. I hypocritically fish out of cans instead.

The wind is up slightly, around 8 – 9 knots, and we're running square just under the poled-out headsail. *Shanti* is slipping along on greased wheels and we're loving it. A giant bubble of happiness fills my chest and gets released in song. What do I love most about this crazy life? I love the challenge of it; drawing on my own resources to hold it all together. The watchfulness that that entails. The solitude, the peace. The push towards acceptance of what is.

There are a few mare's tails in the perfectly blue sky, so perhaps more wind is on its way. Or perhaps not.

1450. Totally becalmed. Once again, perhaps it's the calm before the perfect 15-knot SE Trade Wind. This heat is stultifying—38 degrees. I'm *so* tempted to jump over.

There's no point in setting expectations, experiencing frustrations, railing against what the present moment brings. Remember, what we resist, persists. Aaaaaah!

We all have dozens of ways of distracting ourselves from now—watching TV, going to movies, reading, talking, etc. For me, out here, most of these are gone. I still prepare meals, generally 3 times a day, perhaps bake bread, listen to the odd audiobook, do the odd French lesson, play my guitar and sing. But mostly it is *Shanti* and the elements that demand my attention, drawing me back into precisely what is happening now.

It is becoming easier to watch my thoughts and their effects. I have noticed that whenever my mind wanders away from the present, I am more likely to make mistakes. Even playing the guitar, which generally keeps me firmly here, a slight mental shift into somewhere else, perhaps a thought of a future audience, a dreamworld of another time, and I forget the chords. I'm grateful for the space in which to notice these things, practically as soon as they happen.

———

Sunday, March 17. The wind I was hoping for didn't come. I motored for 4 hours until 1945 last night, then left it to a quiet drift so I could sleep. It might be the last chance for a while. I woke at 0500, sensing a zephyr of wind shifting *Shanti's* motion. I raised the main and gybed the headsail, which seems to have helped a bit. I resolved to work harder on the sails today.

0915. I have done the laundry and washed myself. It's already way too hot to do much more and the subversive sweat is dripping like an ice-cream, intent on undoing my brief moment of bodily cleanliness. Thank God for the Caframo fan that I stabilized by screwing onto a wooden breadboard and have running on full speed day and night, 24/7. The small handheld fan that Luke gave me is also a whirring hum of thanks. Occasionally, he comes to mind as I lie in my bunk with this cooling breeze an inch away from my face. I'm definitely more sentimental than normal, feeling ever so grateful for his support, almost to the point of tears. Perhaps it's because everything out here is so much larger than life; perhaps because of the deep appreciation of life itself or the possibility that I may never see my loved ones again.

There are masses of birds off the bow, especially the vivid white ones wearing bright red lipstick. *Shanti* must be pushing fish for them to catch. Later on, more, different birds arrive— smaller white ones that squeal like anxious piglets. They are not the soaring sea birds like the great albatross but are from nearby land. They have busy wings that flutter more than flap and their movements are much less graceful.

Day 45, 0600. The wind is doing its best to blow more than 4 knots but not succeeding, so the engine has to go on to get us safely through this danger zone.

At 0900 we are passing between Raraka and Katiu atolls, just 6 miles from Raraka. I can see it quite clearly, even though it is so low-lying, little more than a clump of palm trees in the ocean. Still, Land-Ho! I wouldn't want to be at the mercy of the wind, drifting through here. Luckily there is enough diesel left to motor the 60 nautical miles through this mine-field. The wind is down to 3 knots. I hope it picks up on the other side for the last leg to Tahiti.

It's a shame not to be stopping at any of these fascinating atolls, but my failing rig is a concern and if I hope to see my family in April, I need to arrive in time to book flights and a marina berth. Even so, this may not be possible, but I'll aim for it anyway. The water through here is the most crystal-clear blue, like a swimming pool on a sunny day. Dozens of small fish are keeping pace with *Shanti*, I'm not sure why. They don't appear to be nibbling weed or barnacles. Perhaps they are using *Shanti* as protection from the birds.

The birdlife is amazing—mainly the small white ones which seem awkward and unbalanced in their flight. There are a couple of large birds with yellow caps, white underbellies and black, bat-like wings. Their tail is bifurcated when open, a narrow plume when shut. They too have a more jerky, uncoordinated action to their flight. I find it fascinating to sit up on the deck (away from the noise of the engine) and watch them.

1420. Wow! Suddenly *all* of the birds have gone. They must have been called home for dinner. I didn't see which way they went.

1520. They are back. First one of the little white jittery ones, then another, then a couple of brown Boobies, then a few more. The Boobies like to circle *Shanti*, eyeing off a potential ride to a more distant place.

1700. I spotted both atolls—Fakarava to the north and Faaite to the south. Wondrous! The gap at the nearest point is only 5 miles wide. The timing could not have been better, as we passed through both gaps in daylight. Lady Luck is still on my side.

The AIS picked up an Australian yacht *Sunflower*, on anchor in Fakarava. I was tempted to go in but at 1800 it's too late. We're still 8 miles off and those narrow, tide-swept passes are not to be trifled with in the dark. Still, I felt a bit sad to motor on by.

Day 46. After waiting until we were well clear of the last danger that any current might sweep a becalmed boat onto, I finally gave *Yani* a rest. The wind was only 2 – 4 knots so we drifted 20 miles overnight. At 0500 I tried changing a few things, wished, prayed, begged, visualised—all to no avail. A temporary 7 knots teased us for half an hour then died to nothing. *Yani* went on again at 0630, sails down; then off at 0720, sails up; then on again at 0815—*ah, fun and games.*

There is a big rolling swell from the SE which is like a gigantic pulsation of the earth's bodily fluids, rising to a good 4 metres of firm rotundity, with no breaking of the surface. Sitting on the top of the crests is like being up in the first Panama Canal lock, looking back over the chasm behind.

1300. Oh dear me. This is not comfortable at all. Motoring slowly through this swell, which has become quite sloppy, *Shanti* is picked up by the front and by the rear and tossed from side to side. What a horrible motion it is. Thank God motoring through the Tuamotus yesterday was over relatively flat water. I expected it would be the same on this side and that the chain of atolls would give some protection, like the Great Barrier Reef in Queensland. But most of this swell is coming from the south now. A little bit of decent wind to sail would be very welcome. But there's only 1 – 2 knots right on the nose.

1730. Again it would be good to have someone else's opinion right now, as I'm not sure what to do. We seem to be motoring more deeply into glassy seas. To cut *Yani* for the night, we could end up going backwards. It's possible to do something with 4 knots from behind, but not with this. I entertained thoughts of just continuing motoring until the fuel was all gone; but then it might be needed at some stage later to charge the batteries, not to mention arriving into a foreign port. No, I think it's best to stop for the night, no matter how uncomfortable. It's such a bad time not to have any communication.

Day 47. Dropping the sails with only the tiniest triangle of headsail out, we hove-to. At first, *Shanti* drifted round in circles. I didn't think *Tilly 2* could handle no forward motion, but when put back in charge, she at least kept the bow pointing in the right direction, which was psychologically reassuring. Bearing away 40 degrees to try and catch the slightest puff of wind, we actually did make 5 miles in that direction until 0200. It was also impressive that I was able to sleep reasonably well until then, despite the rolling. I woke to rain and wind (12 knots from the north), so unbacked the headsail and re-set the now-struggling *Tilly 2*. At last—decent wind!

Power is becoming an issue with thick cumulonimbus shrouding the sky and not quite enough wind to inspire *Blewy*. Meanwhile, it's time to check the oil, empty the anti-siphon overflow, mop up under the engine sump, compress more plastic rubbish and dig out an oil jug and funnel. I used last night's rain collection for a personal sweet water wash. Luxury! It's a rare thing to catch any rain whilst sailing, as the bimini catchment area is usually flapping up and down in the wind, so it only works when becalmed. There's more rain now, maybe enough to wash my hair. Double luxury!

1145. The wind is up to 15 knots, which may just be from the passing rain squalls. *Blewy* is doing her magical amp-generating trick and the batteries are up to 12.9V. I'm thinking of slowing down (would you believe?) to arrive in daylight, but figured it was more prudent to continue as we are until tomorrow, just in case. So far, we have saved half a day's fuel.

I can hardly believe it. There's a possibility of arriving in Tahiti tomorrow, on my estimated date of arrival, which would be miraculous. Just last night I was contemplating being becalmed out here for the next few weeks, which could still happen. I must try not to count my chickens or fat Booby birds too soon. But regardless—I was just overwhelmed by an unexpected sense of achievement, the first for me on this voyage. We're not there yet, but WOW—how awesome would that be, sailing into Tahiti after all this time? Remembering the exhilaration I felt sailing my beautiful J40 up the Tamaki estuary in New Zealand, my childhood sailing-ground, lifting my eyes to my father's clifftop home, with an inner shout of *Hey dad, look at me!*—well, this comes close. A quiet infilling of the soul. It's nowhere near the end of the circumnavigation, but the near-completion of this past 7 weeks' alone at sea is the closest I've come to patting myself on the back.

One should never speak too soon. At 2000 last night, Day 48, we were hit by a massive storm cell. I had been watching dense black clouds to the north, wondering what they might bring. Well, they brought the lot! Winds well over 35 knots, driving rain and the same terrifying lightning and thunder that I will never get used to. I donned a heavy-duty jacket and once again, was soon soaked through to the skin.

It was a wildly flapping, chaotic struggle getting the mainsail down to the third reef in the darkness, but gradually *Shanti* regained her footing and took off, with no thought of where. Hanging on to the tiller, surfing the broiling froth was exhilarating, very different from the last time. Perhaps it was being on the home stretch, rather than in the middle of nowhere, perhaps it was reconnecting with that moment of peace amidst the turmoil, but I didn't know whether to cry or sing. At last, we were moving!

For another couple of hours, we raced on through the darkness, only giving the briefest thought to any other boats that may be in the way. It was impossible to see anything ahead and none of the local Copra boats used AIS, so we really were running blind. My only hope was that they might see my lights and avoid me. Sometimes one must simply trust to luck.

The booming thunder immediately following the lightning made me realise the storm cell was directly above and we were running with it. I was too wet and cold to ride this through the night so gybed the main and lashed the helm to starboard. *Shanti* rounded up to a more docile, hove-to stance. What a mess I was in, soaked through, shivering with cold and adrenaline. Pitch blackness was everywhere apart from when rent by the brilliant flashes of lightning. I should have known we weren't going to make it into port without at least one more thrashing.

Just as I thought it was done, a gigantic boom of thunder punched my heart like an electric cattle prod and I was literally lifted off my feet by the shock of it; Thor having the last word. The rain was still falling but *Shanti* was left wallowing in 2 knots of wind. I sat cowering from the rain for a long time until the adrenaline subsided. Then a heavy exhaustion enveloped me. I felt as if my innards had been scooped out like a deboned chicken. Somehow, I managed to get through the night without any sleep and at first light started the engine.

1000. There are still lots of black clouds around. I have had it! Last night the precariousness of my situation struck me, being out here alone with no communications. Even with only another 90 miles to go, there's no assurance of getting help if I need it. I felt prepared to motor the remaining distance, or as far as the fuel lasted, just to get there. It doesn't matter if we arrive in the middle of the night. I just want to get there.

The wind is up to 8 – 10 knots, so we are sailing again, albeit much more slowly. I just have to play it by ear and work with what is.

1300. *Oh no!* 14 knots SW, right on the nose, from the very direction we have to go. Unbelievable! Motoring into this is going to increase fuel consumption. The sight-glass shows the level of diesel is only an inch or two from the bottom. And all the jerry cans are empty, so that's all there is. I try to work out how long it might last, but the base of the tank curves to fit the shape of the hull so it's impossible to know. All I can do is keep on keeping on, until I can't.

1730. 55 miles off, I can make out the jagged peaks of the twin islands that are Tahiti. It's going to be another sleepless night for me. I hop up and down the companionway steps a hundred times or more, checking the chart, checking the land, checking for other boats, keeping an eye on the black thunderclouds, wondering which way they are heading. No more storms tonight, please.

Day 49. Friday, March 22, 1030. We are still motoring but I'm too nervous to feel excited. There is a small marina tucked in behind a reef that tempts me, but I keep going. I need to be somewhere near the airport if I am to fly out of here. I know I'm pushing my luck, but it's so close now.

Approaching the Passe de Papeete, a narrow gap in the encircling reef, I called Port Control on the VHF radio. I couldn't believe it when a French-accented voice asked me to stand-by while some traffic moved. Doesn't he realise we're on our last drop of fuel? How much more inconvenient will it be for everyone, if I break down mid pass?

My French is not good enough yet to argue the point, so I turned back out to sea and waited. Way off in the distance, I spotted a squat, stumpy red cargo ship slowly approaching. After an interminable 10 minutes, he was finally through, only to be followed by another, and then yet another leaving the port. Aie yai yai!

Finally, permission to enter was granted, but with her barnacle-encrusted hull, *Shanti* was moving very slowly. Tide and wind were producing a choppy turbulence and I could see waves breaking over the reef that seemed extremely close to the starboard channel marker. I could hear crackling from the VHF that sounded a little like someone calling *Shanti* but couldn't release my iron grip on the helm as

I battled to stay on track. My left ear suddenly became aware of a low rumbling sound and for a moment I imagined it was *Yani* gasping her last. It grew louder and louder, and then, as I glanced behind, I saw the bow wave of a massive *Vodafone* ferry settling down off its foils. At that point, I'm sure my heart leapt overboard.

Within the reef, all was calm as we slowly motored toward the anchorage. Navigating the winding channel means following the line drawn on my electronic charts, which means standing at the tiller, holding my iPad close. It has a waterproof case, but still shouldn't be doused in a tropical downpour. Looking at the ominous banks of dark clouds gathering I prayed that the rain would hold off.

Several airport runways cross over the inner lagoon, and I was asked to radio for permission to transit each of them. Then I might be told, "you have 5 minutes to get to the next runway", or again, I would have to wait as the monstrous belly of a Jumbo jet practically scraped my mast. I'm sure the Port Captain was getting frustrated by me, as he called a couple of times to make sure I understood. All rather nerve-wracking, exacerbated by not having slept for the previous two nights. *"Merci beaucoup"* was all I could say. So much for all those French lessons.

As I lay on my unmoving bunk, the day before flying back to Australia, I reflected on the past 7 weeks. It was certainly an interesting challenge spending that much time alone at sea. I'm not sure what it's done to my head but I feel changed, no longer sweating the small stuff. It's paradoxical how the small things are both unimportant and at the same time, most quintessentially vital.

Chapter 19

Four Single-Handers

Returning to *Shanti* is usually a great pleasure, but this time I felt quite low. It was obvious to me what had happened. I had spent the previous 49 days and nights alone at sea on that interminable passage from Panama to Tahiti, arrived exhausted, and before my feet had steadied on the land, had immediately jumped on a plane home. There had been no time to establish contact with even one friendly face, and now I had returned to that void.

But it wasn't time to linger. I needed to do what had to be done and get moving again. Matt, the local rigger, arrived more or less as arranged and replaced the lower shrouds. He did a good job and I was glad I hadn't waited for the replacements to be sent from Cape Town, or I'd still be waiting.

I collected my duty-free alcohol (Absolut vodka at $US6 a bottle, and likewise quality French wines) and walked to Carrefour for the last time to spend the last of my Polynesian Francs. Peculiarly for me, I used them to buy a new dress instead of more provisions—perhaps the influence of shore life, where shorts and T-shirts don't constitute everyday attire.

An old friend who happened to be in Tahiti invited me out to dinner and I felt I had nothing decent to wear that wasn't all crumpled or smelling of diesel. The month ashore had ironed a few creases out of my face and I was beginning to feel halfway human again, at least in terms of outward appearance. Alan generously splurged on a fancy meal and quality French wine in one of the better shorefront restaurants. He has bought himself a cheap old boat to do up, which gives him a break from his shore life in the UK. We pondered how Brexit would alter the utility of our British passports. Mine at least got me into this country without needing a costly visa.

My next passage should be relatively short, with my initial destination being Suwarrow in the Cook Islands and then Fiji. It was 1530 before I finally got away and the fading hours of daylight were spent motoring in a windless rolling swell. After clearing the island's wind shadow a strong sou' easterly soon had me reefing down. These were the first few days of 25-30 knots that I was counting on to get me off to a flying start. A 75 mg capsule of Stugeron held my queasiness at bay, but still, it was an uncomfortable first night and I couldn't relax.

Seeing the thunderheads of dark clouds rimming the horizon put the panic in me, remembering the last beating that had been dealt. I dropped the main entirely and furled to a pocket-handkerchief of headsail in readiness, and was glad I had. The Society Islands of Bora Bora and Raiatea are well known for these squalls. As the rain began pelting down and the violent gusts tossed *Shanti* like a toy, it was back to hanging on till it passed.

A few bright lights on the shore pricked the darkness as the landlubbers settled into their evening with family, safe and sound within their solid shelters, and I was struck by a rare loneliness. Such is the price of having split my journey to go home for a few weeks, just long enough to get a taste of that warmth and to miss it so much more deeply.

The rest of the night and all of the next day continued with much of the same, wearing me down lower than any other time before. Perhaps it's because I know I'm on the home leg now, and a part of me just wants to get there. I don't have a lot of interest in sight-seeing in foreign ports. "What's the good of being alone in paradise?" someone once asked me. This feeling is exacerbated by having spent such a joyous time with a handful of other cruisers in the Caribbean, and now, since transiting the Panama Canal, I find myself completely alone. This will change I know, further down the track, as I re-enter the more populous South Pacific islands, and slow down to enjoy them.

We're making very slow progress now. The frequency of the storm cells makes it prudent to remain reefed down, and when they pass, *Shanti* is left wallowing, with sails slatting noisily in 3 or 4 knots of wind. Storm cells are like giant vacuums that suck up the air from all around, gathering it into a concentrated blast, then laughing at the upturned turtle left floundering helplessly in its passing shadow. At that time I can either turn the key and motor for an hour seeking wind or drop everything and drift. And this is not even in the forecast calm days ahead. I know the wind is going to drop right out in another day or so.

I woke up to relative quiet, no sails slatting, no rolling or lurching, and clear blue skies with 12 knots of breeze just aft of the beam; in short, a glorious morning, with *Shanti* gliding along as if on a well-oiled track. But nothing stays the same for long, and before midday, the beatific breeze was just a memory left in the wake of the churning propeller. As with the passage through the Tuamotus, the proximity of reefs dictated motoring for the next 4 hours, until well clear. Luckily the wind picked up sufficiently to sail through the night, so I was able to get some sleep.

Day 5. The sky is hiding behind a white shroud, and weeping gently. We have 8 – 10 knots of wind on the beam, giving us smooth sailing. Later in the morning, dodging ominous dark clouds, I furled in half the headsail, just in case. They passed uneventfully, once again leaving a windless sea adorned with a lively confusion of waves. The batteries were low, so an hour of motoring pushed us into the new arena of 6 knots right on the nose. Having expected this, I didn't mind giving away 20 degrees and hardened up sails to enjoy a rare beat to windward. Lunch was a salad with boiled eggs. Sadly all of the Carrefour supermarket tomatoes have gone off in only 5 days.

1430. The sun has come out to play, putting some charge into the batteries and more cheer into the day. This makes it easier to tolerate the wind dropping to 3 knots and the sails slatting uselessly. In local sailing we say, give it the "ten-minute rule" before making any changes. Out here, it's more like the "hour rule".

1440. OK, that's long enough—turn the key. Fuel conservation need not be so strict on a shorter passage, although there'll be no more available until Fiji.

1600. Nothing stays the same for long. Back to sailing again, on a glorious 8-knot beam reach. Oh yeah!

1745. A brief storm cell shot through, out of an almost clear blue sky. Then a great double-arced rainbow spread right over the top of *Shanti* from one side to the other. I certainly do see some incredible sights out here.

Last night *Shanti* didn't know what to make of it, to such an extent that I was almost ready to drop all sails and just sit it out. I tried every trick in the book, getting up every 10 minutes, as yet again, it all changed. In the end, I tried that old favourite that often works—motoring for an hour to escape this black hole, which can extend a mile or a hundred. One never knows, but it's worth a try. It worked, and by 0200 I was finally free of duty to close my eyes for a few hours. I woke to a radiant, clear blue sky and *Shanti* skating daintily over an untroubled sea. Oh, the joy of 8 knots of breeze on the beam! It was a perfect morning for a wash, laundry and bread-making, as *Shanti* drew parabolic curves across the course.

Is there some kind of predetermined trade-off of a gorgeous day for a lousy night? The entire rim of the horizon was on fire with a shimmering white glow, occasionally shot through with staccato orange and red flares, as if some angry god was hurling fireballs into the sea. I want to curl up and hide under my bunk, only the ship's stores are already cowering there. I managed to get a few hours' rest, but by dawn, the wind had completely gone. The big black cumulonimbus encircling *Shanti* had sucked it up again, so I resigned myself to a few more hours' motoring in a rolly sea.

A Sunday arrival at Suwarrow now seems out of the question after sitting still in one place for half the night, but this morning, with full sails back up, a 12-15 knot northerly, *Shanti* is galloping along as if she smells the home pasture. So who knows?

Day 9: It seems as if I'm going to have to get used to this constant change. I hove-to again all night and there was no decent wind until 1400 the following day. This mentally prepares me for an extra day or two, or however many it takes, with the understanding that it can be just as pleasant out at sea as in a harbour. Heaving-to is kind of like anchoring in the middle of the ocean, sans anchor.

What is it with this urge to arrive? I'm only planning on stopping for a few days anyway. Really, is it worth it? A part of me just wants to keep going, or even to stay out here indefinitely, but I have not provisioned for that. And I ask myself, is this some kind of self-punishment? At times I just want to scream. I don't know why. Tired?

Day 11: This morning it's about another 45 nautical miles to go to Suwarrow; an awkward distance, not quite close enough to make it in before dark. It will be a new experience, heaving-to on the doorstep of the destination. To be on the safe side, I will allow about 15 - 20 miles off. That means parking at around 1500 this afternoon. Giving *Shanti* a good clean, I'm so hot and sweaty; her cleanliness is inversely proportional to my grime.

What the …....?

Shanti is jiggling up and down on the spot, preparing to settle for the night. The setting sun is burnishing the copper sky; the ubiquitous dark clouds are thin vapour trails, posing no immediate threat. Suddenly, a brightly-coloured sail appears over the horizon. Another yacht! My excitement is tinged with mild annoyance. Another yacht, on my ocean! It is the first I've seen for I don't know how long—perhaps ever—and it feels very strange, accustomed as I am to the vast expanses of nothingness encircling me. Being this close to landfall, it shouldn't be so surprising, but being so far off the main cruising routes, I hadn't expected it.

I go below and try calling them up on the VHF radio: *"Catamaran, approaching Suwarrow; here is Shanti, Shanti, Shanti; do you copy?"* but get no response. They have no AIS identification and are moving fast, hopefully continuing on. I don't want to have to worry about bumping into another boat that's parking nearby, drifting God knows where in the night.

As darkness blacks out the world, a faint red light in the distance changes to green and I know they have tacked and are re-entering my patch of sea. *Dammit.* That means no sleep for me tonight. I stand outside for a long time, mesmerised, trying to judge their proximity. It's impossible to tell. I briefly entertain unsettling images of waking to find a hard object suddenly alongside. The thought of it gives me goose-bumps. I'm not ready for any such close encounters.

Checking the chart, I note we are drifting at about 2 knots southward. Overnight, this could add a further 15 miles distance from landfall, which would not be good. I experiment with dropping the main and backing the headsail on the opposite side, which sets us northward. To maintain the current position, it will be necessary to alter the hove-to side every few hours, so it's just as well I wasn't counting on getting any sleep.

A slight drizzle was smudging the milky pre-dawn light and *Shanti* was still more or less in the same spot as where we had originally parked. There was no sign of the catamaran which I had long since lost sight of. I had plenty of time to do a gratitude meditation, giving thanks for an uneventful night before beginning the approach to the island.

Cautiously entering the shallow pass, threading my way through the bent-over sticks marking the edges of reefs, I rounded the back of Anchorage Island. I dropped the anchor close to shore and watched it descend through the translucent water. Standing at the bow, gazing around, I inhaled deeply, savouring the particulate-free air. Oh my God! What a magical place, swathed in aquamarine tranquillity. It truly was every bit as stunning as I'd been led to believe, reminding me of the pristine Cocos Keeling Islands. Another picture-postcard tropical island, nestled beneath its own sun-drenched, clear blue skies. All this, just for me! Well, almost.

I hadn't expected there to be any other yachts in the anchorage, apart from perhaps the catamaran, so I was surprised to find another two. The nearest and largest yacht had a second dinghy tied behind, which I assumed belonged to the resident Ranger. I waved.

Shortly after, two men approached *Shanti* in a large rubber-tubed dinghy. I assumed the one with a cap and backpack to be the Ranger, come to collect my $US50 fee, but he turned out to be from the catamaran. He introduced himself as Captain Denis and asked if I would like to go ashore with them (which was about the extent of his English). The older Frenchman who had been cruising for 25 years and had slightly better English, said it was the first time he had encountered 4 single-handers in the one anchorage—two French, one German and lastly, one Australian, me. All that could be seen of the German was an empty dinghy following a snorkel in the middle of the bay. The Rangers were not due to arrive for another month, so we had the place to ourselves.

Tired as I was, going ashore was too good an offer to refuse. *"Oui, oui, merci!"* I grabbed my sandals and jumped into the dinghy.

Put a single female among long-distance solo sailors and they can't help but skite. I was already impressed by the lean, tanned physique of Captain Denis, but he had to go further, hauling the heavy dinghy up the beach with biceps bulging. (*Regardez-moi!*) He frolicked about as gleefully as a child in an adventure playground, taking photos of everything in sight. It was obvious he was showing off on my behalf.

The uninhabited Rangers' hut, the tiny book exchange, the freshwater tanks, the overgrown gardens were all intriguing—more so, the weather-beaten statue of the famed survivalist, Tom Neale, who lived alone here, writing about it in his autobiography, *"An Island to Oneself."* Isolated from human contact and especially medical aid eventually undid him, but his love of this magical place captivated his soul for decades. I could well understand why.

Denis seemed intrigued by the smallest thing, a moving shell, a tiny hermit crab. A queen-sized hammock strung between two palms was an invitation to lie down together, which I demurely declined. It was too soon for such familiarity, no matter how much affinity fellow cruisers share in remote places. *Je me demande— why am I so mingy with my affection?* But there was still Luke to consider. That loyalty, however misplaced, has kept me to myself all these years. But now, the closer to home I got, that 'unavailable' banner was slipping. Who knew what the future had in store, but it was as if there was a fish-hook in my side with a thin line to nowhere. If only I could just be here, now, free to enjoy...

The Rangers' hut has an open-sided veranda with a wooden table and benches, perfect for sharing a pot-luck meal and drinks. Denis arranged to pick me up later, so I had time to bake a loaf of bread and gather some victuals for the soiree. The four of us sat around the long table which Denis had set with a tablecloth and all the accoutrements of fine dining, including candles and crystal glasses. (It's obvious that he lives on a catamaran, where breakages are less likely than on a monohull).

By request, I brought my guitar along and was glad that I had learnt a few songs off by heart. The others joined the chorus of the best-known numbers. Then Denis took the guitar and impressed me further by playing some beautiful French songs. He played well and sang with feeling. His friend, Guy has a rich tenor voice and set up a counter harmony, to which I added some high trills. The German sailor, Frank, spoke English well. Having someone to share a conversation with rounded out the evening perfectly.

Frank is also sailing around the world alone, in a similar-sized boat to *Shanti*. He meanders at a more leisurely pace, never turning the engine on. Like *never!* I admire that tenacity. He has been here for a couple of weeks already and sat out some strong blows, riding surf-like waves spilling over from the ocean side of the island. Other, bigger boats in the lagoon were damaged, one having its bow fittings buckled and the foredeck holed. It is not always as perfectly serene here as it is now, so again I count my blessings.

I hadn't noticed at first, but the boom on Guy's boat is broken in half. One of those nasty storm cells caught him unawares a few nights ago, causing an accidental gybe. On a 50' yacht, the stress of this is far greater than on my tiny rig. He plans to leave soon for repairs in Samoa. The general preference amongst the others is to head to Western Samoa rather than American, it being less costly, less bureaucratic and a better anchorage, so I will too. Magnificent as this uninhabited island is, supplies are non-existent, so the time to stay and play is limited.

Je me demande, what is wrong with me? I'm lifting my anchor.

The past few nights were the most fun I've had in a long time. But I'm shaking like a debutante, my pulse pounding in my ears as I rush to escape. It has gotten too intense too quickly. Last night, when Denis brought me home, he asked if he could come aboard for a new guitar string to replace one of his that broke, and perhaps a nightcap. *Bien sûr. Pourquoi pas?*

I poured a couple of glasses of Amarula liquor, made from the fruit that the South African elephants get high on, while Denis fitted his new string. For another hour or so, we drank and took turns playing the guitar and singing. No matter how tired I am, singing is the one thing that can keep me up way past bedtime. The night wore on until it became obvious that flirtation was challenging pragmatism, shifting up a level, to either be dealt with or ignored.

I gave the cue by putting down the guitar and standing up. Denis moved closer for a goodnight hug, which turned into a lingering embrace. Slipping my top off one shoulder, he began nuzzling my neck, softly murmuring my name in such a sensual accent that I melted. It was all I could do to say, *"Non, non"* and push him away. The faintest groan told of my intense arousal. But I could not.

Denis took the rejection well. Standing in the dinghy alongside, guitar in hand, under the full moon, he sang, "I can't get no satisfaction."

I laughed and sang back, "Though I tried, and I tried, and I tried..."

After he was gone, I lay in my bunk, so full of longing it was painful. *Why not?* I asked myself. What harm in it, just a moment of tenderness and human intimacy, so desperately needed. What kind of fool am I to reject it? My body and mind were awhirl with conflicting feelings, but after I settled, I felt I had done the right thing, not for Luke's sake, but for my own, to preserve some sense of loyalty, even if misplaced. Who knows if there is any future relationship for us, but for now, he is still looking out for me, being caring and supportive. I value that sense of having someone, no matter how distant, to care about whether I live or die.

I spoke to Frank on the VHF radio. He is 17 miles behind me, also adrift. His boat is heavier than *Shanti* so doesn't do as well in these light conditions. I have no idea where the catamaran is, last seen disappearing over the horizon many miles ahead. I could envy that speed but quickly forget that. We each have our own ship to sail.

I'm enjoying this quiet time alone. It's helping me to get clear on things, such as who I am, where I am going and what do I want. I forget these things so easily. (Where's that little notebook I started, with notes on what's what?) Reflecting on the past is of some help in placing the jig-saw puzzle pieces. There are recurring patterns, like familiar clouds in an otherwise totally blue sky. And even though they are ephemeral, they leave a tinge or residue in my constitution that leans me more readily one way or another. What do I know?

Everything changes; nothing stays the same—and yet I still cling to the "good" and reject the "bad". But nothing outside of me—not the weather, the waves, the rain, the discomfort—is inherently "bad" or "good". It is always my thinking that labels them thus and thereby colours my reaction to them.

Day 4. Very little wind—surprise! I had thought I might make it in to Apia by Wednesday but now it's looking more like Thursday. Still, my original estimate was for about a week to do the total of 520 nautical miles and I shall be lucky if it's only that, with these calms.

I got soaked through at 0300 when a westerly storm cell hit, with driving rain and wind. At least we sailed for a few minutes, even if in the wrong direction.

Day 5. 235 miles to go—nothing really. We're motoring into a headwind of 2 – 4 knots. To motor now allows for the possibility of arriving on Thursday morning, but so what if it's Friday. What's the rush? I think of Frank, now many miles behind, who doesn't burn diesel at all. I'm sure his attitude is not at all destination-driven and he happily waits out the lulls.

How would it be if there was no destination? Like sailing around the world non-stop, with nothing in between leaving and arriving back at the start. Then there would be no turning the key, ever. Just sit and wait patiently (or not) for the wind to come, which it always does.

I have this thing of wanting to make landfall in daylight and preferably in Customs' working hours. But now I know it's possible to heave-to the day before arrival or sail around in circles through the night. I realise that a big part of my wish to make good progress is due to the appointment I have on June 20, for the excision of the BCC from my nose. Making appointments for set dates is never a good idea. There are absolutely no absolutes out here.

Wednesday, May 22. I decided to burn some diesel (of which I still have plenty) and try to make it into port tomorrow. We drifted for 10 hours overnight. There's no wind this morning, or at least 2 knots on the nose. So the trusty little *Yani* has been ticking away since 0530 and will most likely have to continue until this evening.

I have done my calculations of how long to sail and how long to motor, but of course it all depends on there being some wind. We may just have to drift to get a few hours' sleep tonight. *Yani* is a trustworthy little diesel, but like all 3 cylinders, she clatters noisily with far from a smoothly balanced purr. Even though I love her for it, she does make sleep difficult. The wide ocean is an undulating, glassy terrain, more like land than sea.

Communication with Luke and the family has been virtually non-existent. I guess it's nice to know it's possible, in the event of an emergency, but what could they do anyway? The Epirb or HF radio would be the first recourse. In another day or so, I will have a local SIM card and regain that communication that most of us take for granted.

Day 8. Hey, I lost a day, somewhere overnight. Today is apparently Friday. Oh dear. How confusing. Where did it go?

I had a few hours' decent sailing yesterday, from 1630 to 0030. Then I decided

I could possibly sleep just as easily with the engine noise as with the slatting and banging of the sails and rig, so turned the key, and am still motoring, 9 hours hence. We're almost there, about an hour away, which is good because I should get to Customs and Immigration in business hours. Watching the chiselled peaks and gutters of Western Samoa, I wonder what today will bring. The future seems so totally unknowable. Do I have any say in it?

Chapter 20

The Pragmatism of Age

Apia harbour is very open and easy to enter. It shallows quickly toward the shore, and when there are a couple of ships or barges anchored, there's not a lot of swinging room. There is a small marina through a narrow pass, but it's not obligatory to berth there. It's not expensive as marinas go, but I prefer to swing to the breeze, especially when it's so hot.

I motored around for a while, checking depths, before dropping anchor. I had prime position, being the only yacht in the bay. It took me another hour of hot work to launch the dinghy and get the outboard on, but I still made it ashore within business hours on Friday afternoon.

There were only about half a dozen boats in the marina, one of which was the familiar French catamaran. Denis wasn't on board, as he'd gone to the Immigration office in town with a woman from a German yacht, to help translate for him.

Theoretically, the Customs and Immigration officials can come out to the anchorage to clear you into the country, if you pick them up in your dinghy. When they saw my small inflatable, they decided against this, explaining that it would be bad for all of us if they sank the boat, large men that they are. Formalities were conducted sitting on the back of a 50' Bavaria yacht owned by a Polish couple whom I had met in Panama. The Biosecurity check was supposed to be carried out onboard *Shanti* so the officials hung about long enough for their boss to believe they had done it, drinking cold drinks, playing guitar and singing. It couldn't have been easier.

Our obliging hosts know hardly any English at all, but are accomplished musicians, having entertained us all at Shelter Bay Marina in Panama, singing some beautiful, traditional Polish songs. A young bilingual crewman has since joined them, which must make their lives so much easier. I can't imagine entering foreign countries without understanding the fairly universally accepted common lingo of English. There are not too many places in the South Pacific where Polish is spoken. Through their young interpreter, I was invited to join them, sharing a taxi tour of the island the next day.

Later in the afternoon, when back on *Shanti* I wasn't too surprised to see a large, familiar dinghy rapidly approaching, with Captain Denis bringing gifts of fresh pineapple. He said the couple on the German yacht had invited us for drinks that evening. The Poles would be there with guitar and I should bring mine too.

It was just starting to rain when I climbed up the back of their boat. Denis wasn't there yet. He arrived later, standing on the dock beneath a large umbrella, crooning, *"I'm singing in the rain …."* Such light-hearted antics are always good for a smile.

There are different styles of sharing "Sundowners" on board boats of different nationalities. The Australian way is to BYO drinks and food to share; the Europeans provide everything. When it's your turn to reciprocate, they come and drink you out of boat and home. I definitely prefer the Australian way, given that I don't carry that much alcohol on board *Shanti*.

On this occasion, we all brought something to share, so the cockpit table was sagging beneath platters of all kinds of delicacies and the wine flowed freely. Somehow, despite the language differences, conversation seemed to flow as well.

After a while, the guitar cases were opened and the music began. Denis insisted I sing something, saying he was my biggest fan. I begged tiredness, having just arrived after a sleepless passage, but was not to be let off. I played my most recently learnt song, *"What's Up"*, by 'Four Non-Blondes', which tests my vocal range with its low and high parts. As I sat there strumming the few simple chords, listening to the rich mingling of voices as all joined the chorus—*"I say hey, yay, yay, yay; I say hey, what's going on?"*—I momentarily saw it from a distance and my heart was like a hot-air balloon rising to the heavens. Timelessness enveloped the moment and it might have lasted forever. I adore this aspect of the cruising lifestyle. No matter how different we might be as people, from so many diverse backgrounds, we all share the same challenge of crossing oceans on small boats. We all know what it's like to have things go wrong in the middle of the night.

En-route here, something broke on one of Denis' engines, making it impossible to turn the engine off. Finally, he closed the fuel supply, but the problem now needed fixing. He would have to stay here longer. Later, when I mentioned the invitation that I had been given to do the taxi tour of the island with the Polish trio, he insisted I wait and go with him. There would be more room in the car. Also, I could help translate—clearly he imagines my French is better than it is.

On Sunday morning our driver was ready and waiting at the marina gate. Denis sat in the front, with the window open, speaking French non-stop into his phone as he shot videos of the passing scenery. The narrow, winding roads were bordered by tall tropical blooms, their vibrant colours vividly edged in stark relief against the cloudless blue sky. So much life bursting forth in pregnant fullness, it was hard for my sea-eyes to adjust.

Our driver suggested stopping to pick up some local take-aways for lunch, but Denis asked if he could find us somewhere more chic to sit down in comfort. The first stop before lunch was a waterfall pool, set in a green-shaded gulley. We changed into our bathers, a little self-conscious at first, then splashed and frolicked in the water in that pre-sexual way of teenagers, testing for mutual attraction. It was obviously there. The slightest touch of bare skin sent tingles down the spine and our laughter echoed around the cool chamber.

Changing back into dry clothes, the tour continued, this time passing through some moist green, densely tropical rain forest. Eventually, it opened out to a broad view of the ocean. No matter how much I revel in the variegated greens and brilliant colours of plant-life, there is nothing like the sight of the ocean to fill me with joy. There it is—my home! It's strange how this identification has crept in. I wonder how long before it fades out.

Bouncing down an unmade dirt track towards the ocean, we stopped for lunch at an exclusive spa resort, complete with leaf-roofed huts and umbrellas encircling a sparkling infinity pool. The adjoining restaurant area was largely uncovered, with life-sized wooden carvings and Bird of Paradise floral arrangements near every table. *Très chic*. The kind of place that makes me want to hold my breath for a moment, so as not to sully the atmosphere. Half a glass of wine is normally enough for me to drop all inhibitions so the rest of the day played out more playfully.

The "Sua Deep Trench" is a popular tourist attraction. Our driver left us to wander off alone for a few hours, telling us, "People fall in love with Samoa, and come back for Some more and Sam-moa." No doubt this little play on words rolls off the tongue to enchant all of his passengers.

The broad stretch of clifftop parkland overlooks miles of spectacular coastline, the wild and free white-water curling and tumbling ashore, fading into the distant mist. This alone would satisfy the soul, but the *piece de resistance* is the 30-metre-wide hole in the ground, the "Deep Trench", formed by a collapsed volcanic caldera. The constant erosion of the lava-field by the pounding surf has tunnelled through, letting the sea enter the caldera in rhythmic pulsations. Concealed amidst thick foliage, it's quite difficult to spot at first and would be easy to fall into, were it not for the surrounding white picket fence.

I changed into a dry one-piece swimsuit, which I knew to be flattering. At first, Denis didn't notice me standing there in my best bathing-beauty pose, towel slung strategically over one shoulder; then looking up, he stopped in his tracks and made all the appropriate sounds of admiration. *Oui, oui monsieur; flattery will get you everywhere!*

He took my hand and we walked together like any happy couple. That simple act of holding hands meant so much to me. It's something that Luke would never do. I was over the moon that Denis sought my hand and held it so warmly. Such small things, yet so immense; a universal token of human connection, perhaps felt more strongly by parents attuned to that loving act of belonging, protection and guidance.

Access to the pool is down a steep, narrow ladder, adding an extra thrill of potential risk. The currents ebb and flow strongly and ropes have been tied between dead tree trunks and boulders for swimmers to hang onto. Like most of the other couples in the surging rip, we clung to one another, laughing all the time. Denis scooped me up in his strong arms as I floated weightlessly on my back. A dark green collar of foliage framed the sky, so high up above. Nothing more was needed to round out that moment of childlike bliss.

Frank arrived the next day. Not running the engine had not added many days to his passage from Suwarrow, and again I questioned my rush. What difference would it make to arrive on Friday or Monday? Would anything have panned out differently? Who knows the effect of the proverbial "butterfly wing" flapping in some distant land?

That night I received a panic call from my sister in Kalgoorlie, in Western Australia, who was sure our father was on death's doorstep. I had already said goodnight to the others and returned to *Shanti*, but suddenly felt overcome with worry. I hesitated to seek solace from the one I felt closest to but tiptoed nervously back to tap on the side of the catamaran. Denis held me in his arms, comforting me like a frightened child, while my tears wet his shirt.

The next morning, I checked out of the country and said my *au revoirs* to new-found friends, with perhaps slightly more than the usual sadness. One never knows when or where we might meet again.

As if understanding my fragile state, wind and weather drew in their horns, finally allowing some perfect SE Trade Wind sailing. The distance of 580 nautical miles to Fiji was covered in one week, giving me plenty of time to reflect. It seems as if my voyage may be cut shorter than expected. I had originally planned to stay in the South Pacific, cruising around the islands of Tonga, Fiji and Vanuatu until the beginning of cyclone season in November. It would have been a kind of indulgence— not part of the perpetual push to get around the world and back. I didn't feel ready for it to be over.

Also, there was Luke, ostensibly waiting for me. I really didn't know what to do about that. A knot in my stomach grew tighter whenever I tried to think about it. I took advantage of the calmer weather to meditate, seeking answers from my intuition. All that served to do was untangle my insides and lay them down in an empty quietude, like a familiar friend. Was that it? Could we simply be friends? Lovers come and go, whereas friendships can last a lifetime. It seemed preferable.

But what were his expectations? Like me, he probably had no idea.

Arriving in Savusavu, I was very fortunate to get the last available berth at the Copra Shed Marina. Watching 'Marine Traffic' from his Australian base, Luke had spotted a familiar 46' yacht, *Blithe Spirit*, and asked his friends to watch out for me. It's amazing how small the cruising community is. I met Sally and Stuart several years ago in the Whitsundays and it was an unbelievable coincidence that they should happen to be here at the same time as me.

Once again, I was grateful to Luke for his help, though this time with mixed feelings. It seemed logical to pull away, to break the bond that has held me in its grip for the past few years. *We are simply not compatible, I remind myself.* There are too many major differences in who we are and what we like to do. Eventually, these things would make both of us unhappy. Still, staying loyal to him has at least kept me clean and free of further complications that might have stopped me along the way.

The more urgent need now was to find out how my father was and to see if I needed to fly out immediately. After buying a local SIM card and making several phone calls to Australia and New Zealand, the crisis seemed to have passed. My sister and I both recognised the transient nature of this reprieve; things could take a downhill turn at any time. With that in mind, I decided to continue homeward, without further detours or delays. This was never, after all, a pleasure cruise, but the fulfilment of a childhood dream to sail alone around the world. Any extra diversions were a bonus, the icing on the cake. Now, I just needed to close the circle.

Leaving the complete stillness of the Marina at Savusavu, it was inevitable that the passage to New Caledonia should test my stomach mercilessly. Twenty knots from the south-east made it a tight beat south down the Koro Sea, a patch of water renowned for its roughness. I held on to my breakfast for a couple of hours before losing it, then continued dry-retching for the rest of the day and night. Sleep was out of the question with that going on, plus all the reefs and islands around.

After about 60 miles it was possible to bear away to the west, making it slightly more comfortable. The one plus was I covered my best ever distance of 140 nautical miles in 24 hours.

At midnight on the fifth day, I was completely becalmed, with the sails once again slatting in the residual swell. While it may be possible to block out some of the noise with earplugs, some of the light with eye covers, I cannot hide from the incessant jerking motion. It's like having someone shove your shoulder rudely, just as you're about to drop off. I have had hardly any sleep over the past few nights and am feeling very strung out.

In the hope of chasing down some wind, I ran the motor for 10 hours but then gave that up, knowing I don't have enough fuel for the remaining distance. Since then we have been drifting with 5 knots dead astern, doing around 2 knots speed over ground. It's such a peaceful change from the engine clatter. I'm expecting another day with more of the same tomorrow.

There has been no word from Denis, but that's OK. I'm feeling relaxed about everything man-related for the first time. What is it all about, after all? Initially, there is attraction, then there is getting acquainted, then the possibilities, the wishes, the desires, the options. There are the practicalities to consider, such as who lives where? Who can live where? It's not so simple. After the "I want you"—then what? In the beginning, it's all very blind, full of impetuous passion and a willingness to overlook any foibles that might later irritate. At what point do we walk away from an unsuitable match? After 10 years or 20 years? Staying single is looking a lot easier. *Amour et sagesse ne vont pas ensemble.* Ah, the pragmatism of age.

———

The lack of wind continued over the next three days and any hopes of covering the 850-mile distance to New Caledonia in one week faded. On Monday, June 24, I ran the motor for 4 hours in an attempt to make slack water at 0830 Tuesday. That had to be adjusted to 0950 Wednesday when I realised I had 1 knot of counter-current. So it was back to a more peaceful night of drifting in the rain.

We're still on track timewise to make 0950 slack water tomorrow. It is important to time the tides right for the entrance through the reef at the Havannah Canal, where the outgoing tide can run up to 8 knots. Slack water at the entrance occurs about an hour after low tide at Noumea, a little like Port Phillip Bay in Melbourne, where the pond continues emptying long after the tide has turned.

I pulled everything out of the cockpit subfloor to investigate the source of all the water under the engine. As suspected, the Volvo "dripless" shaft seal that I had replaced in Cape Town was leaking badly, at the rate of about 10 litres an hour. I tried getting some grease into it. If that doesn't work, I will have to haul *Shanti* out of the water again somewhere to replace the seal before continuing.

The weather forecast that I had downloaded before leaving Fiji showed strong sou' westerlies coming, which I hoped had changed. Wind right on the nose was the last thing I needed when entering the surrounding reefs of New Caledonia. Meanwhile, I found I had drifted backwards overnight. That's got to be one of the most demoralizing lacks of progress. I can handle making the pitiful distance of only 20 nautical miles when it's at least in a forward direction, but going backwards really sucks.

The heavy rain continued so I was shut in down below, everything was damp, and I had a new experience—cold!!! For the first time in months, it was necessary to wear a jumper and use a blanket. Returning to Australia in the middle of winter was not at all appealing.

I pressure-cooked some chickpeas, totally fogging up the cabin. Not such a smart idea. *Shanti* is mooching along at 1.5 knots with 8 knots of wind from directly behind. All rather dismal if I think about it. Once again, I see that the "problem" is not the wind or rain or sea, but is within me and my reaction to it. If only I could drop the expectation of getting somewhere by a certain time, I'm sure it would all be much more enjoyable. Better still, if I could accept rainy, cold, windless days with the same equanimity as warm, sunny, perfect 15-knot SE-Trade Wind sailing days. Perhaps, it's because they, like a tantalizingly rare jewel, are so scarce and therefore more highly valued.

I did the calculations for time and distance to go, even to the extent of inserting waypoints at smaller intervals, so I had some idea of where I was supposed to be by when. These things never work out quite the way expected but I still devote a lot of time and energy, as if that might have some influence on the outcome. The sleeplessness of this short passage was becoming worse than on the 7 weeks from Panama to Tahiti when exhaustion finally laid me out. *Je me demande,* how much more of this can I take? For some reason the sea was extremely restless, tipping *Shanti* from ear to ear, so all sails had to be dropped while we rolled to and fro on the same spot. The motion was relentless and I found myself longing desperately for just a moment of stillness. This was the worst it had been for the past week so I knew some stronger wind was coming. I could hardly wait.

At 0600 it came in with a vengeance, gusting up to 32 knots. The seas quickly built up and huge rollers kept on whacking us broadside. Approaching an unfamiliar coastline, seeking a pass through reefs is nerve-wracking enough on a good day. There is often a disparity between the charts and the actual, so I'm hopping up and down the companionway steps a hundred times, wishing I had a waterproof chart plotter at the helm. In the end, the only thing to trust is actually eyeballing what's in front of me. It doesn't help when the pouring rain whitewashes everything like a thick fog.

The AIS showed that there were two other boats nearby, both much bigger and faster, dashing to make the pass at slack water. It was only when they were practically upon me that I could make out the ghostly shape of their sails. They were gone in a flash, so it was pointless to rely on following them in. The best I could do was note the brief trace of their AIS track. From this, I could see that they stuck to the very centre of the Havannah Canal, where the outflowing current is strongest. It's possible to avoid this by passing near the Goro lighthouse, but it was too dangerous to go so close to the breaking surf when I could scarcely see *Shanti's* bow.

These are the times when I can't help but wish it was different. I know I asked for wind, but it seems to be either none at all or far too much. Am I never content? But this blow is harsh, and I ask *Why now?* Of all times for a gale to blow and the rain to pour and the waves to push and shove. My whole system is on red alert.

Tilly 2 needs constant adjustments, just to stay on the line of approach through the pass. Generally, she tracks more surely than hand steering, but this is testing her to the limit. I need to be free of the tiller, to be able to jump down the companionway steps to check the course on the computer, then back outside, straining to see our actual position through the thick obscurity of the rain. Tide and wind and waves constantly push us off course. Ten degrees to port, fifteen to starboard, back to port. Ai yai yai! Just get us through this, please.

Entering the pass an hour before slack water, we still had 2 knots of current running against us. *Yani* was roaring away at high revs, pushing hard, churning and sliding. Just when I thought we were good, suddenly we were within roaring distance of the reef and the crashing surf seemed certain to claim us. I grabbed the tiller and shoved it hard across, right into the face of a huge wave that stopped us dead. *Yani* spluttered and missed a beat, along with my heart. *Please don't die now!*

There was no time to check fuel or lines or filters or any of the other things that I know to do. All I could do was pray she'd keep going and somehow manage to claw our way back to safety. Inch by inch, breath by breath, heartbeat by heartbeat, we pushed against wind and waves and tide. My eyes were blinking back either rain or tears or both. A lot of water was sloshing about the cabin floor from the leaking shaft seal but it would have to wait for calmer waters.

Even after passing a long way inside the encircling reefs, the waves were still surprisingly just as vicious, dealing out short and sharp blows. Wasn't it supposed to be protected inside? Perhaps not in such stormy conditions. There were still many more miles ahead before finding a peaceful refuge. We motored on, punching slowly through the chop. My whole body was still shaking and I lacked the fortitude to even consider changing anything.

Eventually, I unfurled a tiny amount of headsail and gave the valiant *Yani* a break. It was such a relief to cut the noise and feel *Shanti* lift to the wind. There were still reefs and islands nearby, all like magnets. With engine stilled and so little sail out, we struggled to gain enough windward ground to clear them, but gradually my confidence returned. *We're OK; we can do this.*

Finally, we cleared the last headland and could ease sheets and bear away. With the wind coming more from behind, the breaking rollers slewed us left and right with their usual challenge, but it was like home territory. We're well used to this downwind slalom ride. I took over steering, holding us as square as possible to avoid an accidental gybe. The tension began to slip from me as the rain eased and the double arcs of a limpid rainbow filtered through the clouds. My lips involuntarily curved upwards in a deeply felt mix of divine pleasure and gratitude.

I considered anchoring for the night in the Baie de Prony but the risk of discovery by the French Border Force is greater there (it is forbidden to anchor anywhere before checking in at Noumea), so I continued on to Baie Blanche, on the lee of Ile Ouen. The wind was still piping strongly down the hillsides and it took nearly an hour to cover the short distance to nearer the shore. Once safely tucked in, it was the prudent option to ignore the rules and get a good night's sleep before continuing on to Port Moselle the next morning. I furled my ragged Australian flag, turned off the AIS to avoid detection as a foreign vessel, and sank into deep oblivion.

"A Frenchman has been asking after you every day," the dark-skinned woman at the Marina office mentioned. "Do you want me to call him?"

The room was still swaying as it always does after first setting foot on land. I stared blankly ahead, my tight grip on the counter, being all there was between me and the floor. The woman kindly handed me a glass of water and sat me down on the comfortable couch. A few minutes later, Denis was beside me, his arm wrapped protectively around my shoulders, helping me read the French *Douane* arrival forms. The tiny print was written in both languages, but for some reason, neither made any sense. Denis practically had to direct the pen for me to fill in the gaps. He seemed thrilled to see me, burbling on in French, telling me how he had sent me many emails (to the wrong, land-based address). Knowing the terrible weather conditions, my silence caused him great *inquiétude*. He was like an over-excited puppy, almost ready to lick my face. I was like a barely-existent marionette whose strings have snapped.

I was glad to stagger back to *Shanti* to await the Biosecurity check, have my remaining food taken and then rest for a few hours. It always amazes me how restorative that short sleep can be. I was feeling half-way human again when Denis called by later to take me out to dinner at the *Bout du Monde* restaurant. Still, I cut the evening short as exhaustion overtook me again. I don't think I stirred an eyelash for the next 15 hours. The following day dawned with all the excitement of being in a new country, a French-speaking country, with a new friend waiting for me.

The changes in the Port Moselle Marina have been huge since I was last here about 10 years ago. There are many more pontoons, nearly all of which are taken up by permanents. The anchorage is perhaps slightly less crowded but full of moored boats. I was fortunate to get a berth on the visitor's dock for 4 nights. Denis had already used up his marina time and had been out on anchor for the past few weeks, waiting for me to arrive. I felt flattered, though still unsure.

The next stop for me would be Australia—home—Bundaberg, and possibly Luke. Would he also be waiting for me? What were his expectations? Nothing had ever been said. Whatever future scenarios we each might envisage were entirely within our own minds. This irked me slightly. I wished we could be more open and discuss these things freely. In the light of such a void, such uncertainty, I pulled back further, reminding myself that in fact, we were not really a couple in any sense of the word. Or maybe I just didn't want us to be.

Nothing is cheap in New Caledonia, not even local food from the nearby market. It's not a great place to get work done but it was an unavoidable pain to have to haul *Shanti* out to replace the leaking shaft seal. Still, the mechanics seem competent even if the shipyard is badly managed. It was a week just sitting on the hardstand waiting for anything to begin. Not as bad as for others; a German couple had already been waiting for over a month for engine parts and kept on getting conflicting stories as to their whereabouts. Very frustrating!

Despite the slow pace and the high costs, I decided it was a good idea to paint the bottom again, as the old antifoul, last done 10 months ago in Trinidad, was wearing thin. So *Shanti* is now looking her best for her return to Australia. That thought is at once exciting and deflating; the end seems to have suddenly leapt forward to be so soon upon me as to be surreal. I can understand the solo circumnavigator, Bernard Moitessier, who after winning the Golden Globe around the world race, didn't stop to receive his accolades, but kept on sailing. They say this strange life at sea can be addictive. Who knows? It is certainly a love/hate relationship, but one that makes me feel more alive than anything else has ever come close to.

I bade my *au revoirs* to Denis as he flew back to France, leaving his catamaran on the hardstand for the cyclone season. He tried to make me promise to visit him but how could I possibly say? My uncertainty annoyed him, and I could understand that in ordinary life, people can ordinarily say yes or no, dependent on practicalities and so forth. But for me, after so many years of trying to live in the present moment, any future plans could only be as speculative as the weather. Finishing what I had set out to do was about as close as I could get to having any immediate direction. After that, who could possibly know? It's clear to me that even if I might wish to make no changes, life will certainly change regardless. It suits me better to wait and watch for the clues it gives at the time.

The panic over my father's wellbeing has subsided; his wife, Tanya now has extra home help, plus her brother from Thailand is staying with them for a couple of months. The BCC lesion on my nose still needs to be attended to in Melbourne, but I have postponed the appointment for another couple of weeks, just in case of delay. I have begun weather watching with the intention of heading back to Port Moselle to re-provision and refill the water and diesel in readiness for departure. All going well, I should close the circle of my circumnavigation and be back in Bundaberg within the next few weeks. And then that chapter of the great adventure comes to an end.

I caught the early morning bus to Port Moselle and ran around to the various authorities to clear out of New Caledonia. That done, the more pressing issue of timing my departure through the reef with the outgoing tide made me set off immediately.

The first two days brought the usual battle with lumpy seas and seasickness, but that settled into some glorious weather with perfect winds, and all was well in my little world.

On Day 6, I was becalmed, which seems to have become something of a habit, and something to just accept, sitting and waiting. So long as I can drop any expectations of an arrival date, this works well. Generally, the wind will return. There are still those niggly little thoughts in the back of the mind about being a sitting duck, immobile in the face of potential disasters, like being run over by a ship, or hit by a newly formed storm, that make me want to move. It's an eerie feeling just drifting without sails through a pitch-black night. Which is best ignored, because the reality is that moving is just as dangerous. As always, it is the mind causing trouble.

Each country has its own distinctive smell. Western Samoa was sweet—not in a heavy, cloying way, but a delicate filigree, like the sweet nectar we children sucked from the trumpet heart of flowers. Australia smells like smoke—the coal-burning fumes of industry. I could smell it for many miles out to sea before I actually saw it. There was a turgidity to the motionless air.

I had just rounded Breaksea Spit at the top of Fraser Island, motoring to cover the last 40 nautical miles, with tiny puffs of wind just starting to ruffle the glassy sea—and then! Dolphins, leaping, spinning, flipping, turning somersaults high in the air in such an exciting display, as if to say *"Welcome Home"*.

After shrieking in delight as each new performance outdid the last, I quelled my excitement and crept quietly back to the cockpit. These magnificent creatures do seem to be attuned to our reactions, almost showing off like young children. A few years ago, a woman in New Zealand, similarly enthralled, died of a heart attack when one crashed through the boat's windscreen and landed in her lap. I'm not sure what happened to the dolphin.

I had just returned to the cockpit when glancing forward, I saw the most enormous humpback whale, right in front of *Shanti*. That was a heart-stopper! Luckily it had the good sense to dive out of the way, and surfaced again nearby, waving a fluke as if to say, *I'm fine thanks*. I watched in silent amazement as several others of these unbelievable giants leapt as miraculously as a jumbo jet getting airborne and breached all around me. An awe-inspiring sight worth sailing around the world for!

Seeing Australia on the clear and sunny horizon, there was no doubt about it—there was definitely a strong sense of coming home. (I still call Australia Home). I was glad to have chosen Bundaberg as the port of entry rather than Brisbane, with its busy shipping channels and shallow waters. Aside from a straight and easy entry, Bundaberg gave me a sense of completion, of closing the circle where I began the solo part of my circumnavigation.

Arriving mid-afternoon on July 30, a gentle breeze was blowing so I had plenty of time to experience the profound mix of emotions rising within me. I couldn't put labels on them all, but I felt the tears that often brim whenever I am deeply moved. Usually, this is a combination of stomach-clenching anticipation, exaltation and disbelief that such a thing could be happening. Like when my young son shoots the winning goal in the last few seconds of his basketball game. Or when small children sing in the school play. Or when bulls charge down the narrow streets and no-one is killed. Or when a baby is born.

Here and now, after allowing the full gamut of sentimentality to reverberate, I am left with a predominant feeling of gratitude. There are so many things to be grateful for. Luck is probably the biggest. I have seen so many others on the wrong side of it, with engine failure, a broken mast, grounding on a reef, or with major health issues. I'm grateful that my health held together, that *Shanti* held together, both of us through some very testing times. Not everyone with this same dream gets the opportunity to pursue it. Not everyone gets to complete it. I was definitely one of the lucky ones.

There was no grand finale when I arrived, no brass band, no flag-waving, no cheering crowds, no cameras; in fact, no-one at all to welcome me back to Australia—which I was glad of.

The one person whom I might have expected to be there was Luke. Often, I had envisaged that delicious homecoming scene, the comforting familiarity, the completion not just of the journey but of my self, with heart and soul and body wrapped up and lovingly put back together again. I felt so in need of connection. In many ways it had constituted a major incentive for me to continue, just to get back home, with no need to leave again.

As it turned out, Luke was only a few miles up the coast on his yacht, but engine problems kept him there. My ambivalence about us made that not such a bad thing. I really didn't know how to be with him, believing we should just accept our differences and finally let it go. How hard that decision! So often he had jostled in and out of my unguarded thoughts.

One thing that there is no shortage of at sea, is time to think. Possibly I spend more time in my head than in my heart and the two don't always sit comfortably together. Once again, I am tossing things over and around, sifting the good from the bad, making excuses and deals. I recognise that there is a wish for things to be as they were in the beginning, in that first intensity of attraction. I also see the frustration that comes from hanging onto that imaginary, perfect person. It is a breeding ground for disappointment.

I tell myself that I belong to no-one and no-one belongs to me—yet I see how I cling to a "special" attachment and wish for its permanence. "Rescue me, complete me, love and adore me, make me happy"—the unwritten abiding expectation which must ultimately fail. Especially so with 'star-crossed' lovers, thwarted in their union from the very start. Oft-times, when all obstacles are removed, only a hollow shell of unfulfilled potential remains. There needs to be at least some reality in it, some practicality, some basic compatibility.

Heathcliff made his life and the lives of all those around him miserable by his monomania, his obsessive, unattainable love for Catherine. Is that what I have for Luke, an unhealthy obsession that has no practicality whatsoever? I use the label 'love' for the depth of feelings I hold, although they are less needy now and more open to pragmatic scrutiny. But how to undo the knot that has tied us for these past few years? I'm sure we both know it is a foundationless match, the incongruity of which we have been trying to ignore.

The comedian Tim Minchin more realistically sings: "If I didn't have you, I'd most probably have someone else." Is it simply the need to love and be loved that is so compelling, rather than the object of one's desire? How many mismatched couples are there out there, clinging to a star that has long since extinguished? No, that's not for me. If nothing else, the unfettered ocean has strengthened my need to be true to myself.

I can see the low slopes of The Hummock in the distance and the first of the leads to the Burnett River. It is both exhilarating and deflating in equal measure. So many mixed feelings are vying for supremacy that they cancel each other out and I'm simply sailing slowly into yet another port. The afternoon sea-breeze is filling in and it's turning into one of those rare, perfect sailing days. A part of me doesn't want this to end.

An unusual sound that I haven't heard for a very long time snaps me out of my reverie. My oldest friend and her husband are calling to give me their congratulations.

"I'm just about to enter the river," I laughed. "Not quite there."

"Well done!" they effused. "We're so glad you made it safely home! At last, we can stop worrying about you."

Once again, I saw that I have caused a lot of concern to my friends and family in pursuing this dream of mine. And I realised with a jolt, that to them, it was over. Looking through their eyes, I would behave myself now and settle down.

This perception was later reinforced by my children and all those who never want me to go to sea again. It was as if there was some kind of circle, not just of closure, but of enclosure, like a fence around a home pasture. Everything could now be wrapped up and put behind me, as if it was just some crazy stunt that I once did, which was now purged from my system, forevermore.

Epilogue

I am not the only one whose future dreams have been put on hold. The whole of the outside world is suddenly as far out of bounds as the Moon. It is like having landed in some weird kind of virtual reality, where a massive curtailment of our freedom to move about has been imposed. The freedom I enjoyed crossing the South Pacific Ocean and re-entering Australia, is now gone.

Having skirted most news for the past few years, it comes as a sudden shock to me. It truly does seem as if I have returned to a world gone mad. Violence, rioting, climate change, huge fires burning out of control are all sideliners to the global pandemic that is bringing the world to its knees.

I am currently living alone in a small brick box in an outer suburb of Melbourne, a city locked-down in a second-wave resurgence of Covid-19. I just celebrated my birthday with a virtual dinner party online. The up-side of this is no-one had to drink/drive home after. The downside is no physical contact, no cuddling my new baby granddaughter. And no possibility of returning to *Shanti* in Queensland.

Life will always present challenges. Our perceptions will affect how we respond to these. I have friends here who are struggling immensely, believing conspiracy theories, chemical warfare, 5G radiation and dictatorships are behind the scenes. Such perceptions must make everything that much harder to bear. Better to ask if anything can be done about it, in this very moment? Or am I screaming at the wind?

The other factor that I am used to dealing with at sea, is the unknown. When will this end? How will it end? Will our world ever be the same again? Change and uncertainty are rocking the boat.

Here is an opportunity to learn that freedom comes from within us, that we can be happy within life, rather than *because* of life. The sea has taught me patience, acceptance of what is, and that it is possible to experience inner peace in the midst of turmoil. The storms, the calms, the perfect 15-knot Trade Winds, the sun and the rain never remain the same for very long. Knowing that challenges will always come, we can differentiate between the actual challenges of the moment and the imaginary scenarios of the mind, the unhelpful thoughts of "what if the boat should sink?" It is a choice we ourselves can make.

Appendix 1 - Glossary

Aft	Towards the back of the boat; see also stern, astern
AIS	Automatic Identification System; method of collision avoidance
Anti-siphon	Introduces air in a pipe to prevent water flowing backwards
Astern	Towards the back of the boat
Astern Propulsion	Backwards movement
Autopilot	Used to steer the boat without a person in control
Bar	A shallow area of sand at the entrance to a harbour
Beam	Maximum width of the boat; "On the beam": side on
Beating	Sailing close to the wind
Berth	A boat's allocated place at a wharf or dock
Bilge	Lowest point inside the boat
Bleed	To let air out of fuel lines
Boathook	A pole, often extendable, with a hook on the end
Boat speed	Speed of the boat through the water, as opposed to SOG
Boom	The horizontal pole at right angles from the mast, to which the bottom of the mainsail is attached
Boot-topping	A narrow stripe painted close to the boat's waterline
Bow	The front of the boat
Broach	To lose control surfing down a wave and turn side on
Broadside	The side of the hull
Buoy	An anchored float for mooring or as a navigation mark
Cleat	A T-shaped piece of metal or wood to which ropes are attached
Clew	Lower corner of the sail, often with an eyelet to tie a rope through
Coaming	Raised border round the cockpit to keep water out
Cockpit	Outside sitting/steering area
COG	Course Over Ground; includes tidal influence or leeway

Companionway	Entrance from cockpit to cabin, usually with steps down
Deck	Flat area running the length of the boat to walk on
Depth sounder	An instrument set in the hull for measuring depth of water
Dodger	Protective structure, usually canvas, between cabin and cockpit
Dock	A structure for boats to tie up to near land
Down below	Below decks, in the cabin
Draft	Depth of water needed to float
Drogue	Towed behind the boat to slow it down in rough weather
Electrolysis	Damage to dissimilar metals due to an electric current
Epirb	Electronic Position-Indicating Radio Beacon
Fore	The front of the boat
Foredeck	Forward part of the deck
Forepeak	The front section of the cabin, often used for storage of sails
Forestay	Front wire that supports the mast
Fuel polishing	To pump fuel through a filter using an electric pump
Furler	Drum with rope wrapped around it to pull headsail in and out
GPS	Global Positioning System, a navigational tool for location
Gunwale	Upper edge of the side of the boat, where hull meets deck
Gybe	To swing the boom to the opposite side, with wind from behind
Gypsy	Part of the anchor winch, used to raise or lower chain or rope
Halyard	Rope used to raise or lower a sail
Headsail	The small triangular sail at the front of the boat; see also Jib
HF radio	High-Frequency long-range radio; see also SSB radio
Helm	The steering wheel or tiller
Heave-to	Using a small amount of sail to "park" the boat
Hull	Body of the boat
Impeller	The rotating part of a centrifugal pump, used to move water
Iron spinnaker	Colloquial expression meaning to use the engine
Jib	The small triangular sail at the front of the boat
Jury rig	A make-shift rig used to keep sailing after rig failure
Katabatic	Wind being funnelled more strongly down a slope
Keel	Extension of the hull that increases stability

Knot	Boat speed. One knot equals one nautical mile per hour
Lazy jacks	Ropes from boom to mast to contain the sail when lowered
Leeward	The opposite side from which the wind is blowing
Leeway	The sideways movement of a boat
Lifelines	Horizontal wires around the perimeter as a safety fence
Liveaboards	People who live aboard their boat
Log	An instrument set in the hull for boat speed or distance
Log-book	A written record of boat's position, conditions, etc.
Luffing up	Pointing the boat directly into the wind
Main (sail)	The large triangular sail attached to the back of the mast
Mainsheet	Rope that pulls the mainsail in or out
Mast	Vertical pole to which the sails are attached
Mooring	A floating object tethered to the sea-bed
Nautical mile	Equals 1.852 kilometres
On the beam	Wind on the side of the boat, at a 90-degree angle
Open roadstead	An exposed anchorage near the coast
Osmosis	A blister in the fibreglass, affecting the hulls' structural integrity
Pactor Modem	An electronic interface between computer and HF radio
Paddle Wheel	See Log; rotates as water passes by, giving boat speed
Pick	A colloquial term for the anchor
Pintel	A bolt or fitting on which the rudder turns
Port	The left side
Pulpit	Railing around the front of the boat
Pushpit	Railing around the back of the boat
Quarter berth	A bunk at rear of the boat, below the cockpit
Raft-up	To tie two or more boats alongside each other
Reef	To reduce sail, using reef-lines or furler
Rhumb line	A direct course between two fixed compass points
Rig	The mast, sails, wires and ropes
Rolling hitch	A type of knot or friction hitch used to resist lengthwise pull
Rudder	A flat piece hinged vertically near the stern for steering
Seacocks	"Taps" in the hull for water inlet, e.g. for toilet or engine
Sheets	Ropes used to control sails; see also Mainsheet
Shrouds	Wires supporting the mast from the side of the boat
Sikaflex	Brand name of polyurethane-based adhesive filler
Slack water	A still point between the rising and falling tide
SOG	Speed Over Ground; includes tidal influence
Spinnaker	A large, light sail flown from the front of the mast in light winds

Spinnaker pole	A long pole used to hold the spinnaker out from the bow
Spreaders	Horizontal bar, usually two-thirds of the way up mast
SSB	Single Side Band radio used for long-distance communication
Stanchion	Upright posts supporting the lifelines, usually about knee height
Stand-by	Wait
Starboard	Right side
Stem	Another word for bow, or an extension of the keel
Stern	The back of the boat
Stugeron	Brand of tablet taken for sea-sickness
Through-hull fittings	Seacocks or other fittings that go through a hole in the hull
Tidal race	A fast-moving tide passing through a constricted area
Tiller	A horizontal bar fitted to the head of the rudder for steering
VMR	Volunteer Marine Rescue
Washboards	Removable "doors" to the companionway
Waterline	The line where the hull meets the surface of the water
Water-maker	High-pressure filtration system to get fresh water from saltwater
Weigh anchor	Raise the anchor
Whisker pole	A pole which is smaller and lighter than the spinnaker pole
Wind vane	Steers the boat using only the wind
Windward	Direction from which wind is blowing

For more images and videos of the voyage, visit shantiatsea.blogspot.com

Appendix 2 - Layout of Shanti

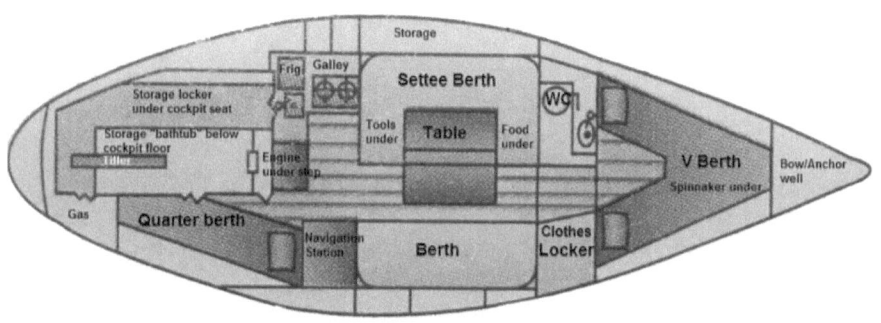

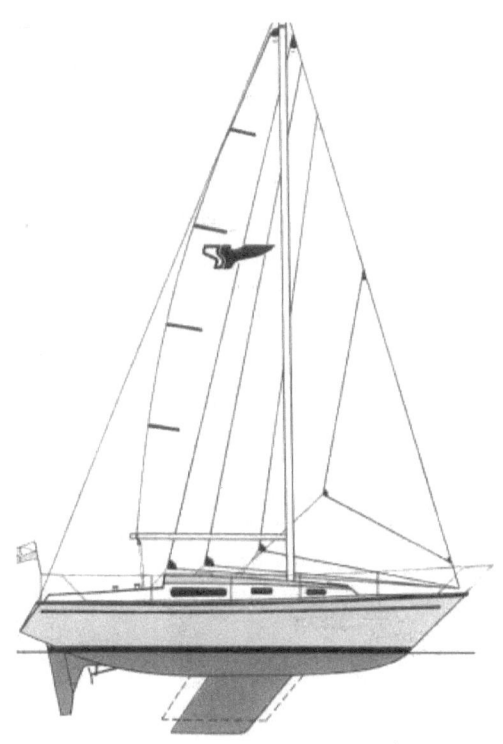

www.ingramcontent.com/pod-product-compliance
Lightning Source LLC
Chambersburg PA
CBHW030528010526
44110CB00048B/783